The Liberal Ascendancy, 1830–1886

British Studies Series

General Editor: JEREMY BLACK

Published

Forthcoming

The Liberal Ascendancy, 1830–1886

T. A. Jenkins

MACMILLAN

First published 1994 by
THE MACMILLAN PRESS LTD
Houndmills, Basingstoke, Hampshire RG21 2XS
and London
Companies and representatives
throughout the world

A catalogue record for this book is available
from the British Library

ISBN 0-333-59247-6 hardback
ISBN 0-333-59248-4 paperback

Printed in China

Contents

List of Tables

Acknowledgements

The Universities of Exeter and East Anglia have provided me with pleasant, temporary berths, which have greatly facilitated the writing of this book, and both have been generous with financial assistance to cover research expenses.

I would especially like to thank Bruce Coleman, whose support helped to get this project off the ground, Geoffrey Searle, who has bravely read the whole book in draft, and Brian Hill, who provided helpful comments on the early chapters. Colin Davis, though not a nineteenth-century scholar, has done more than a little to aid the completion of this book by kindly lending me his word-processor.

I am also grateful to my students, at Cambridge, Exeter and East Anglia, for giving me numerous opportunities to try out and refine my ideas: if this book proves to be of use to other students, it will be in large part thanks to them.

The author and publishers wish to thank the following for permission to use copyright material:

The British Library for material sourced to their collections; Lord Clarendon for the extracts from the Clarendon MSS deposited in the Bodleian Library; the Earl of Derby for the extract from the Derby MSS deposited in the Liverpool Record Office; Devon Record Office, on behalf of Lady Margaret Fortescue, for the extract from the Fortescue MSS; the Clerk of the Records, House of Lords, for the extracts from the Brand Papers; Maurice A. T. Rogers for the extracts from the Rogers MSS deposited in the Bodleian Library; the Royal Historical Society for the extracts from *The Parliamentary Diaries of Sir John Trelawny, 1858–65*, ed. T. A. Jenkins; the University of Birmingham Library for the extracts from the Chamberlain MSS; the University of Southampton Library, on behalf of the Trustees of the Broadlands Archives, for the extracts from the Broadlands MSS.

Every effort has been made to trace all the copyright-holders but if any have been inadvertently overlooked the publishers will be pleased to make the necessary arrangement at the first opportunity.

Introduction

Little explanation is required for attempting to provide an up-to-date account of the history of the 'Liberal Party' in its heyday between 1830 and 1886. During this time, 'Liberal' governments were in power for a total of thirty-nine years, more than two-thirds of the whole period, and such was the electoral dominance of the Liberals that there were only two occasions – in 1841 and 1874 – when their Conservative opponents succeeded in gaining an overall parliamentary majority. The Liberals, of course, were *the* party of the left-centre, and it was not until the early decades of the twentieth century that their position came to be challenged by the newly created Labour Party. This latter subject, however, has been the one to which the most attention has been devoted by historians since the 1960s: the question of whether the decline of the Liberals and the rise of Labour was inevitable, or else whether it was the result of accidental circumstances, has provoked a strongly contested debate made all the livelier by its obvious implications for our perception of political developments during the 1970s and 1980s. By contrast, the period in which the Liberals enjoyed a more or less unchallenged position as one of the two main parties of State has been comparatively neglected, perhaps because of its lack of modern resonance. In the last decade or so, however, the situation has begun to be remedied with the appearance of a number of important monographs, many of them obviously highly specialised. If it remains surprising that no general survey of the Liberal ascendancy has previously been written, it can at least be said that the project now seems feasible in a way that would not have been true even a few years ago.

Another reason why the Liberal party in the nineteenth century has always been such a forbidding subject for undergraduates is that what was known about the Liberals showed them to be patently a diverse, and often highly fissile, coalition of interests. An air of confusion and uncertainty all too easily enveloped the subject, in consequence. For example, there is still no agreement amongst historians as to precisely when the 'Liberal Party', as such, actually came into existence, and dates as widely separated as 1835, 1846, 1859 and 1868 all have their advocates. (It will already have been noticed that I sometimes find it necessary to refer collectively to the 'Liberals', or the 'Liberal Party', in recognition of the fact that these terms were not universally used by contemporaries throughout the period covered by this book – but one must call them something.) Similarly, there continues to be a great deal of controversy over such a fundamental question as the causes of the great Liberal schism of 1886, which marked the end of the party's long period of political and electoral hegemony.

The inspiration behind this book lies not in a desire to assert that matters are really simpler than previous scholars have made out, but in the belief that it should be possible to unravel the tangled threads of Victorian Liberalism and weave them into a fairly discernible pattern. The approach adopted in this book, therefore, is to identify the various components of the coalition which came together under the umbrella issue of parliamentary reform, in the early 1830s, and to consider their respective ideologies, what they represented in the constituencies, and how they interrelated. It will then be possible to trace the shifts that took place, over time, in the complex equation involving the various groups which have been defined – none of which was entirely homogeneous, as will become clear – and to see how these changes were reflected in the development of Liberal ideology. Central to the whole process will be the assessments of the roles of leaders such as Russell, Palmerston and Gladstone, which will look at the ways in which they related – and sometimes did not relate – to the different elements of the Liberal coalition.

While there is no escaping the real difficulties in comprehending the nature of the nineteenth-century Liberal Party, the effort required can bring its full rewards. The Liberals, after all, succeeded to an extraordinary extent in combining traditional social groups with newer, highly dynamic ones – whether they be Whigs and radicals, landed and industrial interests, or church and chapel – to create a potentially formidable political force. It therefore seems reasonable to argue that, in spite of the problems they frequently encountered, the Liberals operated as a more effective broad coalition of the 'left centre', at least until the 1880s, than the Labour Party has managed to be since the 1920s. For this reason alone, the era of the Liberal ascendancy would seem likely to repay a careful study.

There are two aspects of this book which require a little explanation. First, particular emphasis is placed on the survival of the Whig tradition of aristocratic leadership, a theme that has recently been explored by a number of scholars working in different areas of nineteenth-century politics. The result is an account which places the Whigs at the centre of Liberal politics, rather than merely charting their supposedly inevitable decline in the face of Cobdenite/Chamberlainite radicalism and 'Gladstonian Liberalism'. Secondly, although some space will be devoted to the intellectual influences on Liberal politicians, it should be noted that this book concentrates on the role of 'ideas' in shaping practical politics and political argument, instead of focusing on the abstract theories of intellectuals. Consideration will thus be given, for instance, to the ways in which the Whigs' conception of their own political function was shaped by the writings of Russell and Macaulay, the influence of Bentham's ideas on radical politics during the 1830s, the importance of the ideology of Free Trade in helping to create a new 'Liberal' identity in the 1840s and 1850s, the significance of concerns about 'democracy' as an influence on Liberal politics from the 1860s onwards, and the way that the question of 'imperialism' contributed to the break-up of the Liberal Party in the 1880s.

What will emerge from this history of the Liberal Party is a picture that is undoubtedly complex, but, hopefully, one that students will find fascinating at the same time. This is one way of saying that what makes the subject so interesting, to my own mind, is the fact that the Liberals' political ascendancy, striking as it may seem in retrospect, was rarely an easy and straightforward process, free of perils; and certainly not one that contemporaries would have regarded as inevitable.

1 The Spirit of Reform

Introduction

The crisis over parliamentary reform, in 1830–2, which culminated in the passing of the Great Reform Act, also ushered in a long period of political dominance by what came to be known as the 'Liberal' Party. This dominance was underpinned, electorally, by the consistently strong support for the Liberals in many areas of the country which had benefited greatly from reform. As part of the 1832 settlement in England and Wales, 64 seats were transferred from small English boroughs to larger ones that had previously lacked direct representation in Parliament, including major industrial towns of the north and midlands, such as Manchester, Birmingham, Sheffield and Leeds, and the populous London districts of Tower Hamlets, Lambeth, Finsbury and Marylebone. The uniform £10 household franchise, which applied to all boroughs, old and new, accounted for roughly 100,000 of the newly enfranchised adult males. For a time, in the early 1830s, the appearance was also given – misleadingly as it turned out – that the English counties, which had gained almost as much from redistribution as the large boroughs, and which had more voters, were similarly committed to the party of reform.

It is important not to forget that a separate Reform Act was passed for Scotland, with consequences that were in many ways more dramatic than in the case of England and Wales. Indeed, the Scottish Reform Act can be said to have given that country a representative system for the first time, dismantling the archaic set of regulations that had previously allowed only about 4500 people to vote, and replacing them with new voting qualifications which, although more restrictive than those for England and Wales, nevertheless increased the total electorate to nearly 65,000. Eight seats taken from small English boroughs were redistributed to Scottish burghs, raising the number of Scottish MPs from 45 to 53. In Scotland, too, the reformed electoral system inaugurated a long period of Liberal hegemony, in this case almost as strong in the counties as in the burghs, which was never seriously threatened until late in the nineteenth century.[1]

However, it is also the case that parliamentary reform, in the early 1830s, served as an umbrella issue, sheltering an otherwise disparate group of political forces with varying aspirations and priorities. Aristocratic Whigs, secular radicals, nonconformists, and Irish repealers (many of them Roman Catholics), had all been able to unite in support of reform, as had certain single-issue pressure groups like the slavery abolitionists, who saw reform as a means towards the achievement of their specific objective. But it was not to be expected that such a coalition would prove to be anything other than fragile when it came to dealing with subsequent political problems. It is necessary, therefore, to analyse the main components of the reform coalition, and the ways in which they related to one another, before we can proceed to study the politics of the post-Reform-Act era.

Whigs

It has often been observed that the government formed by Earl Grey, in November 1830, which carried the Great Reform Act, was more aristocratic in its composition than almost any other administration of the nineteenth century. Of the thirteen Cabinet ministers, nine sat in the House of Lords, and the remainder consisted of an Irish peer, the heir to an English peerage, a landed baronet and a major Scottish landowner (Charles Grant, later raised to the peerage as Lord Glenelg). Privately, Grey acknowledged that his instinctive preference was for members of the aristocracy rather than commoners, and indeed he asserted that one of his 'essential objects', in constructing the government, had been 'to show that in these times of democracy and Jacobinism it is possible to find real capacity in the high Aristocracy'.[2]

In political terms, however, this thoroughly aristocratic government was far from being homogeneous in its composition. Four members of the Cabinet, Palmerston, Melbourne, Goderich (later Earl of Ripon) and Grant, were 'Liberal Tories', who had broken from the 'Protestant' leadership of the Duke of Wellington in 1828; yet, paradoxically, a fifth minister, the Duke of Richmond, was an 'ultra Tory', who had been alienated by Wellington's subsequent surrender over Catholic emancipation in 1829. This obvious coalition dimension to Grey's government ought not to obscure the equally important point that those who might more conventionally be described as 'Whigs' did not constitute an entirely distinct group. For instance, the Lord Chancellor, Brougham, and the Earl of Durham, were considered to be much more radical in their leanings than colleagues such as Lansdowne and Carlisle, who had a greater affinity, personally as well as politically, with ex-Tories like Palmerston, with whom they had served in George Canning's short-lived 'broad-bottom' administration of 1827. At a social level, too, there were a number of different circles among the Whigs, the most famous being that centred on Holland House, where Lord Holland, the nephew of Charles James Fox, regarded himself and protégés like Lord John Russell (who entered the Cabinet in June 1831) as representatives of a tradition of 'pure' Whiggery so rigorous in its criteria that few – not even Earl Grey – were considered to be quite up to the required standard.[3]

The absurdly exclusive mentality of the social clique at Holland House suggests a need for scepticism about the use of narrow definitions of the term 'Whig'. Lord John Russell, in published works such as *An Essay on the History of the English Government and Constitution* (1821), may have endeavoured to assert the existence of a continuous commitment to the defence of the liberties of Englishmen and opposition to the threat of arbitrary monarchy, on the part of a group of aristocratic families stretching from Lord Shaftesbury in the late seventeenth century, through Sir Robert Walpole, and down to Fox and his heirs. As with most political myths, this view of the Whig past contained just enough truth in it to avoid being ridiculous. The reality, however, was often a good deal more mundane. In spite of the superficial survival of party terminology, this could not disguise the fact that at certain times, notably in the era of Walpole and Pelham, those calling themselves Whigs had reached a comfortable accommodation with the Crown and became the political 'establishment' of the day. Nor should one exaggerate the continuity of Whiggery in terms of its personnel. Few even of the families associated with the Glorious Revolution of 1688 were entirely constant in their allegiance to the Whig cause thereafter (Russell would not have welcomed any reminder of the political record of his ancestor, the fourth Duke of Bedford, who had supported George III's favourite, Lord Bute, in the 1760s), and some descendants of revolution Whigs, such as Shaftesbury, Newcastle and Argyll, had become staunch Tories by the early nineteenth century. Conversely, some of the great names of nineteenth-century Whiggery were relatively recent converts to the cause: an obvious example is Charles Grey, the future second Earl Grey and Whig Prime Minister, who became politically attached to Charles James Fox in the 1780s, but who was from an old Northumberland family with no previous Whig connection

That there should be such fluidity in the personnel of Whiggery is perhaps not surprising when we remember the political vicissitudes experienced by this party. For instance, *Mr* Charles James Fox – a curious idol indeed for such an aristocratic party! – had seen his following reduced to a small rump in the 1790s, when the so-called Portland Whigs rallied to the government of Pitt the Younger, at a time when the nation seemed to be threatened, both externally and internally, by the contagion of revolutionary ideas emanating from France. A slow process of rebuilding then took place during the 1800s and 1810s, with a number of Portland Whigs, such as Spencer, Minto and Fitzwilliam, retracing their steps, together with fresh recruits to Whiggery, such as the Fortescues and Barings. From this perspective, therefore, the admission of five former Tories into Grey's Cabinet of 1830 represented not a serious dilution of the pure Whig stock, but a further valuable infusion of political blood. Whiggery can only sensibly be defined, then, as a tradition of aristocratic leadership of the reform movement, and should not be considered as the exclusive property of a specific group of aristocratic families.

Perhaps the real significance of the notion of an enduring Whig tradition lay in the way that, whatever its historical inaccuracies, it nevertheless provided the growing body of opposition Whigs during the early nineteenth century with a powerful sense of inherited political identity. According to Whig ideology, as it had been refined by this time, the historic role of the aristocracy had been to act as the guardians of liberty, mediating between the conflicting but equally perilous pretensions of the Crown, on the one hand, and the populace on the other. Only the aristocracy, through their possession of landed property – the true guarantee of independence and therefore of liberty – could effectively resist the encroachments of an arbitrary monarch. It was helpful for the opposition Whigs of the early nineteenth century, whatever the precise history of their own families, to feel themselves part of a proud tradition dating back to the first Whigs of the seventeenth century, who had opposed the sinister designs of the Stuart Kings, Charles II and James II, and whose principles had survived through later generations of Rockingham and Foxite Whigs, who sacrificed their political careers in daring to challenge George III's exercise of the Royal prerogative.

What seems to have gradually changed, after about 1810, was that,

with the incapacitation of George III and the political weakness of the
Prince Regent (later George IV), vices hitherto attributed to the over-
weening ambitions of the Crown were transferred more and more to
that portion of the ruling class which was coming increasingly to be
identified with 'Toryism'. This is not to deny the importance of the
considerable personal antipathy that existed between George IV and
the Whigs, which clearly helped to ensure the latter's continued exclusion from office. It is, nevertheless, indicative of the way Whig attitudes
were developing, that the repressive measures adopted by Lord Liverpool's post-war government, including the suspension of habeas corpus,
the passing of the six acts, and culminating in the notorious Peterloo
massacre of 1819, were considered to be the work not of an arbitrary
monarch, but of entrenched 'Tory' ministers who had shown themselves to be only too ready to violate the liberties of the people in the
selfish interests of the governing elite. By the 1820s, in consequence,
there was a growing consensus, especially amongst the younger generation of Whigs, like Althorp and Russell, that a measure of parliamentary reform was necessary if the existing system of government was to
be saved from itself. Finally, in 1830, even the 'Liberal Tories', and the
'ultra-Tory' Duke of Richmond, joined with the Whigs in the conviction that reform was imperative for the sake of the stability of the
country, and that the government of the Duke of Wellington, in setting
its face against any such measure, itself constituted a threat to the preservation of strong government and social order.

It is now widely accepted by historians that, in passing the Great
Reform Act of 1832, Earl Grey and his colleagues had no intention of
releasing the aristocracy's grip on the levers of political power. While it
was perceived to be necessary to remove the worst abuses of the old
electoral system, such as the 'rotten' boroughs, and to extend the franchise in order to attach the sober, industrious, respectable 'middling
classes' to the constitution, the object was to strengthen and preserve
the existing institutional arrangements rather than to undermine them.
Furthermore, the Whigs' analysis of the world dictated resistance to the
crude ideas of democracy being propagated by some of the more
extreme radicals. The unfettered liberty of the masses was believed to
pose as great a menace to social order as that of a tyrant King, and it
was therefore essential that the people should be encouraged to accept
their natural subordination within an hierarchical social structure. A
sensibly restricted electorate, exhibiting legitimate deference – what the
Whigs liked to call 'rational liberty' – to an aristocracy which had

redeemed itself by the wisdom of its actions, was the object of the
authors of the Great Reform Act. To a young Whig MP like Charles
Wood, Earl Grey's son-in-law, the measure, when first introduced in
March 1831, appeared to be 'an efficient, substantial, anti-democratic,
pro-property measure'.[4]

This characteristically Whig blend of reformism and conservatism is
nicely illustrated by the attitude of Lord Milton (the heir of Earl Fitzwilliam), in the autumn of 1831, when it became certain that the
House of Lords would reject the Reform Bill: 'For my own part I am
ready to take the most decisive measures, viz: *to pay no taxes till the Bill is
passed.*' Interestingly, however, when it came to the possible creation of
new peers in order to force the measure through, Milton's views were
more ambivalent. He confessed that he had 'no objection provided you
can find as many people with 2,000£ a year – my objections are not to
the creation of *peers*, but to the creation of *poor peers*, who are as injur-
ious to the constitution of the H. of Lds as the rotten boroughs are to
that of the H. of Cns'.[5]

In the eyes of the Whigs, aristocratic government was not simply a
one-way process of gradual surrender to pressure from the people: an
authoritarian strand in Whig thinking insisted that the ruling elite possessed its own reservoir of political wisdom, and therefore had its own
vital input to make to the process of government. This continued will
to govern was undoubtedly reinforced by the climate of religious reviv-
alism which had influenced so many younger members of the aristocracy during the early decades of the nineteenth century. Whether it
took the form of evangelicalism, as in the case of Althorp, Milton and
Ebrington, or a more subdued broad-churchmanship of the kind represented by Russell, Duncannon, Hobhouse, Morpeth and others, a
strong sense was conveyed of the moral rejuvenation which so much of
the ruling class was experiencing at this time.[6] For these serious, earnest
young aristocrats (some of whom were liable to be shocked by the irre-
verence and profanity of the older generation of Whigs, such as Grey
and Holland), an essential feature of the parliamentary-reform exercise
was the rendering of those who traditionally wielded power in the State
more worthy of their privileged position.

If anything, it would appear that the reform crisis of 1830–2 actually
encouraged an upsurge of aristocratic candidacies for election to the
House of Commons. More than one hundred individuals connected to
the aristocracy put themselves forward in the reform interest at each of
the three general elections held in these years, including representatives

of 'Grand Whig' families like the Cavendishes, Russells and Howards, but also many members of families who had previously taken little part in politics during the long Tory regime. Aristocrats even enjoyed considerable success in the larger boroughs, and in industrialised county constituencies such as the West Riding, where Lord Morpeth was elected in 1832. Possibly it is true that some of these aristocratic candidates acquired a taste for the rough and tumble of populist electioneering, as in the case of Augustus Moreton, the son of Earl Ducie, who was described as travelling about in Gloucestershire kissing women and shaking hands with paupers. At the very least, there seems to have been a hard-headed appreciation of the importance of members of the aristocracy taking the lead at popular gatherings in order to prevent them from falling into the hands of radicals.[7]

Patronising and self-serving as the Whigs' image of themselves may appear to the modern mind, it has to be remembered that there was, as yet, no appreciation that the country was undergoing a process of continuous economic change, which would ultimately so transform the nature of British society as to undermine the landed basis of the aristocracy's power. The Whigs were certainly conscious of the remarkable growth of commerce and industry that had occurred over recent decades – indeed, they had often been the beneficiaries of it themselves, through their ownership of mineral deposits and urban land – but no-one yet spoke of an 'industrial revolution', with all that that might imply for the long-term position of the aristocracy. This explains why it was that for some years after 1832 the Whigs were able to describe the Great Reform Act as a *final* settlement, a once-for-all adjustment of the system of parliamentary representation designed to give full satisfaction to legitimate grievances.

From the point of view of the maintenance of political stability, at any rate, it seems fair to conclude that Earl Grey's government served as a safety valve for the country at a time of acute agrarian and industrial distress, as well as of political turbulence on the continent of Europe. It was of the utmost significance that in Britain the ruling class was not politically united, and that a substantial minority, including some of the greatest magnates in the land, such as the Duke of Bedford, the Duke of Devonshire, and Earl Fitzwilliam, were sufficiently detached from the system of government that had prevailed up to 1830 to be willing to sponsor a major reform of it.

Nor was it the case that Whig ministers expected the Reform Act of 1832 to mark the complete end of the process of political change in

Britain, however cautiously they might wish to approach the future. Earl Grey's view was that the government and its supporters should endeavour to 'promote and . . . encourage a quiet and moderate course of conduct', while avoiding 'extreme and violent changes'. It was necessary, he felt, to put 'a drag-chain on the wheels, which if impelled with too rapid a motion, it may be impossible to stop, till we are precipitated into ruin'.[8] Clearly, there was no desire to maintain a perpetual state of popular agitation of the sort that had helped the Whigs to force through their Reform Act against the wishes of the King and the House of Lords, but equally there was no expectation that the reform process could realistically be halted entirely.

On the contrary, as the efforts of the leader of the House of Commons, Lord Althorp, during the sessions of 1833 and 1834, illustrate, the momentum for further reforms remained strong and was not always dependent upon extra-parliamentary pressure to sustain it. The Whigs, in other words, showed that they were well abreast of the new economic ideas and social concerns of their age. Althorp was one of a number of Whigs who had been influenced by the writings of the political economists, such as Adam Smith and David Ricardo, and it was ultimately due to his determination that the Poor Law Amendment Act of 1834 was carried. The punitive aspects of this measure, which embodied the principles of less eligibility and an end to outdoor relief, have rendered it notorious in modern minds, but it ought to be remembered that it was enthusiastically supported by most of the leading radicals of the day, like Grote and Hume, as well as by Sir Robert Peel and the bulk of the Conservative opposition. Moreover, the act was passed in the belief that it would serve to invigorate the economy, creating employment and raising wage levels, and that in this way an escape might be found from the dire Malthusian prediction of a crisis of over-population. Althorp's attachment to the principles of political economy was not, in any case, dogmatic, and it was he who was primarily responsible for the Factory Act of 1833 (often referred to as 'Althorp's act'), which imposed restrictions on the employment of young children. It was also largely through Althorp's initiative that the system of government grants for elementary education was introduced in the same year, reflecting the growing concern about the insufficient provision of school places. In the case of the abolition of slavery throughout the British Empire, also implemented in 1833, the government clearly was influenced by an extra-parliamentary campaign but, equally, Althorp's own motives seem to have been chiefly humanitarian. As Althorp's record suggests, the Whigs were possessed of certain genuine ideological principles, as well as a healthy share of pragmatism and humanitarian concern, and their conduct cannot be dismissed as purely reflexive, responding only to pressure from without.[9]

Superficially, Grey and Althorp, the two leading figures in the government of 1830–34, could hardly have presented more contrasting personalities. Grey was a man prone to extreme fluctuations of mood: unquestionably one of the outstanding orators of his age, he thrived on the praise that this could bring; but he was equally liable to periods of deep pessimism, manifested most famously in his virtual abnegation of all leadership during the politically inauspicious 1820s. To describe Grey as an 'Olympian figure' would be a proper use of that clichéd phrase. Althorp, too, acquired a remarkable degree of authority as a parliamentarian, but in his case this was achieved not through eloquence or outstanding debating talents, but because he embodied the sort of personal characteristics that were so appreciated by the House of Commons as an assembly. Physically he was stout, pot-bellied, and with a reddened complexion, and above all he had an honest face – altogether a typical specimen of the foxhunting squire (which indeed he also was). Personally, his manners were straightforward, 'manly', kind-hearted, conciliatory and humorous: it was his obvious frankness and simplicity, and absence of pretentiousness, that was so appealing. In spite of their temperamental differences, however, the crucial quality that both Grey and Althorp brought to public life was a reputation for absolute integrity and disinterestedness. It was well known, and a matter for admiration, that they had taken office reluctantly, and out of a strong sense of public duty. Each in his own way embodied the finest aristocratic virtues of 'character' and 'honour', something that was still valued, and valid, long after 1832.[10]

Radicals[11]

The general election held late in 1832, once the changes enacted by the Whigs were in operation, produced an overwhelming majority for the supporters of the Reform Act, who filled something in the order of 500 out of the 658 seats in the new House of Commons. However, while the first edition of *Dod's Parliamentary Companion*, published in 1833, shows that the majority of these MPs professed an attachment to 'Whig principles', and a willingness generally to give ministers their confidence, there remained a considerable number who clearly could not be regarded as automatic adherents to Earl Grey's government. This was particularly apparent in relation to the question of further parliamentary reform. *Dod* listed 130 MPs as 'reformers', a label which denoted the feeling that the principles of the Reform Act 'might with advantage be extended', and 12 other MPs seem to have held similar views although they were given no political label. A further 24 MPs, described as 'radical reformers', were deemed to be more emphatic in their belief that the Whigs' measure was insufficient. Interestingly, a separate estimate by the Government chief whip yielded a broadly similar result, reckoning on 34 confirmed radicals and 123 'Men mostly agreeing with Althorp in opinion . . . but upon whom we cannot depend on so entirely to sacrifice their own opinions.'[12]

As these figures suggest, it is impossible to categorise politicians into precise groups, but it seems reasonable to suppose that a figure of between 150 and 160 may be taken as a rough guide to the parliamentary dimensions of what was a very broad spectrum of 'radical' opinion. (Just how broad this spectrum must have been is also indicated by the fact that *Dod* listed another 51 MPs as 'moderate reformers', although no definition was provided of what these men stood for.) The impulse for reform, after all, emanated from a number of sources. There was an established tradition of popular radicalism, dating back to the eighteenth century, and two prominent 'democrats', William Cobbett and Henry Hunt, were among those returned to the House of Commons in 1832, although both men were near the end of their lives and they made little impact at Westminster. (That so few MPs of their kind were elected is a good illustration of the fact that no dramatic change in the social composition of the House of Commons occurred as a result of the Reform Act – the 1832 elections confirming, in Althorp's view, that 'the people will not choose Blackguards'.[13]) It is quite likely, on the other hand, that some advocates of further reform were simply being carried along on the momentary tide of excitement in the constituencies, and did not have deeply held convictions on the matter.

At the forefront of this diverse body of reforming opinion we can nevertheless identify a group of 'Philosophic radicals', many of whom had been personally associated with the philosopher Jeremy Bentham (1748–1832) during the 1820s, and who were to give to the cause of reform the articulate expression and intellectual distinction which it possessed in the decade that followed. A gallery of fascinating personalities includes Sir William Molesworth and Charles Buller, both Cornish landowners, George Grote, a wealthy London banker, John Arthur Roebuck, a lawyer, T. Perronet Thompson, a retired army General, H. G. Ward, a newspaper proprietor, and William Ewart, Joseph Hume and Henry Warburton, all of whom had been merchants (the latter was also the proprietor of a lunatic asylum). Inspired by Bentham's utilitarian philosophy, – a rationalist system of thought based on the belief that the value to a community of its political, social and legal institutions could be judged scientifically, by the extent to which they promoted human happiness, – these radicals were therefore confident in their contention that man-made solutions to the reform or design of such institutions were readily attainable. Accordingly, these heirs to the legacy of the eighteenth-century 'age of reason' were impatient in their rejection of conservative doctrines derived from an unquestioning respect for the 'prescriptive' claims of established institutional arrangements.

It would be artificial to seek to present a clearly defined 'programme' supported by all of the philosophic radicals, let alone by the whole of the heterogeneous body of radicals in parliament, but it is still possible to point to certain key issues which formed part of a widely held radical analysis of the shortcomings of post-reform society in Britain.

An immediate focus was provided by the principle of household suffrage for parliamentary elections, in place of the £10 borough and forty-shilling county franchises laid down by the Great Reform Act. This proposal had the advantage that it could be supported equally by those who only wished to see a limited expansion of the electorate, as well as by those, like Grote and Roebuck, whose ultimate ideal was universal manhood suffrage. Whether representation was to be accorded to all adult males, or only to the heads of households, the belief was that only a system in which all individuals (or alternatively all families) were represented, could ensure that there was an identity of interests between MPs and the community. In addition, there was widespread acceptance of the need to further increase MPs' accountability to their constituents by repealing the Septennial Act of 1716, which required general elections only every seven years, and during the 1833 session of parliament a resolution by Charles Tennyson in favour of a three-year limit was only defeated by 213 votes to 164, with the Whig Ministers – not for the last time – being rescued from an embarrassing defeat by the assistance of the Tories.[14] Above all, however, in the eyes of many radicals, was the necessity for the secret ballot in elections, as a means of liberating voters from improper influence, and this issue was to be particularly associated with the name of George Grote, who raised the matter regularly in parliament, attracting 106 votes in 1833 and 155 by 1837.

For the hard-core of philosophic radicals, at least, such modifications of the electoral system were regarded as merely a prelude to a wide-ranging assault on the numerous bastions of a privileged ruling elite, including the House of Lords, the Church of England and the military establishment. The aristocratic domination of government, indeed, was considered to be at the root of all the evils that the radicals sought to eradicate. Whether the problem was extravagant government expenditure, partiality in law making, the involvement of Britain in unnecessary foreign wars, or the corrupting effects of the extensive system of government patronage, all could be attributed to the pervasive influence of the aristocracy within the various branches of the State. The most immediate impact made by the radicals was in the area of government expenditure. As Grote had put it in his election address to the City of London, in 1832, 'The oligarchical interest hitherto predominant in our legislature have kept up an exorbitant scale of public expenditure, fruitful in corrupt influence, and oppressive as well as demoralising to the nation.'[15] The 1833 session of parliament was therefore notable for a series of assaults on the Whig government by economically minded radicals like Joseph Hume and Edward Ruthven, who enjoyed some success in forcing reductions in the number of pensions and sinecures paid for by parliament.[16]

Central to the fulfilment of the aims of the philosophic radicals was the provision of universal elementary education, which would ideally be offered on a secular basis in order to remove the pernicious influence of the Church of England. Education was an essential precondition for the creation of a rational, independently minded citizenry of the sort dreamed of by the radicals. Through 'the irresistible extension of knowledge', as General Perronet Thompson saw it, the people would gradually shake off the antiquated institutions which continued to hold them down – in Thompson's own view, the end result of this process would be the creation of a republic. Whatever the eventual outcome, the prospect was held out of a continual improvement in the state of British society. In the words of William Ewart, writing in 1837, 'the prevailing policy of this great Country must be, to render its laws and institutions less feudal and oligarchical than they are at present, as society rises more and more in advance of those institutions'. This is not to suggest that the radicals anticipated an eventual state of complete social equality; but at least the extension of education would, as Thomas Duncombe saw it, make the working men better workers.[17]

Despite their claims to be the true representatives of 'the people', it has to be remembered that the philosophic radicals were influenced not by the concept of natural law, and therefore of the inalienable rights of man, but by a purely utilitarian analysis of the need for a broader representative system. Universal (or household) suffrage was deemed necessary as it seemed the only way of securing good government, not because it was intrinsically a good thing in itself. Furthermore, most of the prominent radicals of the 1830s had backgrounds in either landed society, the professions, or commerce, and they tended to be strongly metropolitan in their outlook: their experience of the growing manufacturing areas, or of the conditions of the ordinary people, were inevitably slight. The significance of all this is that it encouraged the radicals to adopt an elitist view of their role as the natural leaders and instructors of the populace, and it is revealing, for instance, that they later reacted with extreme hostility and contempt towards the pretensions of Chartism, and the style of independent, extra-parliamentary agitation for which that movement stood.[18] A somewhat cold, abstract personality like that of the scholarly Grote seemed concerned only with promoting efficiency in government, rather than being actuated by any real sympathy for ordinary human beings and their sufferings. According to Grote's vision of a rational system of government:

> Legislators . . . must be men of first-rate intelligence, whose discussions would rectify and elevate the whole tone of political reasoning throughout the Country – men in whom the accident of birth and connection would be eclipsed by the splendour of their personal qualities, identified in heart and spirit with the happiness of the middling classes, and no less qualified by laborious completion of their own mental training, to serve as an example and an incentive to aspiring youth.[19]

The philosophic radicals frequently expressed contempt for the Whigs, an effete class of aristocratic legislators whose inevitable demise was looked forward to so that there might at last be a clear-cut battle between Tories and radicals: a confrontation between darkness and light was preferable to stumbling around in the confusing half-light of Whiggery.[20] And yet, ironically, the radicals were to prove ineffective in parliament, in the long-term, largely because of their own anti-party instincts. The very concept of 'party' was associated, in the radical mind, with the rival and equally corrupt aristocratic factions, Whigs and Tories, and the object of reform was therefore seen to be the creation of a purer political system in which there was no place for parties. Pinning their faith in the salutary effect of the spread of enlightened, 'progressive' opinions, which would naturally come to prevail in parliament, only limited attempts were made to organise a group of radicals in the House of Commons. In any case, a man such as Grote, to whom many looked as a leader for the radicals, was temperamentally unsuited to the task. Their strongly metropolitan character and anti-party attitudes combined to produce the impression that the philosophic radicals were a rather dilettante set of politicians.

Furthermore, the reality of the situation in many constituencies clearly called for co-operation between local Whigs and radicals rather than a fight to the death. The maintenance of a united Whig–radical front to resist the Tories was encouraged by the prevalence of two-member constituencies within the post-1832 electoral system, which meant that it made sense to run, in harness, candidates from the Whig and radical sections of a community in order to maximise their support. Such co-operation was not always easily achieved, and relations in particular constituencies were liable to break down from time to time, but it remained an important feature of politics in major provincial towns such as Manchester, Leeds, Birmingham and Leicester, as well as in industrialised county constituencies such as the West Riding of Yorkshire, where a balance had to be struck between urban and rural interests.[21] In fact, the preoccupation of many local businessmen with their own affairs often led to the representation even of urban constituencies being left in the hands of members of the traditional ruling class, who possessed the leisure and the financial independence which enabled them to assume the heavy responsibilities of an MP: thus, in Halifax, the representation remained in the hands of a local landowner, Sir Charles Wood, throughout the political vicissitudes of the period 1832–65, while in Bradford, the four MPs who represented the constituency between 1832 and 1841 were all 'Anglican landed gentlemen'.[22]

Nonconformists

Another important component of the coalition of forces that had gathered under the Whig umbrella, during the political crisis of 1830–2, was hardly represented at all – in terms of personnel, at least – in the reformed House of Commons. No more than a handful of protestant nonconformists were elected to parliament during the 1830s, and yet no-one was in any doubt as to the political impact made by the chapels in the wake of the so-called 'evangelical revival' of the late eighteenth and early nineteenth centuries. It is true that the most dynamic of the nonconformist denominations, the Wesleyan Methodists, tended to be rather conservative in its general outlook, and many of its members eschewed involvement in politics altogether, but the early decades of the nineteenth century had also witnessed a rapid growth in the membership of two of the older sects, the Baptists and the Congregationalists, who, along with smaller but tightly knit groups like the Quakers and Unitarians, had a much stronger association with political radicalism. Even under the pre-1832 electoral system, as recent research has demonstrated, the growing power of nonconformity was making itself felt in some of the more open constituencies,[23] and by the late 1820s it was sufficiently well organised at a national level, through the Committee of Protestant Dissenting Deputies (in which the Wesleyans also participated), to be able to campaign successfully for the repeal of the Test and Corporation Acts – those seventeenth-century penal statutes which had excluded nonconformists, in principle at least, from holding public office.

Once the repeal of the Test and Corporation Acts had been secured, the Dissenting Deputies joined in the agitation for parliamentary reform, which was seen as an essential instrument for securing decisive action on an issue long dear to the hearts of nonconformists, the abolition of negro slavery. Beyond this, however, there remained an agenda for further constitutional reforms, which reflected a continuing sense of grievance at the surviving forms of discrimination suffered by nonconformists – untouched by the largely symbolic gesture of abolishing the Test and Corporation Acts – and which the enhanced electoral power conferred on nonconformity by the Great Reform Act, ensured would be brought to the forefront of politics. This agenda, articulated by a re-formed United Committee of Protestant Dissenting Deputies (which did not include the Wesleyans), in a manifesto published in May 1833, raised such questions as the exclusion of nonconformists from the ancient universities, the Anglican monopoly over the registration of births, marriages and deaths, and the requirement that nonconformists must contribute towards the upkeep of the Established Church by means of the Church rate.[24] To some nonconformists, at least, what lay at the end of the road was the whole question of the status of the Anglican Church as the Established Church of the nation. As we shall see later, the Whigs' attempts to address some of these nonconformist grievances were to colour much of the politics of the 1830s.

The picture that emerges from case studies of the new industrial towns is one in which the electoral impact of nonconformity was magnified by the limited provisions of the Great Reform Act, and by the slowness of the transition to large-scale manufacturing production. Levels of adult male enfranchisement were usually between 10 and 20 percent, and the proportion of 'working class' voters within the total electorate was very small, often no more than about 5 per cent in the 1830s.[25] Evidence from surviving pollbooks, which were kept in the days of open voting and often provide details of the occupations of the electorate, suggest that 'Liberal' support was strongest among groups like craftsmen and retailers, while merchants and manufacturers tended to divide more evenly between the Liberal and Conservative sides (the 'professions' and the drink interest were more inclined towards the Conservatives).[26] Thus, in Bradford, where a Reform Society was founded in 1835, the original 'directors' included '33 worsted merchants and manufacturers, 9 shopkeepers, 2 gentlemen, 2 schoolmasters, 2 innkeepers, a journalist, whitesmith, upholsterer, mechanic, bookkeeper, shoemaker, machine-maker, ironmonger and architect'.[27] Furthermore, it was precisely amongst such people that nonconformity was likely to be strongest, for, as recent research has emphasised, it is a mistake to associate the spread of religious dissent with the expansion of an urban, factory proletariate, trained into docile habits by the 'opiate' of religion. On the contrary, those attracted by nonconformity were more likely to be craftsmen, tradesmen and artisans, rather than unskilled factory hands, men for whom religious dissent was an expression of social independence from traditional forms of social discipline.[28] This reinterpretation of the character of nonconformity has gone hand-in-hand with an increasing awareness, by historians, of the gradual nature of the economic and social changes brought about by the 'Industrial Revolution'. It is now appreciated that large-scale, factory-based production did not become the norm in most industries until late in the nineteenth century. In an environment where small-scale producers and retailers still flourished, so too did nonconformity and a political commitment to the 'Liberal' cause. The general rule seems to have been that nearly all nonconformists, as in the case of Leeds, were 'Liberals' of one shade or another, and that many members of local Liberal elites, for example in Bradford, were nonconformists – usually belonging to the older, more radical sects.[29]

Nor is it only to the new industrial boroughs that we need to look for the nonconformist voter. Bearing in mind the point that industrial production was not typically based upon large-scale factory units, and that many electors in the new boroughs were craftsmen, tradesmen and artisans, it is important not to exaggerate the differences between these boroughs and other, much older ones, which we do not normally associate with the 'Industrial Age'. In fact, the more widely diffused property within the older boroughs meant that although their populations were smaller, they contained a disproportionate number of £10 householders able to qualify for the franchise. Thus, the 29 English boroughs with the largest registered electorates, of 2000 or more, consisted not only of the likes of Manchester, Leeds and Sheffield, but also of Bath, Chester, Exeter, Norwich, Worcester and York – towns which often had a firm tradition of nonconformity, particularly among their supposedly 'pre-industrial' craftsmen and tradesmen. Similarly, with the 35 English boroughs of 'intermediate' size, having registered electorates of between 1000 and 2000, we find such places as Bedford, Cambridge, Colchester, Gloucester, Maidstone, Yarmouth, Shrewsbury, Ipswich and Brighton, rubbing shoulders with Bradford, Stockport, Sunderland, Salford, Bolton, Oldham and Wolverhampton.

It is also important not to overlook the smaller English boroughs, those with registered electorates of under 1000, which were, after all, the most numerous category of boroughs in the post-1832 system. Whereas the largest boroughs returned 58 MPs, and the intermediate boroughs elected 63 MPs, the small boroughs accounted for 202 MPs. Many of these small boroughs, of course, were those that had survived the changes made by the Great Reform Act, but they were by no means always under the total control of local landowners, and the newly enfranchised £10 householders sometimes contained a significant nonconformist element, for the same reasons that applied in the larger boroughs. This was true of Tavistock, in Devon, nominally a proprietary borough of the Duke of Bedford, but a constituency where, in practice, it was found to be expedient to divide the representation (it was still a two-member seat) between a nominee of the Duke and a more radical Liberal acceptable to the townspeople, who was willing to espouse a number of nonconformist causes such as the abolition of Church rates. The following picture of a small Liberal constituency relates to a market town in Oxfordshire:

The leaders of the Banbury Liberals were drawn entirely from the town's middle class: attorneys, a family of bankers, wool merchants, grocers, bankers, chemists, drapers, tavernkeepers, printers and ironmongers. Most of the shopkeepers were leading men in their trades, with shops on the principal streets. All of the principal religious denominations in the town were included, though the proportion of Nonconformists was higher than in the town as a whole.

In the southern coastal town of Poole, in Dorset, one of the few small constituencies for which detailed information regarding voting behaviour and religious affiliation is available (relating to the period 1841–65), it emerges that the various nonconformist sects constituted a 'sizeable minority' of the population, that most nonconformist voters were in such characteristic occupational groups as retailers and craftsmen (i.e. 'respectables'), and that their voting behaviour shows an overwhelming preference – 82 per cent – for the Liberals.[30]

One of the recurring themes of this book will be the remarkable social gulf that separated what came to be known as the 'Liberal Party', at Westminster, from the interests and forces in the country which it purported to represent. Such a gulf would not have been sustainable, however, unless there had been genuine bonds of sympathy between the parliamentarians and the electors. The large body of radicals in the reformed House of Commons contained few nonconformists, and some radicals, such as Grote and Roebuck, were actually freethinkers; but the injustices inflicted upon a group in society, because of their religious beliefs, by a selfish and corrupt 'Establishment' which was already a target for radical criticism anyway, naturally encouraged a certain community of sentiment. Equally, a religious creed which stressed the direct relationship between man and God, rejecting the interposition of such human agencies as a Pope or a State-controlled Church, was intrinsically individualistic and potentially even democratic in its political implications (particularly through the evangelical emphasis upon the possibility of *all men* finding salvation, not just the 'elect' few), and it therefore fitted in well with the 'Liberal' concern for civil as well as religious liberty.

More importantly, perhaps, the nonconformist cause made a valuable contribution to the broadening of the Whigs' political identity. The fact that, historically speaking, the Whigs felt themselves to be victims of the unrestricted prerogative power of the Crown, had engendered a sense of alienation from the political 'Establishment' during the half-century before 1830. Ostracised from power themselves, this experience doubtless encouraged the Whigs to identify with and champion the cause of other social groups suffering from similar disabilities. The notion of a consistent Whig attachment to the cause of religious liberty, since the seventeenth century, may have been another figment of Lord John Russell's imagination, but his success in moving for the repeal of the Test and Corporation Acts, in 1828, was easily represented as a reaffirmation of what the Whigs would look back upon as an unswerving support for the rights of nonconformists. In this way, the commitment to 'religious liberty' assisted in the process by which the Whigs gradually moved away from their eighteenth-century vendetta against the Crown, and obsession with 'secret influences' behind the throne, and towards a wider concern with the civil rights of other groups in the nation, which were being denied by an incorrigible Tory 'Establishment'.

A quite different situation existed in Scotland, however, and the link between Whiggery and nonconformity there requires a separate description. In Scotland, of course, the Established Church was the Presbyterian Kirk, which enjoyed a status that was in certain respects more favourable than that of the Church of England (it had, for example, its own annual General Assembly, with powers to legislate for the Kirk). Nevertheless, there was growing support in the country for religious groups which, although themselves Presbyterians, were in dissent with the Established Kirk for reasons which were political – mainly to do with the question of the control of lay patronage – rather than theological. By 1839 the main dissenting group, the United Secession Church, had a membership of over 250,000, roughly equivalent to one-tenth of the total Scottish population, and although in 1835 only one Scottish MP was a dissenter, the electoral reform of 1832 had undoubtedly made the dissenters a significant force in many constituencies. The main dissenting grievances focused on their exclusion from teaching posts in schools and universities, and on their liability to the annuity tax (the equivalent of the English Church rate, levied in certain burghs including Edinburgh). They were also strongly opposed to any increase in the State endowment of the Established Kirk for the purpose of building new churches, something that was urgently desired by many members of the Kirk. This paradoxical situation, in which a State Church was opposed by a dissenting Church of the same religious denomination, placed the Whig governments of the 1830s in an invidious position, as they had no wish to alienate either side. The inevitable result was a paralysis of government policy, with the Whigs being unwilling to make concessions to the dissenters, but equally unable to give the Kirk the extra financial resources that it required.[31]

Irish Repealers

The broadening of the Whigs' perspective during the early part of the nineteenth century, which we have already noted in relation to English nonconformity, was also influenced by the passing of the Act of Union between Great Britain and Ireland, in 1800, and the consequent problem arising from the persistence within the new United Kingdom of discriminatory legislation against Roman Catholics. Indeed, the cry of 'Catholic Emancipation' was to provide a common cause for all shades of Whig opinion thereafter, supplying the essential cohesion, for example, for the alliance of Foxites and Grenvillites after 1801. Following the Tory capitulation over Catholic Emancipation, in 1829, the leader of the Catholic Association in Ireland, Daniel O'Connell, proceeded to throw his energies into the general movement for parliamentary reform. He did so, however, because he saw the Reform Act as a means towards the fulfilment of his ultimate goal, the repeal of the Act of Union and the restoration of Ireland's own parliament. At the general election of 1832, according to *Dod's Parliamentary Companion*, 41 MPs committed to O'Connell's programme of repeal – a few of them expressing certain reservations – were returned by Irish constituencies. The cause gained vital added momentum, at this time, from the mounting resentment felt by the Irish people towards the Anglican Church of Ireland, an alien institution in a predominantly Catholic land, whose right to levy tithes and a Church cess (or rate) provided an obvious target for O'Connell and his followers, and a useful leverage in the political battle for repeal of the Union.

Another recurring theme of this book will be the disturbing, dissonant effect of the 'Irish Question' on the evolving 'Liberal' politics of Great Britain. Quite distinct in its economic, social, religious and cultural identity, Catholic Ireland was to pose an enduring challenge to the 'Liberal' values which predominated in Britain, contributing all too frequently to the disruption of Liberal governments. In fact, none of the components of British Liberalism, analysed above, was able to relate easily, or with very much sympathy, to the Irish people and their grievances, once the question of Catholic Emancipation had been dealt with. The roots of the difficulty lay partly in the economic back-wardness of Ireland, with all its attendant problems; but more impor-tant was the fact that the Irish cultural identity was shaped by a force which was considered to be fundamentally 'illiberal'. It was the Cath-olicism of the Irish, the fact that they were in thrall to a 'reactionary' and alien religious potentate, that so repelled British Liberals, confirm-ing and reinforcing the deep-seated racial contempt which had for long characterised the relationship between the two islands. Thus, while it is true that a minority of radicals, some forty or fifty in number,[32] opposed the coercive measures applied to Ireland by the Whig govern-ments in the early 1830s, regarding them as an unacceptable manifes-tation of the power of the State impinging on the liberties of individuals, this did not mean that there was any real sympathy for the Irish people themselves behind the radicals' standpoint. The underlying hostility of most radicals towards O'Connell and the Repeal Party was to become clear early in 1835, when an attempt to form a party of seventy or eighty radicals, independent of the Whigs, fell through owing to an unwillingness to accept Hume's and Warburton's view that O'Connell should be included in their number. As one radical MP put it, 'I could not usefully belong to a *sub-division* of the Liberals which numbered O'Connell among its members, however willing I may be to co-operate with him and his immediate friends as part of the *general body*.'[33] Such sentiments were likely to be even more pronounced in the case of the nonconformists, who, naturally enough, on religious grounds, tended to be antagonistic towards a party inspired by Popery. The support given by the Committee of Protestant Dissenting Deputies to the cause of Catholic Emancipation, in the late 1820s, as part of its wider campaign for the removal of all religious disabilities, therefore proved to be a sign of an ephemeral rather than an enduring alliance between British nonconformity and Irish Catholicism.

With regard to the Whigs, the social unrest in Ireland during the early 1830s, focusing on opposition to the payment of tithes, revealed the limits to their libertarian ideology. The problem was not that the Whigs were unwilling to embark upon major reforming legislation, as is evident from the Irish Church Temporalities Act of 1833, an important measure which streamlined the Church of Ireland and abolished the Church cess. But an exasperated government discovered that its efforts had done nothing to reconcile the Irish people. In their darker moods, this realisation confirmed the feeling amongst Whig leaders like Grey and Althorp that the Irish were not really fit for liberty. Indeed,

Althorp had expressed the opinion, sometime earlier, that 'The population of Ireland is not sufficiently advanced in civilization to make it desirable that they should have any very great preponderance in the Legislative Assembly of a highly civilized State.'[34] Confronted with a threat to property in the form of a campaign against the payment of tithes, Grey's government responded with what was to become a familiar formula of repression combined with gestures of conciliation. While the Whigs were prepared to recognise the differentness of the Irish, and the need for special legislation to deal with their problems, which would not have been considered appropriate for Britain, the 'Irish Question' was never comprehended as one involving a separate nationality with a legitimate right to recognition. For the Whigs, the 'Question' was perceived instead in terms of how best to integrate Ireland more fully into the United Kingdom, and consequently the need to maintain law and order (what the Whigs would have considered to be 'normality') was usually found to be the most pressing requirement of government. It would be easy to condemn the Whigs for displaying blind stupidity towards the problems of Ireland, but it should be remembered that Irish nationalism itself, throughout the nineteenth century, displayed considerable ambiguity in its attitudes towards the connection with Britain.

The Crises of 1834–5

Disputes within Earl Grey's government over the conduct of Irish policy were sufficiently serious to provoke a major crisis in May 1834, the repercussions of which were to do more than anything else to shape the course of British politics for the remainder of the decade. The resignation of four Cabinet ministers, Stanley, Graham, Richmond and Ripon, was in fact the culmination of a long-running battle between Stanley and Lord John Russell, concerning the direction of Irish policy, which was clearly inseparable from the personal competition for supremacy between these two rising stars of the Whig front-bench in the House of Commons. At issue was the principle of whether the State was entitled to appropriate for lay purposes (such as education) any surplus revenues of the Established Church of Ireland, something that had been vaguely embodied in clause 147 of the Irish Church Temporalities Bill of 1833, but subsequently dropped in order to ease the bill's passage through the House of Lords. However, Russell had insisted on reasserting the principle of lay appropriation in a dramatic intervention during the parliamentary debate on the Irish Tithes Bill of 1834, a move which finally provoked the breach with Stanley and his associates. There were undoubtedly genuine ideological reasons for the resultant Cabinet split: the Stanleyites were all High Churchmen, on the more moderate wing of the government generally, who had accepted the redistribution of revenues *within* the Irish Church involved in the bill of 1833, but could not agree to the confiscation of any of its revenues for non-Church purposes; whereas Russell represented a more thoroughly erastian, broad-church position, which regarded lay appropriation as a useful opportunity to pursue a conciliatory approach towards the Roman Catholics, perhaps eventually leading to State endowment of the Catholic clergy. As will be seen, however, the significance of lay appropriation was to be more symbolic than practical, and it ultimately served as a device by which Russell and a clique of like-minded colleagues sought to preserve their right to guide the religious policies of the governments of Grey and, from July 1834, his successor, Lord Melbourne.

The alarm created by the Irish Church question also extended to a higher quarter, and it was to be the underlying cause of King William IV's 'dismissal' – it amounted to that – of Melbourne's administration in November 1834. Melbourne's proposal that Russell should replace Althorp (who had succeeded his father as Earl Spencer) as leader of the House of Commons, was objected to by the King on the ground of Russell's particular identification with the principle of lay appropriation, and the Prime Minister's consequent offer of his ministry's resignation was readily accepted. Sir Robert Peel was then commissioned to form an alternative government, in spite of his hopeless numerical disadvantage in the House of Commons. Aided by the King's willingness to grant a dissolution of parliament, Peel and his followers gained about 100 seats at the general election held early in 1835, marking a substantial recovery by what was coming to be known as the Conservative Party. Especially noticeable was the fact that the Conservatives recovered a slight majority in the English counties (73 seats out of 144), as well as making gains in English boroughs of all sizes. Even in the largest boroughs the Conservatives captured a few seats, though, with the exception of Leeds, these tended to be in the older, more established urban centres such as Bristol, York, Exeter, Newcastle and Hull. No doubt this Conservative revival was due in large part to a natural restoration of traditional electoral influences once the turmoil of the parliamentary-reform crisis had subsided,[35] but this process was certainly assisted by the opportunity afforded the Conservatives to capitalise on the Whigs' association with the various 'subversive' doctrines of the radicals, nonconformists and O'Connellites, which could be presented as threatening the privileges of the Established Churches of England and Ireland.

In spite of these considerable gains, Peel was still unable to command a reliable parliamentary majority, and by April 1835 he had been forced from office after suffering a series of defeats in the House of Commons, compelling a reluctant monarch to take back the Ministers whose services he had dispensed with only five months earlier. The restoration of Melbourne's government, with Russell now as Home Secretary and clearly the dominant figure in the Commons, was facilitated by the meetings held at Lichfield House, in February–March 1835, at which Whig, radical and O'Connellite MPs agreed to co-operate in order to secure the removal of Peel. This so-called 'Lichfield House compact' has been described by Norman Gash as 'in fact the point of origin for the Victorian Liberal party'.[36] But we should be careful not to exaggerate the extent of the new-found unity of purpose amongst the various 'Liberal' groups, for the 'compact' was confined solely to an agreement to combine so as to turn out Peel's ministry. Beyond the decisions to oppose the re-election of the Speaker of the Commons, Spring Rice, and to support Russell's motions on the Irish Church question, including a reaffirmation of the principle of lay appropriation, no pledges were made by Russell – the only Whig leader to address the three Lichfield House meetings – regarding the policies of a future Whig government.[37] In so far as anyone made real concessions it was O'Connell who, in spite of being kept at arm's length by the Whigs, promised to help reinstate them in power without receiving any firm guarantees about the treatment of Ireland other than the restated commitment to lay appropriation. And yet, during the debate on the Address in the House of Commons, O'Connell declared that he was shelving his demand for the repeal of the Act of Union.

It could be argued, therefore, that King William, by dismissing Melbourne's government in November 1834, helped to provoke a false appearance of unity between the Whigs and their radical and Irish allies, as the Whigs were forced to enter into formal communications with these groups in order to secure a return to power. Certainly it is the case that Peel regretted the King's action, believing that, given more time, the Whig government would have disintegrated as a result of its own internal divisions and quarrels, a process which had, after all, led already to the resignation of the Stanleyites in May, and to the retirement of a despairing Grey in July. Instead, the King's clumsy use of the Royal prerogative had stung even moderate Whig leaders like Melbourne and Lansdowne into accepting the necessity of some sort of understanding with the radicals and O'Connellites in the House of Commons. However, while from a long-term perspective the Lichfield House meetings appear to mark the beginnings of the 'Liberal Party', it can only be said that the 'birth' was a dangerously premature one, and that it was not at all clear at the time that the infant would survive.

The Second Melbourne Administration, 1835–41

During the months preceding the formation of Melbourne's second ministry, Lord John Russell had been anxious to ensure that the replacement for Peel's government should consist of the 'Whiggest part of the Whigs',[38] and it is certainly true that Melbourne's government was even less 'radical' in its composition than his previous one. Lord Brougham, for instance, always an uncomfortable colleague at the best of times, and one who had gained fresh notoriety through a series of inebriated public speeches during the summer of 1834, was excluded from office by Melbourne, as was the tempestuous Lord Durham ('Radical Jack'), a potentially serious thorn in the Prime Minister's side, whom Melbourne was relieved to be able to despatch to St Petersburg, as British Ambassador, shortly afterwards. More importantly, in the eyes of Whigs like Earl Grey, and also of the King, it became clear that Melbourne had no intention of offering O'Connell a seat in the Cabinet, as had previously been rumoured.[39]

In a reassuring letter to Grey, Russell expressed his confidence that he and his colleagues would be able to 'hold our own Whig course'.[40] We are surely entitled to suppose, however, that what Russell really meant was that the ministry would pursue the policies which he had in mind for it. Clearly, the constitutional crisis of 1834–5 had done much to enhance Russell's standing amongst the Whigs, while at the same time it had weakened the position of his main rival, Stanley. Not only had the divisive question of lay appropriation been at the heart of the dispute with the Crown, but it had also provided the basis for the Whigs' restoration to power, as it was the defeat on Russell's motion reaffirming the principle of lay appropriation that had finally brought down Peel's government. In the heated circumstances of the time, lay appropriation, an issue on which most other leading Whigs had hitherto been lukewarm, became a focal point for all those who considered themselves to be victims of the Royal prerogative. Whether consciously or otherwise, Russell, by reasserting the primacy of this issue, was able to perpetuate the rift with Stanley and his followers, rendering increasingly unlikely that rapprochement which many other Whigs, such as Grey, would have been glad to see take place, and ensuring that the dividing line in politics remained firmly drawn in a place that best suited Russell's own prospects.

Irish policy was one sphere in which the hand of Russell was particularly apparent in the years that followed. His influence was strengthened by the presence in Dublin, as Lord Lieutenant, of one of his closest political allies, Lord Mulgrave (later Marquess of Normanby), and in the Cabinet, of another friend, Lord Duncannon, an Irishman who had previously acted as a line of communication between the Whigs and O'Connell. Thus, during the 1836 and 1837 sessions of parliament, renewed efforts were made to settle the tithe problem, although the insistence that these bills should contain a provision for the lay appropriation of surplus Church revenues ensured their defeat in the Conservative-dominated House of Lords. The Whigs' persistence with this controversial principle, in spite of the fact that O'Connell himself had made it clear, in 1836, that he no longer attached great importance to the matter, tends to confirm the suspicion that lay appropriation had become primarily a political symbol designed to preserve an insuperable obstacle to any reconciliation with Stanley. It is perhaps no coincidence that by the time the Tithes Bill finally passed, in 1838, shorn of its provision for lay appropriation, Stanley and his followers had already firmly entered the Conservative camp. Whatever the government's motives may have been in this respect, from O'Connell's point of view it must have appeared that, with the Tithes Bill being pressed, a reform of Irish Municipal Corporations in prospect, and a sympathetic administration in Dublin willing to show generosity in its distribution of patronage to Roman Catholics, he had been right to postpone the question of the repeal of the Union. It is likely that repeal remained O'Connell's long-term objective, but he was prepared to pursue a temporary strategy of using the threat of a renewed campaign for repeal as a leverage in order to secure other objectives. The message that was, interestingly, being conveyed in confidence by O'Connell to an English Whig MP, in the mid-1830s, was that he had been 'not anxious so much for Repeal in itself, but . . . that the agitation about it [might] be the means of obtaining a good and mild Government for Ireland'.[41]

While a certain amount of scepticism seems appropriate when assessing the motives of the Melbourne government in its efforts to appease the Irish – Russell himself, after all, detested Catholicism as a religious creed, and, if anything, rather hoped that the removal of legitimate Catholic grievances would help to strengthen Protestantism in Ireland – there is less reason to doubt the sincerity of the Whigs' attempts to conciliate nonconformists in England. The broad-church, latitudinarian instincts of many of the most influential Whig ministers, hostile as they were to the extreme clerical pretensions of High Church Anglicans, and distrustful of any form of religious dogma, encouraged a genuine belief that, by removing the surviving vestiges of social inferiority attached to nonconformity, there was a realistic prospect that many nonconformists might eventually be reconciled to a more truly national, and functional, Church of England. (But it was imperative, from the point of view of the erastian Whigs, to maintain State control over the Church of England, and Russell had therefore stated his overall strategy in the following terms: 'our object is, if possible, to conciliate the Dissenters, and having framed our measures with that end, strenuously to resist the separation of Church and State'.[42]) In this spirit, a series of measures was enacted in 1836, including the abolition of the Established Church's monopoly of the registration of births, marriages and deaths, and the granting of a Royal Charter to London University (one of its constituent Colleges, University College, being a non-denominational body). The Tithe Commutation Act, of the same year, was also welcome enough in principle to nonconformists, although it was in fact primarily conceived by the government as a sop to the farming interest. Arguably, the most valuable of the measures enacted by the Whigs was one whose benefits were again not confined to nonconformists. On returning to office in 1835, the Melbourne administration had acted promptly on the recommendations of a highly partisan committee, set up two years earlier, by creating an elective system of local government for the 178 Municipal Corporations of England and Wales. The monopoly of control of many Corporations by Anglican cliques was thus broken, and nonconformists were afforded a real opportunity to participate in the local government of the towns, in place of the often merely theoretical right granted by the earlier repeal of the Test and Corporation Acts. In Leicester, for example, the first municipal elections under the new system produced an overwhelming majority for the 'Liberals', and the successful candidates included twelve Unitarians, twelve Baptists, ten Congregationalists, three Quakers, two Wesleyan Methodists, and a member of the Countess of Huntingdon connection.[43]

Nevertheless, another highly contentious issue remained, that of the legal requirement for nonconformists to pay Church rates, and this proved to be a major stumbling block for the government. The problem from the Whigs' point of view was not the principle of abolishing the rate, which was actually proposed by them in a bill of 1837, but that the aggressive nature of the campaign being conducted in the country by nonconformist groups made it increasingly difficult for the Whigs to present their plan as being in the best interests of the Established Church. The Whig argument, that by removing the irritant of Church rates the standing of the Church of England would be enhanced, was not easy to sustain when prominent nonconformists were seeking to link the issue with the wider one of Church disestablishment. Eventually, the abolition bill became bogged down in the House of Commons (a number of Whig MPs opposed it, and the second reading was only carried by five votes), and the government had effectively abandoned it before the death of the King necessitated the dissolution of parliament.

The general election in the summer of 1837 demonstrated clearly the perils facing a Whig government that had come to be identified too closely for its own good with militant nonconformity, while at the same time being smothered by the warm embrace of O'Connell and the Roman Catholics. In the circumstances, it was all too easy for Conservative candidates to exploit the cry of 'the Church in danger', alleging a systematic Whig attempt to subvert the national Church through a sordid political alliance with the Church's enemies at both ends of the religious spectrum. It is particularly significant that such alarm about the direction of Whig policy seems to have extended to many Wesleyan Methodists, who desired neither the disestablishment of the Church of England nor concessions to the claims of Roman Catholics, and whose defection in some numbers to the Conservative side on this occasion illustrates very well the diversity of the 'Liberal' coalition and the difficulties facing the Whigs in trying to hold it together.[44] This pro-Anglican backlash in the constituencies helped the Conservatives to sustain their remarkable electoral recovery begun in 1835, although it is significant that their net gains were confined almost entirely to the English counties (where they now held 99 out of 144 seats) and smaller boroughs (98 out of 202). In consequence, the government's overall parliamentary majority, which had been so vast in 1832, was now reduced to approximately 30 seats.

One important feature of this decline in the Whigs' position had been the gradual alienation of a number of its more moderate supporters in the House of Commons. In attempting to legislate in order to satisfy the demands of various sectional elements within the reform coalition, the Whig governments of Grey and Melbourne had throughout run the risk of forfeiting the confidence of moderate MPs who were increasingly dismayed by the evident fact that the Great Reform act had not put an end to the pressure for major organic change. Robert Stewart has identified at least 31 MPs who, having supported the cause of reform in 1832, became Conservatives at some stage between 1833 and 1837, the most prominent of these being the ex-Cabinet Ministers, Stanley and Graham.[45] Thus, by 1837, defections in the House of Commons, as well as Conservative gains at two general elections, had contributed significantly to the erosion of support for Melbourne's government.

In a famous summary of the dilemma confronting Whiggery in the late 1830s, Lord John Russell referred to 'that very old difficulty of Whig administrations, that their friends expect them to do more than is possible; so that if they attempted little, their friends grow slacker, and if they attempt much, their enemies grow strong'.[46] It is indeed ironic that, while the Whigs found themselves being castigated for their policy initiatives directed towards nonconformists and Roman Catholics, they gained little advantage from the firm stand taken against other questions of radical reform. At the opening of the new parliament, in the autumn of 1837, Russell acquired his nickname of 'finality Jack' through an offensive speech defending the Reform Settlement of 1832, in which he declared himself strongly against any further extension of the franchise, and also explicitly rejected calls for the introduction of a secret ballot and triennial parliaments. This uncompromising stance was primarily directed against the parliamentary radicals, and was probably encouraged by the fact that the radicals had suffered a number of casualties at the general election. (According to the *Annual Register* for 1837, it was estimated that only 80 radicals and Irish repealers *combined* were left, compared with 150 in 1835.) Furthermore, with the emergence of Chartism as a serious, and potentially revolutionary, force in the country, during 1838–9, it was inevitable that the Whigs' commitment to 'finality' would be reinforced. In a public letter to his constituents at Stroud, in May 1839, Russell thus sought to dissociate the Whigs still further from the 'party of movement', by emphasising the dangers of reopening the whole issue of constitutional reform at a time of social turbulence. Instead, the electors were urged to rally to the 'true Whiggism' of the government.[47]

The Whigs were undoubtedly strengthened in their determination to resist pressures for further reform by the attitude of the leader of the opposition. So long as Sir Robert Peel judged that his followers lacked the strength and cohesion necessary for him to form a stable, alternative government, his own best interests were served by a tacit arrangement whereby he would, if necessary, give the Melbourne administration his support so that it might repel the advances made by its own radical back-benchers. By encouraging the Whig ministers to pursue a moderate course, which could be endorsed by the opposition front-bench, the hope was that the extremes both of 'democratic' radicalism and of ultra-Toryism could be effectively contained. There had, in fact, been occasions as early as 1833 when Peel had found it expedient to come to the rescue of a Whig government in danger from its own supporters, but he appears to have pursued a more systematic policy later in the decade. For instance, during the early months of 1837 Melbourne's government was confronted with a spate of radical motions concerning such issues as the secret ballot, the abolition of the property qualification for MPs, the removal of bishops from the House of Lords, and the repeal of the Septennial Act, and, as the *Annual Register* observed, 'on all these divisions on constitutional questions, the Ministers were altogether dependent upon the tories for the stand they were enabled to make against their more liberal allies'. On Tennyson D'Eynecourt's motion against the Septennial Act, indeed, 'the number of Whigs and reformers who voted with Lord John Russell did not exceed 29'.[48] Following the general election later the same year, Peel continued to administer aid to the Whigs when appropriate. Ian Newbould has pointed to several episodes, between the autumn of 1837 and the spring of 1839, where Peel saved the government from embarrassing defeats on a range of issues, including not only electoral reform, but such matters as the abolition of negro apprenticeship in the West Indies, and C. P. Villiers' annual motions against the corn laws.[49]

Another element in the political equation making for a more unambitious Whig policy was the dramatic transformation that had taken place in the Whigs' relations with the Crown, following the accession of Queen Victoria in June 1837. While William IV was still alive, the memory of the humiliating events of 1834–5 had ensured that there was little cordiality between monarch and ministers, and it was obvious that the King would gladly have seized any opportunity to rid himself of them permanently.[50] With a young and politically inexperienced Queen on the throne, however, it became possible for the Whigs to identify themselves much more positively as the ministers of the Crown, basking in the warm glow of Royal favour. The key to this was the close personal relationship which developed between Victoria and Melbourne: the one, a fatherless girl-Queen, who had hitherto led a solitary existence and was desperately in need of some sort of paternal guidance; the other, a widower with no surviving children, who obviously responded with instinctive gallantry to the onus falling on him to help Victoria to cope with her constitutional responsibilities. Melbourne, in fact, assumed a role closer to that of a personal confidant than that of the head of a Cabinet composed of partisan politicians. Nevertheless, the political advantage to the Whigs of their newfound and unaccustomed Royal favour was obvious, and was certainly milked for what it was worth at the general election of 1837, in which the 'Royal card' was probably of some benefit to government candidates in the larger boroughs.[51]

Melbourne's close attachment to the Queen, and the relative quietism of his ministry in its later years, have contributed to an impression of the nature of the man that is potentially highly misleading. A superficially indolent manner, and an unenthusiastic approach to all political questions, have been too easily mistaken for evidence of apathy and even a lack of ambition. In reality, Melbourne should be seen as the exemplar of a characteristically aristocratic code of conduct, which feigned indifference to the pursuit of power and personal glory (Lord Hartington, later in the century, was another representative type), and dictated that high office in the State was to be accepted only out of a sense of duty and personal honour. Moreover, the frankness and absence of dogmatic opinions that helped to make Melbourne's such an attractive personality, also concealed an underlying cynicism about the conduct of political affairs, which could lead him to go surprisingly far in the direction of reform when he deemed this appropriate. Melbourne enjoyed the power derived from holding office, and was prepared to do what was necessary in order to retain it. The record of his second ministry in its early years, after all, compares favourably with that of later 'Liberal' governments, when we consider such important measures as the Municipal Corporations Act of 1835, the Dissenters' Marriages Act of 1836, and the willingness to attempt a settlement of the vexed question of Church rates – something no other government was to dare to touch for the next thirty years. Equally, however, Melbourne was more than willing to settle for a 'stationary system' of government,[52] where this seemed possible, and no doubt such an arrangement was better suited to his temperament, enabling him to concentrate on the more congenial task of instructing the young Queen in sound (Whig) constitutional principles. For radicals like George Grote, meantime, there was nothing to be done but express disgust at the course taken by the Whigs:

> The Whig Government has been, ever since the accession of our present Queen, becoming more and more confirmed in its Conservative tendencies; in fact, it is now scarcely at all distinguished, either in its leanings or its acts, from Peel and his friends . . . Lord Melbourne's majority is a very inconsiderable one, and he maintains himself in the House of Commons chiefly by making use of the Radicals against the Tories, and of the Tories against the Radicals . . . A few years' enjoyment of power and patronage has inspired the present Ministry and their supporters with all those faults which used to be the exclusive attributes of the Tories . . . Toryism is regaining its ascendancy, and we must before long have a thorough Tory Ministry: even that will be a slight improvement, rather than otherwise, upon our present state, when we have both a Conservative Ministry and a Conservative Opposition.[53]

The peaceful accommodation, for the time being at least, between the Whigs and O'Connell only served to intensify the instinctive radical contempt both for the government and for the Irish leader.

Of course, the Whigs' delicate balancing act could only last for as long as Peel was prepared to allow it to, and in May 1839 he effectively declared war on the government by attacking its autocratic handling of an insurrection in Jamaica. On a vote in the House of Commons, the Whigs' majority was consequently reduced to just five. Although the ministers decided to resign, they were soon called upon to resume their offices after the Queen's refusal to change any of her ladies of the bedchamber (all good Whigs) caused Peel to decline the commission to form a government. Victoria's wilful behaviour may thus have given Melbourne and his colleagues a renewed lease of power, but, deprived as they now were of the insulating effect of Peel's assistance, the fundamental dilemma had to be faced of how best to redefine the relationship between the Whig tradition and its motley coalition of allies in parliament and in the country at large. And yet, the electoral revival of Conservatism, and the growing confidence this gave not only to Peel but to Conservative-dominated institutions like the House of Lords and the Church of England, ensured that any new policy initiatives by the Whigs would face a formidable opposition. Thus, Russell's attempt, in 1839–40, to modify the system of State grants for elementary education so as to distribute the funds more evenly between Anglican and nonconformist schools, aroused such a storm of protest from the Church of England and its supporters that the government was forced to retreat and implement an alternative measure that was largely satisfactory to the Church. Similarly, when a Municipal Corporations Bill for Ireland was eventually passed, in 1840, it had been so emasculated by the House of Lords that it became, in some of its provisions, a reactionary measure.

The increasing state of paralysis afflicting Melbourne's government had scarcely been relieved by the decision, in 1839, to make the question of the secret ballot an open one, as this was little more than a belated recognition of the fact that a clear majority of their own back-benchers were already committed to such a measure. All the Whigs were doing was to rectify the anomaly whereby, for some years, they had been resisting the wishes of most of their own supporters. Even so, the government was not pledging itself to act on the matter, and no positive steps were forthcoming. It was not until 1841, in the ministry's dying months, that a significant new course of policy was sketched out in relation to freer trade. The severe economic depression, beginning in 1837, had resulted in a loss of government revenue, and therefore a sequence of budget deficits, from 1839. In an attempt to stimulate trade, provision was consequently made, in F. T. Baring's budget of 1841, for a reduction in the import duties on timber and sugar, while a separate proposal was adumbrated (but never carried) for the replacement of the sliding-scale of import duties on corn by a modest fixed duty, which would have amounted to an overall reduction in the level of protection afforded to British agriculturalists.

It is difficult to understand the rationale behind the view of some historians that the Whigs' movement on the questions of the secret ballot and the corn laws was in some sense qualitatively different from their earlier reforming measures, and that it either indicated the bankruptcy of the Whig tradition, or else represented an abnegation of the true Whig principle of 'moderation'.[54] An alternative view would be that the Melbourne government's tentative steps in the direction of Free Trade, in 1841, can be seen as proof of the continuing evolution of Whiggery, along lines that were to be of the utmost significance for the subsequent development of a 'Liberal' ideology, as will be seen in the next chapter.

For the immediate future, however, any measures regarded as posing a threat to the landed interest, like the proposed fixed duty on imported corn, were certain to have the effect of weakening still further the prospects for the Whigs in the English counties. When a general election was held, in the summer of 1841, the Conservatives duly won all but 20 of the 144 seats in this category, and gained a slight majority (111 out of 202) in the smaller English boroughs. On the other hand, the Whigs and their allies remained the dominant force in the large English boroughs with electorates of over 2000, winning 43 out of the 58 seats, and to a lesser extent also in the medium-sized boroughs with electorates of between 1000 and 2000, winning 34 out of the 63 seats. Scotland also continued to return a majority of 'Liberal' members (31 out of 53), but in Wales only 10 out of 29 seats were won by Liberals. At a time when the effects of industrial depression were being acutely felt, the agitation by the anti-corn-law league was growing, and in a few northern boroughs an alliance between Tories and Chartists was operating, it is perhaps surprising that the government did not suffer more electoral damage than was in fact the case. Edward Ellice, a former Whig chief whip, expressed the opinion that the fixed-duty scheme had saved the government from a far worse defeat than was actually suffered.[55] This assessment possibly needs to be qualified by bearing in mind that in some mercantile constituencies the reductions in the duties on sugar and timber were unpopular with the West Indian and Canadian traders, and that in the City of London many financiers were still hostile to the idea of free trade.[56] Whatever the overall effect of the Whigs' policy, the general election ended in a decisive defeat for the government. Peel emerged controlling some 367 of the 658 seats in the new House of Commons, and he was easily able to turn the Whigs out of office when parliament met in August.

A Liberal Party?

The question that remains to be considered is to what extent an identifiable 'Liberal Party' can be said to have come into being by the time of Melbourne's defeat in 1841? It is the opinion of many historians, most notably Norman Gash, that the 1830s in fact witnessed the emergence of the 'modern', competitive two-party system in Britain.[57] According to this view, it became clear after the passing of the Great Reform Act that the traditional bases for the maintenance of governments, Royal favour and patronage, were no longer sufficient for the task. The patronage system had been steadily eroded as a result of successive measures of 'economical reform', since the 1780s, while the monarchy, under George IV and William IV, lacked the prestige and authority enjoyed by George III. Whereas, in the past, Prime Ministers appointed by the Crown were then able to construct a majority in the House of Commons, from the 1830s onwards it was to be the ability to control a majority in the Commons in the first place that determined who would be Prime Minister. As William IV in 1835, and Victoria in 1841, discovered, it was no longer possible to retain in office, simply through personal preference, ministers who could not command a Commons majority. Organised party, in other words, had become the indispensable basis for carrying on both the government and the opposition, and as part of this process of political polarisation, taking place during the 1830s, the truly 'independent' MP virtually vanished from parliament.[58] In his most recent statement on the subject, Gash has stressed the greater homogeneity of parties which, he believes, occurred at this time, involving on the one hand the foundation of the modern Conservative Party, under Sir Robert Peel, and on the other the successful absorption of the radical and O'Connellite MPs by the Whigs, to create another new political entity: 'Long before 1841 the sting had been drawn from both the independent radical and the Irish nationalist parties. A recognisable Liberal party was actually in being.'[59] The Liberals, it is argued, were united by a basic, common philosophy of political action, and this was underpinned by the simultaneous development of a new, central party organisation, the Reform Club, founded in 1836 as a counter to the Conservatives' Carlton Club, and serving a similar purpose as a social and political headquarters for Liberal M.P.s. At the same time, the Reform Club acted as a centre for the co-ordination and assistance of the numerous local registration associations that had grown up in the constituencies since the Great Reform Act, which had required for the first time that registers of electors be compiled annually.

While this interpretation undoubtedly has much to commend it, and certainly cannot be rejected in its entirety, the picture it presents is arguably overdrawn and in need of substantial modification. It has recently been shown, for example, that the Crown did not withdraw from an active role in politics after the 1830s, and that indeed the marriage of Victoria to Prince Albert of Saxe Coburg, in 1840, was to lead to attempts to restore the authority of the Crown through the adoption of new methods.[60] This was to have important implications for the future cohesion of political parties, as will be seen in later chapters. Furthermore, the prevalence of bloc-voting in the House of Commons during the 1830s has also been called into question: while it seems to have applied on certain major parliamentary divisions, usually those involving the fate of a ministry, it is not nearly so apparent when a wider range of issues is examined. As Ian Newbould has shown, using 38 divisions on major policy issues in the parliament of 1835–7, only 20 per cent of the Melbourne government's nominal supporters actually voted consistently with their leaders, whereas as many as 40 per cent of these MPs voted *against* their own government on more than 10 per cent of the divisions analysed. If we go further and examine every House of Commons division in the parliament of 1835–7, it emerges that nearly three-quarters of the government's supporters voted against it on more than 10 per cent of occasions.[61] These findings seriously undermine the notion of a House of Commons that was becoming increasingly polarised along strict party lines, as has usually been argued. That notion is also weakened by the observation, made earlier, that there is a good deal of evidence of tacit collusion between the government and opposition front-benches at various times during the 1830s.

One of the greatest of contemporary sources, the diaries of Charles Greville, clerk to the privy council, who was on close terms with Lord John Russell, certainly confirms the impression that the Whig government and its supporters had yet to be welded into a homogeneous body. At the beginning of the 1839 session of parliament, for example, Greville estimated that there were '267 Government people, including the Irish tail; 66 Radicals, 5 doubtful', in the House of Commons.[62] The situation after the general election of 1841 and the formation of Peel's Conservative government was in some respects worse, for as Greville assessed it:

> when the 300 men who compose the opposition consist of three distinct sections of politicians, the great Whig and moderate Radical body, owning John [Russell] for their leader, the ultra Radicals fol-

lowing Roebuck, and the Irish under O'Connell, and that the Whig leader abhors the Roebuck doctrines, can hardly be restrained from attacking O'Connell, and is resolved to be meek and gentle with his Tory antagonists, it does seem as if Peel's difficulties, whatever may be their nature or magnitude, would not be principally derived from the compact union of his opponents.[63]

It is perfectly true that the parliamentary radicals had diminished in number during the course of the 1830s, and that some, such as Grote, became disillusioned with politics, but the continued presence of men like Roebuck, Hume and Duncombe would ensure that there was no greater unity between Whigs and radicals after 1841 than there had been before. Indeed, the election for Stockport, in 1841, of Richard Cobden, the most prominent leader of the anti-corn law league, was a sign of the beginnings of a fresh infusion of radicalism into the parliamentary ranks, which was to be of great importance for the future. As regards O'Connell and the Irish repealers, it is also perfectly true that the tentacles of Whig patronage had gained a firm hold on many MPs, but, as the two entries from Greville's diary indicate, a significant change had taken place in the relations between O'Connell and the Whigs. Whereas in 1839 the 'Irish tail' was counted as part of the government's support, by the time of the 1841 general election O'Connell's frustration with the increasing paralysis of Whig policy towards Ireland had caused him to relaunch his campaign for the repeal of the Act of Union, a move which brought him into bitter conflict with Whigs like Russell. The renewed agitation for repeal was, as events were to show after 1841, of an increasingly extreme nature, and the movement was ultimately to get out of the control of O'Connell himself.

If the radical and Irish-repealer components of the reform coalition were to continue to be beyond the reach of Whig discipline, the same point applies equally to the nonconformist movement outside of parliament. Disappointed by the failures of Melbourne's government over such issues as Church rates, the tendency was for most nonconformist groups (with the exception of the Wesleyans) to become more militant in their campaigning, which was increasingly directed against the principle of an Established Church. The Whigs' education settlement of 1840 was also to provoke a growing intransigence in nonconformist attitudes, which inclined towards the 'Voluntaryist' principle that there should be no State interference in education, and, as G. I. T. Machin has observed, 'the growth of Voluntaryism increased the fragmentation of the Liberal party'.[64] Nor were matters any better in Scotland, which had its own distinctive political disputes, for although the fear of Chartism had driven the dissenters into the arms of the Whigs, and so weakened the position of the secular radicals at the time of the 1841 general election, this was not to be an enduring alliance. On the contrary, the dissenters (who were Voluntaryists) were horrified at the way the Whigs had also angled for the support of the Free Church Presbyterians (who were not Voluntaryists), and therefore resolved to secure their own representation in parliament in the future. As the historian of Scottish politics has summed the situation up: 'the 1841 general election did not herald the dawn of an era of Liberal unity, and the threat of rupture seemed if anything greater afterwards'.[65]

In order to restore at least a little clarity to what is obviously a highly complicated subject, it may be helpful if we move away from the assumption that the emergence of a two-party system must necessarily be associated with a greater homogeneity of political opinions on each side. If it is accepted, instead, that the existence of a broad spectrum of opinions within a political group, or 'party', is not only quite normal, but potentially even a source of strength as well as of weakness, then we need have no difficulty in accepting the proposition that there was a tendency towards a two-party system during the 1830s. These parties, however, were loose coalitions rather than highly regimented armies voting together on a regular basis. However, the fact that at least on some key parliamentary divisions a high level of consistency of voting for one side or the other was achieved, suggests that basic party allegiances did exist amongst most MPs, even if this was not converted into consistent support for one party or the other on the whole range of political issues. In short, we need to have more limited expectations of what party allegiance meant in the 1830s. As for the problem of cross-bench collaboration between the party leaders, designed to resist unwelcome pressure from the political extremes, it is important to realise that this was not a unique feature of the politics of the 1830s, but a fairly common parliamentary device right up until the 1880s:[66] such collaboration does not, therefore, provide an argument against the existence of parties as such.

That party allegiances were comparatively lax is perhaps not surprising when we remember that the majority of MPs were gentlemen amateurs, for whom politics was only one of several occupations, and who in most cases were men of independent financial means who did not owe their seats to the party leaders, and often were not personally ambitious for office. In such circumstances, it was inevitable that there would be limits to the amount of discipline that could be exercised by leaders and whips. The so-called 'Lichfield House Compact' of 1835, whereby the Whigs, radicals and repealers agreed to act in concert in order to remove Peel from office, but without any detailed agreement being reached as to the policies that the next Whig government would pursue, in many ways exemplifies the necessarily restricted nature of party affiliations at this time.

Whig attitudes towards party organisation, in the period 1830–41, certainly reflected their rather limited assumptions about the relationship between the parliamentary leadership and the rank and file. In terms of House of Commons management, the early 1830s seems to have been a particularly chaotic time, with little co-ordination of the efforts of the leader, Althorp, and the chief whips, Edward Ellice followed by Charles Wood. Althorp, indeed, inclined to the view that the formal organisation of MPs, through the whipping system, was an undesirable thing, and that the government ought to rely on its ability to secure majority support for its measures as a result of rational debate. Only an attitude such as this can account for the fact that a government which, on paper, possessed a massive parliamentary majority, experienced great difficulty in carrying legislation, and was even prone to defeat on important issues such as the malt tax, in 1833. Some improvement in the efficiency of parliamentary management probably did occur later in the decade, after Althorp's retirement, and as the Whigs' nominal following was whittled away by the general elections of 1835 and 1837, which encouraged greater cohesion. Yet poor whipping still seems to have been a major factor, for example, in the narrowness of the government's majority on the Jamaica debate, in May 1839.[67]

Party organisation for electoral purposes was tainted, in the eyes of many Whigs like Melbourne, by its frequent association with political radicalism, and this engendered considerable suspicion of a man like E. J. Stanley, chief whip from 1835 to 1841, whose close connection with the Earl of Durham undermined his standing with his own party chiefs. The generally negative attitude of the Whigs was especially noticeable with regard to the creation of central bodies for the promotion of political and electoral organisation. Both the Reform Association (1834) and the Reform Club (1836) were established as a result of radical initiatives. In the case of the Reform Club, which was intended as a new social centre for MPs, the prime movers came from the ranks of the philosophic radicals, such as Grote, Hume and Molesworth, and, while it is true that many Whigs were induced to join the club in order to prevent it from being dominated by the radicals,[68] it is evident that it did not, at this stage, establish itself as the party headquarters in the same way as the Carlton Club had for the Conservatives. The highly exclusive Brooks's Club long remained the social centre for Whiggery. Indeed, as late as 1869, we find the then Liberal chief whip writing to Gladstone, concerning changes that he was planning, as follows: 'The Reform Club is now re-organising itself as a *political* body & is trying under your banner to unite both sections, in this it differs from Brooks' '.[69] The Reform Association, founded by the Earl of Durham for the purpose of promoting the spread of registration societies in the constituencies, seems to have been an even more unofficial body. Joseph Parkes and James Coppock, the two radical lawyers who in effect acted as party agents, operated from offices in Cleveland Row, but, for the few years of the Reform Association's existence, it remained distinct even from the Reform Club.[70] By 1841, Parkes for one had come to despair of effective work being done in the realm of party organisation. The contrast with the close relationship between the Conservative leader, Peel, the Carlton Club, and the party agent, Francis Bonham (who was appointed personally by Peel), is striking indeed. In the field of party organisation, as in that of policy and personnel, all the signs were that, even in 1841, the Whigs had declined to come to terms with the forces unleashed by the Great Reform Act, and it was by no means clear that they really wanted to.

NOTES

1. Norman Gash, *Politics in the Age of Peel* (2nd edn, Brighton, 1977), is the authoritative work on the new electoral system in Great Britain.
2. Grey to Princess Lieven, 9 November 1830, in E. A. Smith, *Earl Grey, 1764–1845* (Oxford, 1990) p. 259.
3. For the so-called 'Grand Whiggery', see Peter Mandler, *Aristocratic Government in the Age of Reform: Whigs and Liberals, 1830–1852* (Oxford, 1990) pp. 44–84.
4. Wood to Grey, March 1831, in Smith, *Earl Grey*, p. 278. See generally, Abraham D. Kriegal, 'Liberty and Whiggery in Early Nineteenth-Century England', *Journal of Modern History*, LII (1980).
5. Milton to Lord Ebrington, 6 and 7 October 1831, Fortescue MSS (Devon Record Office, M/1262) FC 87.

6. Richard Brent, *Liberal Anglican Politics* (Oxford, 1987), explores this theme.

7. See Mandler, *Aristocratic Government*, pp. 72–6, for this paragraph.

8. Grey to Edward Ellice, 11 January 1833, in Smith *Earl Grey*, p. 300.

9. See E. A. Wasson, *Whig Renaissance: Lord Althorp and the Whig Party, 1782–1845* (New York, 1987) pp. 248–321.

10. Smith, *Earl Grey*, pp. 261–2, 324–7; Wasson, *Whig Renaissance*, pp. 177–84.

11. As will become clear, contemporaries often used the term 'reformer' rather than 'radical', in the 1830s, but I have normally used the latter term, for the sake of consistency throughout this book.

12. Charles Wood to Grey, 31 December 1832, in Abraham F. Kriegal (ed.), *The Holland House Diaries* (London, 1977) p. 461, note 12.

13. Althorp to the Duke of Richmond, 12 December 1832, in Wasson, *Whig Renaissance*, p. 252. Cf. S. F. Woolley, 'The Personnel of the Parliament of 1833', *English Historical Review*, LIII (1938), which also estimates that only 86 out of 658 MPs had backgrounds in business, probably less than the figure for the pre-reform parliament.

14. *Annual Register* (1833) p. 225.

15. Mrs Grote, *The Personal Life of George Grote* (London, 1873) pp. 71–3.

16. *Annual Register* (1833) pp. 159–63.

17. L. G. Johnson, *General T. Perronet Thompson* (London, 1957) p. 186; W. A. Munford, *William Ewart MP, 1798–1869: Portrait of a Radical* (London, 1960) pp. 188–9; T. H. Duncombe, *The Life and Correspondence of Thomas Slingsby Duncombe* (London, 1868) vol. 2, pp. 198–200.

18. For example the radical MP for the large working-class constituency of Finsbury; S. S. Sprigge, *The Life and Times of Thomas Wakley* (London, 1897) pp. 312–14.

19. M. L. Clarke, *George Grote: A Biography* (London, 1962) pp. 38–41.

20. For example, Molesworth to his mother, 19 February 1835, in Mrs Fawcett, *Life of the Right Hon. Sir William Molesworth, Bart.* (London, 1901) pp. 73–4.

21. Derek Fraser, *Urban Politics in Victorian England* (London, 1976) pp. 198, 212–13.

22. D. G. Wright, 'A Radical Borough: Parliamentary Politics in Bradford, 1832–1841', *Northern History*, IV (1969) p. 148.

23. John A. Phillips, *Electoral Behaviour in Unreformed England* (Princeton, 1982).

24. G. I. T. Machin, *Politics and the Churches in Great Britain, 1832–1868* (Oxford, 1977) pp. 42–3.

25. J. A. Jowitt, 'Parliamentary Politics in Halifax, 1832–1847', *Northern History*, XI (1976) p. 173 and note 7.

26. See Fraser, *Urban Politics*, esp. pp. 228–30.

27. Wright, 'Bradford', p. 151 and note 104.

28. Alan D. Gilbert, 'Methodism, Dissent and Political Stability in Early Industrial England', *Journal of Religious History* (1978–9).

29. Derek Fraser, 'The Fruits of Reform: Leeds Politics in the 1830s', *Northern History*, VII (1972) p. 105; Wright, 'Bradford', p. 150.

30. T. A. Jenkins (ed.), *The Parliamentary Diaries of Sir John Trelawny, 1858–*

1865 (Royal Historical Society, Camden Series, 1990) pp. 2–19; B. S. Trinder (ed.), *A Victorian MP and his Constituents: The Correspondence of H. W. Tancred, 1841–1859* (Banbury Historical Society, 1967) p. xviii; T. A. MacDonald, 'Religion and Voting in an English Borough: Poole in 1859', *Southern History*, V (1983).

31.   Machin, *Politics and the Churches*, pp. 112–21.

32.   Abraham D. Kriegal, 'The Politics of the Whigs in Opposition, 1834–1835', *Journal of British Studies*, VII (1968) p. 69, note 21.

33.   William Clay to Harriet Grote, 20 February 1835, in Mrs Grote, *George Grote*, p. 99.

34.   Althorp to Lord Ebrington, 14 December 1831, Fortescue MSS, FC 87. For other examples, see Kriegal, 'Liberty and Whiggery', p. 272.

35.   Ian Newbould, *Whiggery and Reform, 1830–1841* (London, 1990) pp. 69–71.

36.   Norman Gash, *Aristocracy and People, 1815–1865* (London, 1979) p. 161.

37.   See Abraham D. Kriegal, 'The Politics of the Whigs in Opposition, 1834–1835', *Journal of British Studies*, VII (1968).

38.   Russell to Lord Howick, 1 February 1835, in I. D. C. Newbould, 'Whiggery and the Dilemma of Reform: Liberals, Radicals and the Melbourne Administration, 1835–9', *Bulletin of the Institute of Historical Research*, LIII (1980) p. 232.

39.   Philip Ziegler, *Melbourne* (London, 1976) pp. 193–207.

40.   Newbould, *Whiggery and Reform*, p. 177.

41.   *Autobiographical Recollections of George Pryme* (London, 1870) p. 231.

42.   Russell to Lord Holland, 24 August 1834, in Machin, *Politics and the Churches*, p. 47.

43.   Ibid., pp. 54–5.

44.   David Hempton, *Methodism and Politics in British Society, 1750–1850* (London, 1984) pp. 206–8.

45.   Robert Stewart, *The Foundation of the Conservative Party, 1830–1867* (London, 1978) p. 109 and Appendix 2.

46.   Russell to Melbourne, 10 August 1837, in Newbould, *Whiggery and Reform*, p. 212.

47.   Ibid., pp. 230–1.

48.   *Annual Register* (1837) p. 126. Tennyson D'Eynecourt's motion was defeated by 91 votes to 87.

49.   Newbould, *Whiggery and Reform*, pp. 214–17.

50.   See *Annual Register* (1837) p. 217.

51.   Ibid., p. 239.

52.   Ziegler, *Melbourne*, ch. 20.

53.   Grote to John Austin, February 1838, in Mrs Grote, *George Grote*, pp. 126–7.

54.   Norman Gash, *Reaction and Reconstruction in English Politics, 1832–52* (Oxford, 1965) p. 184; Newbould, *Whiggery and Reform*, pp. 319–20.

55.   Ellice to Joseph Parkes, 16 July 1841, in Brent, *Liberal Anglican Politics*, p. 298.

56.   *Annual Register* (1841) p. 144.

57.   See Gash, *Reaction and Reconstruction*, chs 1, 5 and 6, for the whole of what follows.

58. D. E. D. Beales, 'Parliamentary Parties and the Independent Member, 1810–60', in Robert Robson (ed.), *Ideas and Institutions of Victorian Britain* (London, 1967); D. H. Close, 'The Formation of a Two-party Alignment in the House of Commons between 1832 and 1841', *English Historical Review*, LXXXIV (1969).

59. Gash, *Aristocracy and People*, p. 163.

60. David Cannadine, 'The Last Hanoverian Monarch? The Victorian Monarchy in Historical Perspective', in A. L. Beier et al. (eds), *The First Modern Society* (London, 1989).

61. Newbould, *Whiggery and Reform*, p. 16 and note.

62. Henry Reeve (ed.), *The Greville Memoirs* (8 vols, London, 1888): 10 February 1839.

63. Ibid., 12 August 1841.

64. Machin, *Politics and the Churches*, p. 110.

65. I. G. C. Hutchison, *A Political History of Scotland, 1832–1924* (Edinburgh, 1986) p. 48.

66. Hugh Berrington, 'Partisanship and Dissidence in the Nineteenth-Century House of Commons', *Parliamentary Affairs*, XXI (1968).

67. Newbould, *Whiggery and Reform*, pp. 24–9.

68. See Gash, *Politics in the Age of Peel*, pp. 402–11.

69. G. Glyn to Gladstone, 19 May [1869], B. L. Add MSS 44347, f. 294.

70. Gash, *Politics in the Age of Peel*, pp. 412–13, 418–27.

2 The Slow Birth of Liberal England

Introduction

Lord John Russell's appreciation of the long-term dilemma confronting Whiggery, in the post-Reform Act era, is apparent in a famous letter to Lord Melbourne, written as early as the autumn of 1837:

> I always thought that the Whig party as a party would be destroyed by the Reform Bill. Their strength lay in certain counties and in close boroughs. The Tories, by the new construction of the House, were sure to beat them in the counties, and the radicals in the open towns.[1]

It is extremely doubtful whether Russell had really taken such a gloomy view of the Whigs' prospects during the heady days of 1832, and allowance has to be made for the natural sense of despondency engendered by the way their parliamentary majority had been dramatically eroded at the general elections of 1835 and 1837, the latter of which had just taken place when Russell wrote. Nevertheless, there remains in Russell's letter an important recognition of the central paradox of 'Liberalism' at the beginning of the Victorian period: that a parliamentary grouping dominated by the landed aristocracy was becoming increasingly dependent for its electoral vitality on support from the urban and industrial centres of Britain. The spectacular successes achieved by the Whigs in the county elections of 1832 had proved to be a temporary phenomenon, and, although the Whigs were never extinguished in these constituencies as Russell seemed to fear, it is true that they were never again to be more than a substantial minority presence. As for the boroughs, Russell was again apt to exaggerate the extent of the Whigs' problems, for they were still doing well in the small – if no longer entirely closed – boroughs, which continued to predominate within the electoral system after 1832; but it was also true that in the larger

44

boroughs the Whigs could usually hope for no more than a position of partnership with the forces of radicalism and nonconformity. By the late 1830s, therefore, it was becoming increasingly clear that the Whigs could not expect to continue to govern simply as an old-style aristocratic connexion. Even taking an optimistic view of the future, it at the very least had to be accepted that, if the Whigs were to survive as leaders of a viable party of government, they needed to embrace more fully the values and aspirations of urban and industrial Britain.

The Genesis of Victorian Liberalism

Paradoxically, the gradual evolution of a distinctive 'Liberal' identity is far easier to explain at the level of broad ideology – some might call it 'party doctrine'[2] – than in terms of developments in party organisation or greater political cohesion at Westminster. In other words, an evolving 'Liberal' mentalité may be detected in the 1840s and 1850s, but this was not to mean the same thing as the creation of a united Liberal Party. This point may best be illustrated by a study of contemporary usage of political terminology. Before the 1830s, the term 'liberal' (almost invariably with a small l) was normally used simply to denote an attachment to a basic set of principles, namely, a belief in the ideals of civil and religious liberty expressed through support for such measures as the repeal of the Test and Corporation Acts and Catholic emancipation. It indicated a general attitude of mind (hence also 'liberality'), and was rarely used as a party label, except by some radicals.[3] During the second half of the 1830s, occasional references may be found to the terms 'Liberal' and 'Liberal Party' (with capital Ls), as collective labels for the alliance of Whigs, radicals, nonconformists and repealers which was analysed in the last chapter, although such usage still tended to be employed mostly by the radicals. If we look at how MPs described themselves in their entries in the annually published *Dod's Parliamentary Companion*, however, it emerges that while the label 'Liberal' was only occasionally used in the late 1830s, it became more common during the early 1840s (75 MPs were using it by 1845), and then rapidly became the most popular label chosen by MPs (163 in the new parliament elected in 1847). Thereafter, few newly elected MPs adopted the older political labels, so that within a few years 'Whigs' and 'Reformers' had virtually disappeared from *Dod*. In the case of *The Times* newspaper, its employment of the collective term 'the Liberals', in place of 'the Whig–Radicals', can be dated precisely to the year 1846.

Of course, the problem with such contemporary terminological usage is that it was largely a matter of fashion: no political leader ever officially sanctioned the use of the new title 'Liberal' in such a way as might enable us to pinpoint and celebrate an official birth-date, and it remains unknown why certain MPs adopted the title earlier than others (it had nothing to do with their voting behaviour on issues like the repeal of the corn laws or the secret ballot). Nevertheless, it does seem to be the case that the widespread acceptance of the terms 'Liberal' and 'Liberal Party' occurred at a later date than that when Sir Robert Peel and his followers began to call themselves 'Conservatives'. And it is surely no coincidence that the great change came about at the time of the political crisis arising from the repeal of the corn laws, in 1846, when Peel's government put an end to the system of agricultural protection with the help of Russell and the opposition. The immediate consequence of this measure was the repudiation of Peel's leadership by the bulk of the Conservative Party, and, following his resignation in June 1846, the formation of a government by Russell,[4] which was dedicated to the preservation and extension of the new 'Free Trade' system. Russell and his colleagues were assisted in their task by the independent support of Peel and a group of his followers who, though usually described by historians as 'Peelites', were listed by *Dod*, appropriately enough, as '*Liberal*–Conservatives'.

It would not be too dramatic to describe the crisis of 1846 as a great psychological moment in British politics, the point at which Russell and the Whigs accepted unequivocally that henceforth the 'Liberal Party', which they led, having taken a clear stand against the policy of protection for agriculture, was to be identified primarily with the interests of urban and industrial Britain. In so doing, vital new common ground was created which helped to provide a fresh source of inspiration, and thus a sense of mutual identity, for the diverse components of what remained in essence a coalition of reforming opinion, of a kind that had been lacking since the days of the fight for the Great Reform Bill. Individuals might continue to think of themselves as 'Whigs' or 'radicals', but all could now accept the generic title 'Liberal', thus demonstrating their shared commitment to the principles of Free Trade.

Some of the Whigs, it is true, being great landowners themselves, had been understandably doubtful of the efficacy of so drastic a measure as the repeal of the corn laws, although by the mid-1840s supporters of this policy included the likes of Lord Fitzwilliam and the third Earl Grey (who succeeded his father, the former Prime Minister, in July 1845). In the case of Lord John Russell, after the general election defeat of 1841 he had gradually moved away from the idea that it was possible for the State to effectively regulate the supply and price of corn by a system of tariffs, a process of self-education which seems to have been assisted by his reading of the classical political economists, Adam Smith, Malthus, Ricardo and McCulloch.[5] Russell's public commitment to the policy of repeal, in his celebrated 'Edinburgh letter' of November 1845, finally removed any possibility of a future Whig-led government seeking to maintain the protectionist system.

From the point of view of the radicals, the policy of Free Trade, culminating in the repeal of the corn laws, represented the triumph of an approach which they had mostly advocated for a good many years. Close links had developed, during the 1810s and 1820s, between the philosophic radicals and political economists like Ricardo, and the dismantling of the elaborate system of protective tariffs thenceforth became an established part of the Benthamite programme of reform. The report of Joseph Hume's select committee on import duties, published in 1840 during the midst of a severe economic depression, was a timely reiteration of the political economists' view that a reduction in tariff levels would serve to stimulate consumption and thus promote trade and employment. Already, in 1836, many of the leading parliamentary radicals had supported the anti-corn-law association, which sought the elimination of protective tariffs for agriculture. However, it was to be the more dynamic, business-oriented anti-corn-law league, a pressure group established in Manchester in 1839, which, through its rigorous *extra-parliamentary* campaigning, would be acclaimed by posterity as the decisive force in the struggle against the 'bread robbery', or 'famine code', imposed by the agricultural monopolists.[6] The particular significance of the League lay in the way that it brought to the forefront of politics the concerns of the manufacturing class as a whole. As a result of the League's activities, there emerged a new generation of radical politicians, the most famous being Richard Cobden and John Bright, whose background in industry distinguished them from most of the philosophic radicals of the 1830s.

At the same time, the cause of Free Trade fitted in well with the world-view of nonconformists, not only because many of them were businessmen – large and small – with a direct interest in low food prices for their workers, but also because of the moral dimension to the issue. Indeed, the campaign against a tariff system designed by an aristocratically dominated legislature for the purpose of preserving their own incomes, seemed to mirror the wider protest of militant nonconformity at the entrenched privileges of that other great institution of the traditional ruling class, the Church of England. For many nonconformists, therefore, Free Trade in the economic sphere became the natural counterpart to the quest for 'Free Trade' in religion, the hope that, at some future date, the State might cease to interfere in spiritual matters by upholding an Established Church, and allow instead all religious denominations to be placed on an equal footing. As was often to be the case in the Gladstonian era, it was the combination of economic self-interest with high moral concern which gave nonconformist pressure its political potency. Some idea of the tone in which nonconformists addressed the Free Trade issue is conveyed by the letters of George Hadfield, a Manchester-based lawyer, written at the time of a by-election, in 1843, in which the anti-corn-law league was active. 'I cannot doubt that [the City of] London will be London still', he wrote to Samuel Morley, a Nottingham hosiery manufacturer and fellow Congregationalist, 'and strangle the accursed power of taxing, for the benefit of the rich and great, the bread of the widow and orphan.' After the victory of the pro-repeal candidate, Hadfield wrote again:

> The triumph of London is truly the triumph of humanity . . . Its influence will affect the world. The spirit of the gospel is one of mutual intercourse and active good-will. The sublime philosophy of our Lord's doctrine is leading us in the right way, and I am full of hope that 'good-will to men' and 'glory to God in the highest' will be extended to the remotest corner of the earth. Men of the world may confine themselves to principles of political economy, but let us look at these things in a Christian light, and we shall soon see who it is that sits at the helm, and is the great Governor over the hearts of men; and who will, by His own power, bring to pass His own purposes.[7]

In the years after 1846, as the Free Trade system appeared to be vindicated by the buoyancy of the mid-Victorian economy, and by the realisation of the extent of Britain's supremacy as a manufacturing nation (evidenced so dramatically by the Great Exhibition of 1851), so it was that the creed of 'Liberalism' acquired its distinctive air of optimism. Indeed, the essential tenet of British Liberalism, for the remainder of the nineteenth century, was to be its confidence in the possibility of *constant* progress, a literal belief that things were improving daily thanks to the magical formula known as Free Trade, which had liberated the beneficent forces of industry and commerce, and spread the blessings of material prosperity through a wide section of society. It is hardly surprising that the maintenance of Free Trade should have remained the pole-star of Liberalism, and that it was capable of providing an emotive rallying-cry for Liberals of all shades well into the twentieth century.

Another aspect of the Victorian cult of progress, which was again peculiarly associated with the Liberals, arose from the relative absence of serious social unrest in Britain after the bleak years of the early 1840s. The prosperity apparently created by Free Trade was an obvious explanation for this, but it could also be regarded, from a broader perspective, as a tribute to the sagacity of Britain's political institutions, which had enabled the Country to avoid the horrors of revolution. Appropriately enough, 1848, the year of revolutions on the continent of Europe, but of the ignominious collapse of the last Chartist demonstration in Britain, was also the year in which the first two volumes of Thomas Babbington Macaulay's *History of England* appeared. As the great exponent of the 'Whig' interpretation of history triumphantly declared in his preface, 'the history of our Country during the last 160 years is eminently the history of physical, of moral, and of intellectual improvement'. In Macaulay's view, the key to Britain's political stability was to be found in the Glorious Revolution of 1688, which marked the victory of the first Whigs in their battle against the arbitrary Stuart kings, and established a system of parliamentary government in which the liberty of the subject was secured. Thanks to this 'preserving revolution', the Country had acquired immunity from the contagion of revolution which had spread through Europe at various times since 1789. Macaulay's *History* did not extend beyond the reign of William III, but it was a logical extension of his interpretation to regard the Great Reform Act of 1832 as a further vindication of the Whig-designed British Constitution, which had once again demonstrated its capacity to adapt itself to changing circumstances. Thus it seemed to Sir John Campbell, a future Lord Chancellor, writing in the 1840s, that the Reform Act had 'wisely remodelled the Constitution, and it is hardly less important than the Bill of Rights'. On reading Macaulay's first volumes, Campbell noted in his journal that:

'I rejoice that such good principles as those which he inculcates should be found in such a popular work. The party of Young Englanders [i.e. Disraeli and his Tory friends] who denounced the Revolution of 1688 as a crime are demolished, and (which is of more consequence) a severe blow is given to the Chartists and the ultra-Radicals'.[8]

It was largely owing to its association with material progress and political stability that mid-Victorian Liberalism also came to be imbued with an ethic of administrative efficiency, which distinguished it sharply, in the eyes of many contemporaries, from its political opponents. The crisis of 1846 over the corn-law question had had the effect of depriving the Conservative Party of much of its ministerial talent, as nearly the whole of the front-bench followed Peel's line, and a number of the most promising of the younger men groomed by Peel, including W. E. Gladstone, Sidney Herbert and Lord Lincoln, gravitated towards the Whigs during the course of the 1850s. Tainted by their attachment to a discredited economic policy, and notoriously lacking in men of first-rate administrative ability, the Protectionist Conservatives (now led, ironically, by the ex-Whig, Stanley) acquired an unhappy reputation for incompetence, which was aggravated by accusations of extravagance and corruption during the brief periods in the 1850s when they were in office.[9] The effect was to confirm the prejudices of Liberals about Conservative governments being by-words for financial laxity and improper practices, and to reinforce assumptions about the superior competence and morality of Liberal administrations.

Lord John Russell's Leadership

If the gradual evolution of a common 'Liberal' identity can best be described in terms of a new ideological synthesis, which embraced the aspirations of the various components of the reform coalition without entirely subsuming them, it is perhaps easier to accept the contention that this process was not matched by any corresponding growth of party unity. One obvious reason for the continued fragmentation of 'Liberalism' throughout the 1840s, and also for much of the 1850s, was that the great defining issue of Free Trade was one that cut across existing political boundaries. The Whigs under Melbourne, it is true, had taken some tentative steps in the direction of Free Trade just before the 1841 general election, but it was left to the subsequent Conservative government of Sir Robert Peel to embark upon a major programme of tariff reductions covering hundreds of commodities, and it was he who therefore gained the credit for lifting the British economy out of depression and balancing the budget. Furthermore, it was Peel who had carried the repeal of the corn laws, in 1846, after Russell's failure to construct a government to deal with the question. The emergent Liberal doctrine of the 1840s and 1850s thus derived, to a considerable extent, from what became the legacy of *Peelite* financial policy.

The picture does not become any clearer when Lord John Russell's attempts at leadership are brought into view. No doubt the difficulties which he encountered were due, in large part, to his own rather awkward personality. Indeed it is hard to imagine a more frustrating character to try to assess, for Russell's personal shortcomings deserve to be mitigated, to a considerable extent, by an appreciation of his genuinely progressive instincts. As a young opposition MP, in 1828, it was Russell who had successfully moved for the repeal of the Test and Corporation Acts; in 1831 he was one of the ministers responsible for drafting the Great Reform Bill; and later in the 1830s he was the driving force behind the policy of conciliation towards nonconformists and Roman Catholics adopted by the Melbourne ministry. All of this amounted to an honourable record as a promoter of civil and religious liberty. He was also capable on certain occasions, though not often enough, of a standard of parliamentary oratory which seemed to rise above the level of the ordinary party politician. Yet his reputation and standing, in the eyes of contemporaries, were more often influenced by another side of his personality, which was proud, aloof, over-sensitive, sulky and peevish. These traits were undoubtedly the product of Russell's intense self-awareness of his aristocratic pedigree, as a scion of one of the greatest of all the Whig families, which encouraged a tendency to think of himself as one of the few surviving representatives of a tradition of *pure* Whiggery stretching back through Fox and Rockingham to the first Whigs of the seventeenth century. We cannot ignore, however, the more prosaic explanation, that Russell was self-conscious about his diminutive physical stature (he was only about 5 foot 4 inches in height). In all probability, it was the case that a sense of physical inferiority served to intensify Russell's aristocratic hauteur. The end product was a leader who, in spite of his indispensable merits as a parliamentarian, conveyed an impression of personal coldness, often seemed unwilling to communicate with either colleagues or back-benchers, and was apt to be prickly in his response to criticism. At the same time, his lack of either physical stamina or force of personality meant that he found it difficult to impose his will upon his colleagues, and was unable to act as a guiding influence on his party to the extent that he would have wished.

True to his Foxite inheritance, Russell was, by instinct, a highly partisan politician, believing in the necessity of maintaining party connexion, and showing a determination to secure the political initiative for a Whig-led Liberal Party. This made it all the more frustrating for him, therefore, when he watched Peel embark upon his great Free Trade experiment. Bearing in mind Russell's typical aristocratic disdain for a man from a 'middle class' background like Peel, it is easy to understand his obvious feelings of resentment and jealousy towards the Conservative leader. A famous *Punch* cartoon of 1845 depicted the situation, with little Johnny Russell (in the playground) looking on in dismay as Peel contrived to perform on all of Russell's favourite musical instruments at once.

The fact that Peel appeared to have successfully pre-empted the Whigs on the policy of Free Trade had serious implications for Russell's ability to exercise authority over the Liberal Party, for it was clear that important sections within the party had considerable sympathy and respect for Peel and his achievements. In 1844, for example, Peel twice ran into difficulty with his own back-benchers, first because of his refusal to incorporate a maximum ten-hour day into his government's Factory Bill, and secondly because of his plan to reduce the differential tariff on sugar from the colonies; but on both occasions he was aided by the support of Cobden, Bright and other Free Trade radicals. As the diary of J. C. Hobhouse, a front-bench Whig, shows, when Lord Ashley's ten-hour amendment was initially carried against Peel's wishes, there were 'about 50 Liberals, chiefly radicals & free traders with Government' (Peel later succeeded in having the amendment rejected), while on the sugar duties scheme, the opposition attack on Peel was 'beaten only by the [anti-corn-law] league'. Not surprisingly, with such indiscipline, Hobhouse found in conversation with Russell that 'he agreed with me that our party were not in a condition to take [over] the government'.[10] Admiration for Peel extended beyond the Free Trade radicals on the back-benches, however, to include a number of Russell's own Whig colleagues. Most notable of these were the third Earl Grey and his brother-in-law, Charles Wood, who were attracted by the possibility of entering a coalition with Peel. There is even some evidence to suggest that radicals like Cobden and Charles Buller would have been sympathetic to such an arrangement. As late as May 1846, during the midst of the corn-law crisis, Grey was noting in his diary:

> This morning in the *Spectator* there is a most ill-natured article (containing however too great a mixture of truth) on Peel's superior qualifications for the leader of a real liberal Govt. over Johnny. . . . It put into my head many visions as to the advantage of a Peel liberal Govt, in which Ld J shd be offered a place but which on his refusing (as he wd do) a good many of us might join. After Church I went to Wood's . . . & discussed this notion with him – he did not think it so visionary as I expected.[11]

Another source of support for Peel, the value of which is not to be under-estimated despite the events of the 1830s, came from Queen Victoria and her increasingly influential consort, Prince Albert. The Crown may have been convinced, by the 1840s, that it was desirable to adopt a position of independence from the political parties, but the object of doing this was to enhance its authority rather than to diminish it.[12] Once the Queen had been weaned off her early preference for the Whigs, she and Albert came increasingly to see in Peel their notion of the ideal Prime Minister, one who strove to pursue policies that were in the best interests of the Country, regardless of considerations of party. Royal favour thus served to encourage that 'executive' style of government which historians have often described as being characteristic of Peel. From the point of view of Russell, of course, Peel's growing status as a 'national' leader could only weaken still further his claim to be the official leader of Liberalism. As we shall see, Victoria and Albert's preference for Peel, and, later, for the 'Peelites', was to be a significant factor in politics throughout the 1840s and 1850s.

Russell's dramatic public declaration of his belief in the need to repeal the corn laws, through the 'Edinburgh letter' of November 1845, addressed to his constituents, must therefore be set in the context of his need to establish some directing control over the forces of Liberalism, which had seemed increasingly liable to dispersion as a result of Peel's own pursuit of 'Liberal' policies. Privately, Russell had been convinced for some time that the corn laws ought to be abandoned, but he had regarded this as a long-term measure, which would have to be accompanied by substantial financial compensation for the landed interest.[13] For the time being, however, irritated at the way Cobden and other

Free Trade radicals were supporting Peel's ministry and making public attacks on the Whigs, Russell had continued to oppose C. P. Villiers's annual motion on the corn laws.[14] Only in June 1845 did Russell finally come out in favour of Villiers's repeal motion, acknowledging that the financial benefits to landowners, derived from the protective tariff, were politically indefensible, and expressing his *personal* opinion that the system could not go on for very much longer. What seems to have accelerated Russell's conclusion that he should take a public stand for immediate repeal was the impending crisis in Ireland, due to the failure of the potato crop, which became apparent during the autumn of 1845.

Peel himself, it is true, was now convinced that the time was ripe for action against the corn laws, but he was unable to secure the unanimous agreement of the Cabinet for such a move. The publication of the Edinburgh letter, at this critical juncture, enabled Russell to pre-empt Peel and seize the political initiative. How far this was the result of careful calculation, rather than of sheer impetuosity, we cannot be entirely sure, but Russell's intervention seemed likely to lay the foundations for future united action by a Whig-led Liberal Party, and thus forestall any further extra-parliamentary agitation by the anti-corn-law league, which would inevitably have focused, however illogically, on the famine in Ireland, presenting this as the consequence of the protectionist system. Russell would doubtless have been encouraged, in this last respect, by the letter from the Free Trade radical, H. G. Ward, thanking him for 'making us a *Party* again'.[15] With regard to the problems in Ireland itself, however, it has to be said that Russell – and also Peel, as it turned out – was open to the charge that he was simply using the crisis in order to further his preconceived domestic political objectives. While Russell continued to assert his desire to help the Irish people, and may genuinely have hoped that his declaration against the corn laws would enable him to reintegrate the O'Connellites into the Liberal coalition,[16] his policy in reality appears to be little more than another symbolic gesture to the Irish, of about the same practical value as lay appropriation in the 1830s.

It is quite possible that Russell had not anticipated that Peel's reaction to the Edinburgh letter would be to tender his resignation and offer support to a Russell ministry for the purpose of implementing repeal. In the event, Russell's attempt to form a government ended in failure, and in circumstances that did little credit to the Whigs. Officially, the reason for Russell's inability to fulfil the Queen's commission was the obstacle raised by Lord Grey's objection to joining a government in which Palmerston was to be Foreign Secretary, but in fact this became a convenient pretext which disguised the wider differences amongst the Whigs. Russell, typically, had consulted none of his senior colleagues before issuing his declaration in favour of repeal, and it soon became apparent, during the course of negotiations for the construction of a government, that there remained considerable Whig reservations about the policy. Lord Lansdowne, in particular, was unwilling to swallow this unpleasant morsel without a very large dose of financial relief to the landowners. The subsequent personal difficulties raised by Grey thus provided Russell with an escape route from a mission that would probably have failed in any case. The fact that a number of leading Whig peers, including Clarendon, Lansdowne and Auckland, made it clear that their position would be untenable in the House of Lords without Grey's support, convinced Russell that he could not proceed.[17] Peel was therefore invited to return to office and attempt to deal with the corn laws himself.

Although Russell and the Whigs emerged from the ministerial crisis of December 1845 with little honour, it may still be argued that, viewed from the purely cynical perspective of party advantage, events had turned out in the best way possible for them in the awkward circumstances created by Russell's premature public declaration. As Clarendon observed, towards the end of the crisis: 'If [our] internal differences serve to make a bridge for Peel's return to office & repealing the C. Laws & smashing his party [Grey] will have rendered good service & not snapped at everybody like a mad dog in vain.'[18] Certainly, by throwing the ball back into Peel's court, and helping *him* to dismantle the agricultural tariffs, the Whigs succeeded in exploiting the situation in order to wreck the Conservative Party. Approximately two-thirds of Conservative MPs opposed repeal, as is well known, and the measure only passed with support from Russell and the opposition, but it is important to note that on the subsequent, fatal division on the Irish coercion bill, which ended Peel's premiership, only about one-third of the Conservatives voted with the opposition. It is by no means clear, in other words, that, but for the defeat on the coercion bill, Peel might not simply have carried on in office, in precisely the same way as he had after the Maynooth crisis in the summer of 1845. By deliberately using the Irish coercion issue in order to bring down Peel's government, the Whigs were able to drive the wedge firmly into the Conservative ranks, denying them any opportunity to regroup in the aftermath of the corn-law crisis. The part played by the Whigs, in 1846, was neither noble nor heroic, but it proved to be highly effective.

In repudiating Peel's leadership, the Protectionist Conservatives had effectively renounced any claim to the Free Trade inheritance, which appeared, in retrospect, to be no less than the prosperity of mid-Victorian Britain. Unfortunately for Russell and the Whigs, while they were thus able to steal some of the credit for the Free Trade achievement from the Conservatives, their political triumph was frustratingly incomplete. The overwhelmingly Whiggish Russell administration, which took office after the fall of Peel, in June 1846, was to suffer from the fact that Peel and his followers, widely perceived as the true authors of Free Trade and the real experts in financial policy, preferred to remain in an independent position. One Whig minister, Lord Clarendon, had urged upon his colleagues the need to include not only the leading Peelites but also Cobden in the new ministry, as a means of broadening the base of 'the Whig party', which, though it still had an essential role to play in 'the true conservative process of reform', was generally considered to be 'aristocratical in its opinions, exclusive in its personnel, and guided by past historical reminiscences rather than by present public opinion'. In fact, according to Clarendon, the Whigs were 'thought to be nearly effete', and therefore:

> A fusion, so far as practicable with some of the Peelite party and some of the extreme Free-traders, would be a symptom that the Whig party recognised that their present position was owing to accident, and not to any general wish of the Country to see them in power. This would at once excite the sympathy and call forth the support of those sections of the community best able to confer strength upon a government under the present peculiar circumstances – in fact, to constitute a government fairly representing the industrial mind and conservative progress of the Country. . . . The Country will not stand still: an impetus has been given to men's minds that cannot be checked: wants and hopes have been excited that must be satisfied; commercial, financial and social reforms have been commenced and must be continued.[19]

However, Cobden was not to be deemed suitable for office at this stage, and none of the Peelites were prepared to accept the offers made by Russell.

Russell's ministry was therefore weakened at the outset because of the feeling that it was a second-best arrangement, and it found itself in the unpleasant position of being almost patronised by Peel and his followers, who were willing to offer limited parliamentary support while enjoying the advantage of being free from the responsibilities of office. It has been estimated that, even after the 1847 general election, the Free Trade Conservatives in the House of Commons numbered over one hundred, enough to give them the 'balance of power', and making them a potentially formidable 'third party' if they were prepared to act as such.[20] Inevitably, this produced an uneasy sense that the Peelites were content to wait in the wings for an appropriate opportunity to seize upon any mistakes made by the Whigs. As Sir Charles Wood, the Chancellor of the Exchequer, put it in a letter to Russell, 'They and we are the rivals for the lead of the great popular party.'[21]

Matters were made worse by the ironic fact that the economic boom of the mid-1840s, apparently inspired by Peel's fiscal programme, had ended in the financial crisis of 1847, which temporarily rendered precarious the whole Free Trade edifice. For the Whigs, it seemed that they were destined to suffer, as in the years 1839–41, as the party identified in the public mind with bad trade and budget deficits: 'the Whigs have as usual fallen on the cycle of depression', was Clarendon's gloomy observation.[22] The economic downturn also meant that Russell's government was not well placed to embark upon a further programme of bold tariff reductions, and though modest progress was eventually made, for example with the repeal of the Navigation Acts in 1849, such achievements were far outweighed by the opprobrium incurred as a result of the decision to renew the income tax in 1848 (this will be discussed later). Thus, the Whigs were left uncomfortably conscious of the possibility that the Peelites, sitting on the sidelines and free of responsibility for taking unpopular policy decisions, might constitute an alternative leadership-corps for the forces of Liberalism, and one that many radicals would all too obviously be ready to support. Lord Palmerston evidently knew how to play on Russell's sensitivities in this respect, warning him, in April 1849, of the disastrous consequences if the government, weak as it was in the House of Commons, were to resign. In such a case, Palmerston thought, the Queen was sure to˙send for her beloved Peel, and Russell would have no choice but to offer Whig support even though he could not, with dignity, take office under Peel himself:

you would be bound almost and obliged to hand your party over to Peel, and to abdicate your own position as Leader in his favour. Our

Radicals would go to him whether you chose or not, and a great many of our independent supporters might do the same, so that at all events you would be left with a much reduced band.[23]

Russell was perfectly well aware of the desirability of broadening the base of his government, as the various overtures made to individual Peelites show, but his Whig pride was still far too great for him to be able to contemplate relinquishing his leadership and allowing a Peelite takeover to occur.

Liberal Diversity in the 1840s

The state of political confusion which characterised British Liberalism during the 1840s cannot be attributed only to the disturbing presence of Peel and the Peelites, however. While it is true that the ideology of Free Trade had created new common ground on which to support all the diverse elements of the Liberal movement, it did not prompt any fundamental redefinition of the relationships between these different elements. Consequently, the tensions that had been apparent in the aftermath of the Great Reform Act were to persist throughout the 1840s, adding still further to the magnitude of the task confronting Russell as he tried to establish an effective command over this unwieldy and frequently unco-operative coalition.

With regard to nonconformity, there was a marked increase in political militancy in the years following the demise of Melbourne's government. It was in 1841 that a new weekly newspaper, the *Nonconformist*, was established with financial support from the Nottingham hosiery manufacturer, Samuel Morley. Under the editorship of a fellow Congregationalist, Edward Miall, the paper helped to propagate the case for Church disestablishment. Both Morley and Miall were also prominent members of the Anti-State Church Association, founded in 1844 and later renamed the Liberation Society, which was to become the outstanding nonconformist pressure group of the Victorian era. The English advocates of disestablishment could also take encouragement, on the face of it at least, from the schism within the Established Presbyterian Kirk in Scotland, in 1843, resulting in the secession of more than one-third of the Kirk's ministers and the formation of the Free Church, which gained considerable support in the large towns and in the Highlands (though it was not opposed in principle to an Established Church). With the forces hostile to the Established Churches growing increasingly vocal, by the mid-1840s, it is hardly surprising that Sir Robert Peel's proposal to increase and make permanent the parliamentary grant to the Roman Catholic seminary at Maynooth, in Ireland, should have provoked such angry protests. Peel's measure was a pragmatic attempt to draw the Catholic clergy in Ireland away from the movement for the repeal of the Union, and as such it received the support of Russell and the Whigs, but the Maynooth grant caused serious offence to those nonconformists who were determined to resist State endowment of any religious sect, Protestant or Catholic.

Another feature of nonconformity in the 1840s was the spread of Voluntaryist thinking, that is to say, the rejection of the idea that the State should involve itself in the provision of elementary education, which should be left instead to the voluntary efforts of the various religious denominations. Such an attitude had been encouraged by the disillusion felt by many nonconformists at the way the Whigs had capitulated to the Church of England in 1840, and it was reinforced by the experience of the Peel ministry's Factory Bill of 1843, which, through its provision for the compulsory education of factory children by the Anglican clergy, seemed to confirm the belief that all State initiatives in the field of education had an in-built bias towards the Church of England. The success of campaigners such as Edward Baines Junior, the proprietor of the *Leeds Mercury*, in forcing the Conservatives to drop their plan, was a significant illustration of the political muscle which nonconformity now possessed. Consequently, when Russell, on his accession to the premiership in 1846, proposed a new Education Bill involving an increase in the size and scope of the system of State grants to elementary schools (most of which were Anglican), this too faced intense hostility from Baines, Miall and many other nonconformist leaders (with the exception of the Wesleyan Methodists). Russell forced his measure through in 1847, but the bitterness which this created was manifested at the general election held later in the same year. The industrial towns of the West Riding of Yorkshire, in particular, saw the political balance between local Liberal groups seriously disrupted by the prominence of the Voluntary issue, with the result that Liberals who supported Russell's Education Act were sometimes driven into temporary alliances with the Conservatives against Voluntaryist Liberal candidates, as in the cases of Halifax and Leeds, resulting in the loss of some otherwise safe Liberal seats.[24] In the city of London, Russell himself, under attack from the Voluntaryists, was placed in the embarrassing position of having to rely on support from local Peelites in order to hold his seat, but his junior ministerial colleague, the nonconformist Benjamin Hawes, was less fortunate at Lambeth.

Such was the pressure exerted on Liberal candidates by non-conformist campaigners, that it was claimed after the general election that 60 Liberal MPs were pledged to oppose any further State endowments of religious sects, and that 26 were committed to the policy of disestablishment.[25]

In Scotland, it was the opposition to the Maynooth grant that proved to be the most potent political issue, for it enabled an alliance to develop between the United Presbyterians (the original dissenters) and the recently formed Free Church, something that would not have been possible on the Voluntary question. The result, in the 1847 general election, was that Whiggish candidates were either swept aside, or else struggled to survive, in those constituencies where a substantial part of the electorate belonged to the Free or Voluntary Churches. Both the sitting Whig MPs in Glasgow, for example, were defeated by anti-Maynooth dissenting candidates, while the most celebrated victim of all was the Cabinet minister, Macaulay, who lost his seat at Edinburgh.[26]

If the Maynooth grant and Education Act episodes exemplify the volatile relationship between Whiggery and nonconformity, they also illustrate the real complexity of the dynamics of the Liberal Party. In many ways, the numerous cross-currents which are thus exposed are more instructive than the familiar socio-economic distinction between aristocratic Whigs and 'middle-class radicals'. For instance, the Maynooth issue emphasises the point made in the last chapter, that there was no natural sense of affinity between nonconformists and Roman Catholics, two important elements in the Liberal coalition who were, in fact, potentially very antagonistic towards one another. Certainly, there can be no assumption that nonconformists were instinctively sympathetic to policies intended to conciliate the Irish Catholics. But the motives which inspired the hostility of the various nonconformist sects towards the Maynooth grant were not entirely the same either, for whereas the older sects tended to see the matter as a simple one of principled opposition to State interference in religion, and denied – perhaps not entirely convincingly – that they were actuated by anti-Catholic prejudice, such prejudice was clearly the main influence on the generally more moderate Wesleyan Methodists, who actually participated in an evangelical alliance that included Tories such as Lord

Ashley. Most significant of all, though, is the fact that Maynooth revealed divisions between nonconformists and the parliamentary radicals, and indeed between the parliamentary radicals themselves. John Bright (a Quaker) was among the 35 Liberal MPs, also including Duncombe, Ewart and Wakley, who opposed the grant in May 1845, but its supporters included Bright's anti-corn-law league partner, Richard Cobden (who was, interestingly enough, an Anglican). Thus Cobden, along with other radicals such as Roebuck, Hume, Villiers, Buller and Clay, found themselves acting with Russell and the Whigs in accepting the grant as an expedient attempt to reconcile Irish Catholics to the Act of Union. A similar division of opinion occurred over Russell's Education Bill, with Bright and Duncombe being numbered among the radicals who supported the position of the Voluntaryists, while Cobden, Hume, Roebuck and others voted with the Whigs, despising, as they did, the Voluntaryists for the way they were creating an obstacle to the creation of a national system of elementary education. Roebuck, incidentally, was to pay for his support of Russell's plan with the loss of his seat at Bath, in the 1847 general election.[27]

The point that ultimately emerges from a consideration of the impact of the Maynooth and education questions, therefore, is that the Liberal Party was a far more complex entity than is suggested by the usual depiction of a simple division between Whigs, on the one hand, and radicals, on the other. Such a convenient fault-line may be detected at certain times and in varying degrees, but what is significant is that, in so far as Maynooth and the Education Bill did divide the Whigs from some of their radical and many of their nonconformist allies, it is the Whigs who appear in the more positive light (to the late-twentieth-century mind, at least) as the advocates of constructive policies. This provides a salutary reminder of the need to resist the natural temptation to conceive of mid-nineteenth-century Liberal politics in terms of a simple scale on which the Whigs are positioned towards the 'right', representing a purely static, unimaginative outlook, whereas Cobden, Bright and other radicals occupy positions on the 'left' of the scale, reflecting their near monopoly of moral virtue and 'progressive' thinking. Too often, in consequence of such simplistic assumptions, there has been a tendency to write off the Whigs prematurely.

On another specifically 'social' question of the day, that of the regulation of the hours of work in textile factories, it is similarly impossible to reduce the political division to one between Whigs and radicals. The Ten-hours Bill of 1847, introduced by the back-bench Tory MP, John

Fielden, was supported by, among others, Russell, Palmerston, Macaulay and Sir George Grey, but opposed by other ministers, like F. T. Baring, Wood and Lord Morpeth (the last two of whom, significantly, represented industrial constituencies – Halifax, and the West Riding of Yorkshire, respectively). A few radicals, such as Duncombe, Bernal Osborne, Brotherton and General De Lacy Evans, supported Fielden's bill, but many others, like Cobden, Bright, Hume, Roebuck and Milner Gibson, were strongly averse to State intervention against the factory owners – with whom some of them, of course, were closely associated. In the field of public health, Lord Morpeth, for the Whigs, had been willing to implement Edwin Chadwick's grandiose scheme for a centralised Board of Health with extensive powers, but it was the widespread opposition to such centralisation, expressed among others by the radical, Bright, that forced the government to modify the Public Health Bill of 1848 into a largely permissive measure. All that can be said at the end, by way of assessment, is that there was at least as much genuine concern within the Whig leadership as in other political groups about the need to address some of the worst problems created by the unplanned processes of industrialisation and urbanisation. If, as has recently been suggested, the implementation of factory reform in 1847 helped to draw what venom was left from the Chartist movement, the credit for this is due in part to the Whigs.[28]

The reputation of Russell and the Whigs has undoubtedly suffered, in the eyes of posterity, owing to their unsympathetic and unimaginative response to an even greater social problem, arising from the failure of the potato crop in Ireland. In retrospect, the attitude shown towards the plight of the Irish appears callous, and betrays the underlying racial contempt felt towards the 'inferior' Celtic people. The Whigs were slow to adopt relief schemes to help tide the Irish over the crisis, and though some valuable measures were implemented during the winter of 1846–7, these were then prematurely dropped. Whig policy towards the starving population was shaped by the fear that, if generous relief were offered, this would only create a situation in which the bulk of the Irish population would be encouraged to become permanent mendicants relying on the British State. In any case, the Whigs were reluctant to abandon the view that it was the responsibility of the Irish landowning class to provide relief for the peasants, not the British State. There was strong opposition in the Cabinet to any measure of tenant right, as a means of restoring stability to Ireland, and, characteristically, the one major measure that was eventually passed, the

Encumbered Estates Act of 1849, was designed to facilitate the sale of estates by bankrupt landowners in order to create a new class of landlords. But, if the Whigs' response to the Irish crisis seems inadequate, the tragic fact for the Irish people, and the one that is most significant from the point of view of this study, is that nowhere within the British 'Liberal' tradition, in its broadest sense (embracing Whigs, radicals and Peelites), was there a clear alternative to the policies pursued by the Russell administration. In fact, the Peelites were inclined to criticise the government for extravagance and inefficiency in its handling of the Irish problem. Many people in Ireland either starved or were forced to emigrate, and the long-term consequence of this experience was a legacy of bitterness which would eventually manifest itself in the form of a new political challenge to British control over Ireland, but in the late 1840s the Irish Question was simply not a major source of division within Liberal politics in Britain.

Cobden and Radicalism

When a rift between Liberals did appear, in the late 1840s, which distinctly involved the Whig leadership on the one hand, and a substantial group of parliamentary radicals on the other, the issue ostensibly at stake was the predictable one of electoral reform. In May 1848, a committee consisting of 51 MPs agreed that Joseph Hume should introduce a motion in the House of Commons calling for household suffrage, a secret ballot, triennial parliaments and equal electoral districts. This so-called 'little charter', the radicals' response to the more far-reaching demands of the Chartists, was defeated by 351 votes to 84, in June. It is important to recognise, however, that underlying this 'new reform movement' was the dispute with Russell's ministry over the question of financial policy. At the beginning of the 1848 session the Chancellor of the Exchequer, Wood, had proposed to renew the income tax (introduced by Peel as a 'temporary' measure in 1842) for a further three years, and to raise the rate at which it was levied from 7d. to one shilling in the pound. This plan, which was designed partly to raise extra revenue to finance a new militia bill demanded by the Commander-in-Chief, the Duke of Wellington, because of fears of a French invasion, provoked vehement protests from radical MPs.[29] Although Wood's proposal was subsequently modified so as to omit the increase in income tax, and allow extra government borrowing instead, ministers still had to beat off an attack from Hume, who sought to limit the extension of the tax to just one year. Significantly, it was after this furious row over financial policy that the radicals launched their new campaign for electoral reform.

The link between the 'little charter' and the question of financial policy is of the utmost importance, because radical support for the former, in the House of Commons, temporarily masked the serious differences of opinion that existed as to which of the two issues should receive priority. Whereas some, like Hume and Bright, considered a thoroughgoing reform of the electoral system to be an essential precondition for any progress in the area of government retrenchment, others, notably Cobden and some fellow members of the 'Manchester school' of radicals, took exactly the opposite view.[30] As was so often to be the case in future, the inability of the parliamentary radicals to unite for very long around an agreed course of immediate action, the product, partly, of personal jealousies and rivalries, as well as of the inevitable tendency for 'earnest' men to show intolerance towards other 'earnest' men with alternative priorities, was to seriously impede the impact of radicalism during the mid-Victorian period.

Cobden's general political outlook is of special interest because it was based on a systematic philosophy which might have provided a coherent basis for radical action. According to the Cobdenite view of the world, the triumph of the Free Trade cause in 1846 represented only the first stage of an assault upon the aristocratically-dominated system of government, which would ultimately revolutionise both domestic policy and international relations. The next step was to curb the financial laxity of a corrupt, extravagant, and worst of all warlike administration, by imposing a rigorous regime of retrenchment. At the end of 1848, Cobden's 'national budget' was published by the Liverpool Financial Reform Association (one of a number of such organisations that had grown up in the provinces in the wake of the protest against Wood's budget), in which he proposed cuts of £10 million, equivalent to nearly one-fifth of total government expenditure, mainly at the expense of the army and navy, in order to finance the reduction or abolition of various customs and excise duties.[31]

It was also Cobden's belief that the extension of Free Trade ideas throughout the world would have a beneficial moral influence, in that by encouraging economic specialisation, and therefore the economic interdependence of States, war between nations would become inconceivable, and the militaristic regimes of aristocratic Europe would be rendered redundant. Whilst the promotion of Free Trade and the spread of international harmony would thus serve to discredit the British ruling class, Cobden's ideal of a new system of government, based upon the values of the middle classes, would finally be achieved through the injection of entrepreneurial methods into the agricultural sector. Far from seeing land and industry as irreconcilable interests, with the former necessarily yielding to the latter, Cobden believed that the manufacturers in the big cities, and a rural middle class of modern, efficient, capitalist farmers, would prove to be natural allies, who might combine in an assault upon the neo-feudalism which had contrived to maintain its dominance both in the countryside and at Westminster.[32]

In Cobden's scheme of things, however, an extension of the franchise, and other adjustments to the system of parliamentary representation, were regarded as suitable objectives only for the long term, rather than as matters which demanded immediate attention. Contrary to Bright and Hume, who saw these reforms acting as a trigger for the wider changes desired by radicals, Cobden thought there was little point in merely increasing the numbers entitled to take part in a system that was dangerously contaminated by the noxious effluent of aristocratic control. To pursue the marine analogy, it was Cobden's view that it was necessary to purify the water first, before any more fish were allowed to swim in it. Cobden's attitude undoubtedly betrayed his fundamental distrust of the working classes. Unlike his ally and friend Bright, with whom indeed relations became strained because of their differences over the priority of franchise reform, Cobden had no faith in the superior political morality of the masses over the aristocracy, and he was not inclined to believe that the electoral system was likely to be cleansed simply by the presence of large numbers of working-class electors. Even when Cobden came round to the view that electoral reform deserved a higher priority, in the early 1850s, he still concluded that the implementation of a secret ballot was the only effective means of combatting the malignant influence of the old ruling elite over the voters, and that such a measure was therefore essential before any thought was given to increasing the numbers who could vote.[33]

There was a practical problem to be faced, in any case, in that the northern industrialists, who had been willing to support the campaign for the repeal of the corn laws, were unlikely to be quite so enthusiastic about a movement dedicated to the extension of the franchise to large numbers of their own employees. On such a policy, as Cobden was well aware, 'We cannot bring the League force with us.'[34] Indeed,

Cobden had been warned by the Manchester businessman W. R. Greg, at the time of the 'little charter' in 1848, that he and other former supporters of the League were:

> almost unanimous in condemning the peculiar time and objects chosen for the new agitation . . . [we] think it far wiser to work with the tools we have than to spend years of contest in obtaining new tools, when our *real work* would still have to be done . . . a large portion of the middle classes will oppose you steadily and to the last on questions involving any radical remodelling of our representative system . . . you will be able to obtain all the *practical* reforms you wish for far sooner than the organic reforms which the Chartists say are necessary preliminaries.[35]

Consequently, as one of the campaigners for electoral reform later recalled, the 'Manchester school' had, on the whole, been 'lukewarm' in its support for the cause: 'Although they voted with us in the House of Commons, they did little more.'[36] Differences such as this, so characteristic of Victorian radicalism, help to explain why it was that the undoubtedly hostile attitude of the radicals towards the Whig leadership of Russell, while frequently damaging, was not inevitably fatal.

Unfortunately for Cobden, the problems which obstructed him in his endeavour to secure widespread acceptance of his vision of the radical future were not confined to the disagreements with other radicals over what should be their priorities. While the idea of enforcing a retrenchment of government expenditure could command much support amongst the parliamentary radicals, for instance, a contradictory impulse manifested itself, as we shall describe in the next chapter, in enthusiasm for the bellicose style of foreign policy displayed by Lord Palmerston, which was obviously inimical both to the idea of limiting armaments and to the wider dream of international peace and goodwill fostered by the Free Trade system. In fact, as Cobden acknowledged in his gloomier moments, it seemed doubtful whether the parliamentary radicals, or the Country as a whole, were prepared to join in a systematic assault upon the insidious network of aristocratic control in all its manifestations. The cunning flexibility demonstrated by the Whigs over such questions as Free Trade had perhaps, after all, proved sufficient to deflect more fundamental criticisms of the system of government. 'It is a formidable task to fight against the aristocracy', Cobden confessed on one occasion, 'when it presents the front of a sham Liberalism, and especially so when we have to deal with a people of such strong aristocratic prejudices, that it would almost prefer to be ruined by lords than saved by commoners.'[37]

The Decline of Russell's Ministry

The chaotic diversity of British Liberalism, throughout the 1840s, should perhaps encourage more sympathy than is usually shown by historians for the predicament of Lord John Russell, as he attempted to steer a pack of truculent and self-willed horses in the same direction at once. Russell's need for a rallying-cry may well help to explain the extraordinary, indeed notorious, step which he took in November 1850 by issuing his 'Durham letter', a letter to the Bishop of Durham denouncing, in the most offensive terms, the Pope's plan to re-establish the Roman Catholic hierarchy in England. Certainly, some of his colleagues had no doubt that, through his contemptuous dismissal of 'the mummeries of superstition', Russell was aligning himself with a strong current of public opinion which was not only outraged by the so-called 'Papal aggression', but also alarmed by the apparently insidious spread of crypto-Catholic, or 'Puseyite', influences within the Church of England itself.[38] It does not appear to have been the case, though, that Russell's action was simply a knee-jerk response to crude, anti-Catholic feeling in the Country, for he had pondered his step for some time before publishing the offending letter. This indicates that there were deeper political calculations behind Russell's move, beyond the obviously profitable pandering to widespread 'Protestant' prejudices.

It is possible to suggest several elements that fit into the political equation as Russell might have drawn it in November 1850. In the first place, the anti-popery cry can be seen as a burning of the boats between British Whiggery and the Irish Roman Catholics, prompted by Russell's growing exasperation with the situation in Ireland. O'Connell had died in 1847, but even before his death his authority in Ireland had been seriously undermined, with the initiative falling to the more extreme nationalists of the 'Young Ireland' movement, notably William Smith O'Brien. An abortive rebellion against British rule, in 1848, compelled Russell's ministry to resort to coercion, including the suspension of habeas corpus. At the same time, the revolution in Rome, and the temporary overthrow of the Pope, finally put an end to Whig hopes that Pius IX might prove to be a more liberal and co-operative pontiff.

Thereafter, it was clear that there was no question of the Pope being prepared to assist the British government by discouraging the Catholic priesthood from becoming involved in the Irish nationalist movement, and perhaps even agreeing to Roman Catholic endowment by the British State.

Apart from his obvious frustration with the problems of dealing with the Irish people and their spiritual leader, other, internal political considerations must have been in Russell's mind when he embarked upon his anti-Catholic crusade. For instance, there was the question of how to wield authority over the radical and nonconformist groups within the Liberal coalition, and on the face of it there could have been no better way to do this than by orchestrating a united stand against the hated Pope and the despised Irish. Then there was the question of how to retrieve some control over his own government – it had never been very strong – at a time when it was being undermined by the conduct of his 'patriotic' Foreign Secretary, Palmerston, whose popularity had only recently been enhanced by his triumph in the Don Pacifico debate. Furthermore, a point that tends to be overlooked, there was the potential threat to Russell's position posed by the Peelite leaders, following Sir Robert's tragic death in May 1850. While Peel had lived, he had shown a general forbearance towards the Whig ministers, and little inclination to force his way back into office quickly, but his ambitious protégés, such as Herbert and Gladstone, were unlikely now to show the same restraint. It is possible, therefore, that one reason for Russell's fostering of the 'papal aggression' protest was that it seemed well designed to repel the Peelite leaders (who were, significantly, mostly High Church Anglicans, tainted, themselves, with suspicions of crypto-Catholicism), isolating them from a Liberal Party identified with Russell's brand of Protestantism.

Whatever his precise reasons may have been, Russell's initiative can reasonably be regarded as an attempt to restore his authority as leader before the process of Liberal disintegration got completely out of hand. In this respect, there can be no doubt that he was unsuccessful in achieving his objective. While Russell certainly managed to alienate those whom he had possibly intended to alienate – the Irish Catholics and the Peelite leaders – the anti-Catholic cry failed to rally the other Liberal groups in the way he must have hoped. It is true that many Wesleyan Methodists were appreciative of Russell's stand, but they had always been the most conservative of the nonconformist sects. Prominent representatives of the older sects, on the other hand, like the Congregationalist, Edward Miall, joined with the Quaker, John Bright, and the general body of parliamentary radicals – secular as well as religious – in denouncing what they chose to regard as a reprehensible manifestation of religious intolerance, directed against Roman Catholics, which was particularly ominous coming from a government that supposedly stood for the principle of religious freedom.

Even before Russell was able to carry through an Ecclesiastical Titles Bill, to penalise Roman Catholic bishops who adopted English territorial titles, the disorganisation of the Liberal Party in the House of Commons had resulted in a humiliating defeat for the government, in February 1851, on the annual motion by Peter Locke King calling for the equalisation of the county and borough franchise qualifications. The painful irony for Russell was that he had already abandoned his position of 'finality' with regard to parliamentary reform, and had indicated a willingness to reopen the question, in spite of the reluctance of his Cabinet colleagues; but his offer – made during the 1851 debate – to bring in a bill the following year, was not enough to satisfy the radicals. With most Conservative, Peelite, moderate Liberal, and Irish Liberal MPs choosing to stay away, a small ministerialist rump of 54 was overcome by the 100 MPs who supported Locke King. It is an obvious sign of the despair felt by Russell at the increasingly impossible position he found himself in, that he chose to resign. However, the Conservative leader, Stanley (soon to become the fourteenth Earl of Derby), was unwilling to form a minority government, and, when the Queen and Prince Albert urged Russell to construct a Whig–Peelite coalition, the repugnance felt by the Peelite leaders towards the Ecclesiastical Titles Bill turned out to be an insuperable obstacle.

Russell and the Whigs were therefore recalled to the helm, but the ministry was in an even more weakened state than before. Finance continued to be a major problem for the government, in spite of the fact that economic recovery was yielding a budget surplus: Sir Charles Wood was able to reduce the duties on timber, coffee, tobacco and paper, but his plan to retain the income tax for a further three years provoked furious opposition from all sides, and in the end it was only possible to renew the tax for one year. The government limped through the remainder of the parliamentary session, putting on the statute book a modified Ecclesiastical Titles Bill, which was an instant dead-letter, and during the autumn Russell fought to secure the concurrence of the Cabinet to a new Reform Bill, involving £5 borough and £20 county franchises. Tensions within the Cabinet were further exacerbated by the fact that one of the leading opponents of the proposed Reform Bill, Palmerston, was increasingly at loggerheads, both with Russell and with the Crown, because of his high-handed conduct at the foreign office. Finally, in December 1851, Palmerston was dismissed from his post, at the insistence of Victoria and Albert. This proved to be a fatal step, for in February 1852, shortly after Russell had introduced his new Reform Bill into the House of Commons, Palmerston scored his famous 'tit-for-tat' by engineering the government's defeat on the Militia Bill. Russell again resigned, and on this occasion Derby was prepared to form a minority Conservative government, with Disraeli as Chancellor of the Exchequer and leader of the Commons.

The chief interest of the brief interlude of Conservative government, from February to December 1852, lies in the way it prompted a closing of the ranks on the part of the various Liberal groups, based for the first time on their common commitment to the defence of Free Trade. While the general election, held in the summer, produced an inconclusive result, the possibility that the Conservatives might seek to restore a protective tariff for agriculture had a beneficial influence on Liberal cohesion in many areas. The constituencies of the West Riding of Yorkshire, where the Voluntary question had had a disastrous impact on relations between local Liberal groups in 1847, provides a good illustration of the emotive power of Free Trade as a rallying-cry which enabled Whigs, radicals and nonconformists to sink their differences.[39] Indeed, the fact that the Free Trade question served to eclipse the Voluntary issue was a disappointment to some nonconformist leaders, and even the *Nonconformist* newspaper reckoned, after the general election, that only 24 Liberal MPs were committed to the Voluntaryist cause, with 25 sympathisers and 15 doubtful.[40] The great exception to this trend was in Scotland, where the Maynooth issue continued to dominate many elections, sustaining the alliance between the United Presbyterians and the Free Church, forged in 1847, which was strong enough to repel the counter-offensive by Whig candidates in most burghs.[41]

Elsewhere, in what proved to be a fairly quiet general election, the most striking feature was the decline of the Peelites, who were reduced to around 45 MPs, having suffered from Conservative exploitation of the no-popery cry. At least, Russell's association with the Ecclesiastical Titles Bill meant that the Whigs were generally insulated from this line of attack. On the other hand, Russell's anti-Catholic stand definitely did harm in Ireland, where the independent 'Irish Brigade', formed as a result of the Durham letter, increased their numbers from 28 to 48

MPs, mainly at the expense of the Whigs, who were reduced to just 15. Taking the United Kingdom as a whole, the loose assemblage of Whig, radical and Irish Brigade MPs accounted for about 319 of the 654 seats in the new House of Commons, so that the Peelites continued to hold the balance of power.

When the new parliament met, late in 1852, Free Trade again provided the stimulus for a combination of Whigs, radicals and Peelites, dedicated to the defeat of Disraeli's budget which, although it made no attempt to restore tariffs, offended against the canons of Liberal financial orthodoxy by seeking to give indirect compensation to landowners for the loss of the corn laws. Ominously for Russell and the Whigs, however, the coup de grace to Disraeli's scheme was delivered by Peel's disciple, Gladstone, in a devastating speech, and after the government's resignation Victoria and Albert were able to exert their influence behind the scenes in order to bring about the long-desired formation of a Peelite–Whig coalition, headed by the Peelite, Lord Aberdeen. Russell found that his position had been weakened because of the dislike felt by many fellow Whigs for his Reform Bill, and because of the personal hostility towards him on the part of the Peelites and radicals. He thus found himself obliged to submit to the indignity of serving in a subordinate capacity in a Cabinet where half the posts were filled by Peelites, in spite of their numerical inferiority in the House of Commons. For a time, at least, it must have seemed that the Whigs' worst fear, that of a Peelite takeover of the Liberal leadership, had been realised.

The Future of Whiggery?

As we shall see in the next chapter, the Aberdeen coalition government proved to be a false start in terms of the evolution of a comprehensive 'Liberal Party', but it is nevertheless usually held to be the case that the failure of Russell's ministry was symptomatic of the failure of Whiggery itself, which had become an obsolete creed, out of step with an increasingly urban and industrial society.[42] This view is open to serious doubt, however. It seems to stem from the assumption that a united Liberal Party had already come into being by 1841, and that Russell and the Whigs, through their own political and personal ineptitude, subsequently failed to hold this party together. But the evidence presented in this chapter suggests a more measured conclusion: that, while Russell's record can hardly be described as successful, it is unreasonable to condemn him for his inability to unite what remained a discordant coalition of groups and opinions, rather than a homogeneous party. British Liberalism, in the 1840s and 1850s, was inherently fissile, and the problems that this caused were not to be confined to the period of Russell's leadership, as Gladstone was later to discover.

We should certainly be wary of the assertion, still found in modern textbooks, that the Whigs had run out of new men by the time of Russell's ministry of 1846–52. It is only necessary to point to the younger generation of Whigs recruited into Melbourne's Cabinet, between 1839 and 1841, notably Morpeth (later Earl of Carlisle), Clarendon and Sir George Grey, whose ministerial careers extended well into the 1860s (Macaulay, another new face, had his career cut short when he lost his seat in 1847); then there was Sir Charles Wood, who entered Russell's Cabinet in 1846, where he was joined in 1851 by Granville, Seymour (later Duke of Somerset) and Fox Maule. These men could not be described as spectacular politicians, it is true, but most of them, along with later arrivals like Sir George Cornewall Lewis, were to become more or less permanent fixtures in a succession of mid-Victorian Liberal governments. So far from being obsolete, it could be argued that Whiggery, by the 1850s, was adapting itself to a changing political climate through its identification with the ascendant ideology of Free Trade, and through its ability gradually to build up a reputation for solid, administrative efficiency. It was for these reasons, indeed, that the Whigs were to continue to serve as an administrative-corps for the Liberal Party right up until the 1880s, and to some extent beyond.

It is indicative of the continued role of the Whigs that, even in the 1850s and 1860s, contemporaries sometimes still referred, in an exclusive sense, to 'the Whig party'.[43] Yet, at the same time, they were equally likely to talk of 'the Whig and Liberal party', or 'the Whigs' as distinct from 'the Radicals whom everybody fears',[44] suggesting that the idea still persisted that the Whigs, while existing as the aristocratic nucleus of Liberalism, embodied for this very reason the views of a wide spectrum of Liberal opinion. That it was never entirely clear, in fact, exactly where the dividing line between Whigs and radicals was to be drawn, is demonstrated by the perplexity of the Peelite, William Waldegrave Palmer, in 1852, who wished to see a 'fusion of Peelites and moderate Whigs', in order to form a government of a conservative character: 'A mere junction of the Peelites with the Whigs would be a very different thing. The combined party would not be divided from Radicalism by any broader line than the late Ministry [i.e. Russell's] were.'[45]

If Russell's style of leadership was at fault, the criticism must be not that he was content to do too little, but that he sometimes tried to do too much. Russell may have failed to preside over that broadening of the basis of his Whig government, aimed at creating a 'government fairly representing the industrial mind and conservative progress of the Country', of the sort urged by Clarendon in 1846, but it is well to remember that such a government would not have been more 'constructive' in its policies. On the contrary, a Liberal government containing a number of Peelites and Free Trade radicals would have been less, not more, likely to be concerned with such questions as the regulation of factory hours, and the Peelites would have strongly opposed any further electoral reform. It was no coincidence that when the amalgamation of all the groups committed to Free Trade was finally achieved, in 1859, it occurred under the auspices of a man who was so moderate in his general political outlook that many did not consider him to be a real Liberal at all.

NOTES

1. Russell to Melbourne, 9 September 1837, in Ian Newbould, *Whiggery and Reform, 1830–1841* (London, 1990) p. 318.

2. Michael Bentley, 'Party, Doctrine and Thought', in Michael Bentley and John Stevenson (eds), *High and Low Politics in Modern Britain* (Oxford, 1983).

3. As the *Oxford English Dictionary* notes, 'liberal' was originally a term of abuse, used by Tory writers like Southey and Sir Walter Scott, against the radicals, in an attempt to equate them with continental nationalists (and thus to imply that the radicals were 'un-English'). However, as with the terms 'Whig' and 'Tory' in the seventeenth century, radicals tended to adopt the label 'Liberal' for themselves.

4. This marked the formal recognition of Russell's overall leadership of the 'Liberal Party', although it had been *de facto* accepted since 1844, when Lord Melbourne had suffered a stroke, ruling him out of contention for the premiership.

5. John Prest, *Lord John Russell* (London, 1972) pp. 190–3.

6. Cobden to George Candy, 'Wednesday' [c. 1842], BL Add MSS 65136, f. 75.

7. Hadfield to Morley, n.d., and 23 October 1843, in Edwin Hodder, *The Life of Samuel Morley* (London, 1887) pp. 77–8.

8. Mrs Hardcastle, *Life of John, Lord Campbell* (London, 1881) vol. 2, p. 204 (autobiography, n.d.); vol. 2, p. 248 (journal, 11 January 1849).

9. Robert Stewart, *The Foundation of the Conservative Party, 1830–1867* (London, 1978) p. 279.

10. J. C. Hobhouse, diary, 18 March, 17 June, 16 June 1844, BL Add MSS 43746.

11. F. A. Dreyer, 'The Whigs and the Ministerial Crisis of 1845', *English Historical Review*, LXXX (1965) p. 534.

12. David Cannadine, 'The Last Hanoverian Sovereign? The Victorian Monarchy in Historical Perspective', in A. L. Beier *et al.* (eds), *The First Modern Society* (London, 1989).

13. Russell to Joseph Parkes, 4 April 1844, in G. P. Gooch (ed.), *The Later Correspondence of Lord John Russell, 1840–1878* (London, 1925) vol. 1, p. 72.

14. J. C. Hobhouse, diary, 25 June 1844, BL Add MSS 43746.

15. Ward to Russell, 29 November 1845, in Gooch (ed.), *Later Correspondence of Russell*, vol. 1, p. 84.

16. Russell to Lansdowne, 27 December 1845, ibid., vol. 1, pp. 98–9.

17. See J. C. Hobhouse's diary of the ministerial crisis, BL Add MSS 47230, ff. 21–41.

18. Clarendon to George Cornewall Lewis, 21 December 1845, Clarendon MSS (Bodleian Library) C532/1.

19. Clarendon's Cabinet memorandum, June 1846, in Sir Herbert Maxwell, *Life and Letters of the Fourth Earl of Clarendon* (London, 1913) vol. 1, pp. 265–7.

20. J. B. Conacher, *The Peelites and the Party System, 1846–1852* (Newton Abbot, 1972) pp. 30–2.

21. Wood to Russell, 14 August 1847, in Gooch (ed.), *Later Correspondence of Russell*, vol. 1, pp. 179–81.

22. Clarendon to Cornewall Lewis, 5 September 1847, Clarendon MSS, C532/1.

23. Palmerston to Russell, 14 April 1849, in Gooch (ed.), *Later Correspondence of Russell*, vol. 1, pp. 193–4.

24. Derek Fraser, 'Voluntaryism and West Riding Politics in the Mid-Nineteenth Century', *Northern History*, XII (1977).

25. Arthur Miall, *Life of Edward Miall* (London, 1884) p. 128.

26. I. G. C. Hutchison, *A Political History of Scotland, 1832–1924* (Edinburgh, 1986) p. 65.

27. See G. I. T. Machin, 'The Maynooth Grant, the Dissenters and the Establishment, 1845–7', *English Historical Review*, LXXXII (1967), for the whole of this paragraph.

28. Peter Mandler, *Aristocratic Government in the Age of Reform: Whigs and Liberals, 1830–1852* (Oxford, 1990) p. 280.

29. See Roebuck to Osborne, 22 February 1848, in P. H. Bagenal, *Ralph Bernal Osborne MP* (privately printed, 1884) pp. 100–2.

30. Cf. Hume to Walmsley, 17 November 1848, Cobden to Walmsley, January 1849, in H. M. Walmsley, *The Life of Sir Josuah Walmsley* (London, 1879) pp. 203–6, 210.

31. See G. R. Searle, *Entrepreneurial Politics in Mid-Victorian Britain* (Oxford, 1993) pp. 51–74, for the financial reform movement. As Searle shows, the financial reformers were themselves divided over the relative merits of the

income tax, some wishing to retain it in order to dispense with all indirect taxes, others desiring its abolition as well.

32.　Cobden to Walmsley, 17 October 1848 and n.d. [1852], in H. M. Walmsley, *Sir Josuah Walmsley*, pp. 209, 267–71.

33.　Cobden to Walmsley, n.d. [1852] and 25 September 1852, ibid., pp. 267–71, 272–5.

34.　Cobden to Walmsley, 20 October 1850, ibid., pp. 210–11.

35.　Greg to Cobden, 11 May 1848, in Derek Fraser, *Urban Politics in Victorian England* (London, 1976) pp. 249–50.

36.　Walmsley's note, 1862, in H. M. Walmsley, *Sir Josuah Walmsley*, pp. 211–12.

37.　Cobden to Walmsley, 17 October 1848, ibid., p. 209.

38.　Clarendon to Cornewall Lewis, 8 November 1850, Clarendon MSS, C532/1.

39.　Fraser, 'West Riding Politics', pp. 227–31; see also Fraser, *Urban Politics*, p. 205, for the case of Manchester.

40.　Machin, *Politics and the Churches*, p. 248.

41.　Hutchison, *Scotland*, pp. 66–7.

42.　Norman Gash, *Reaction and Reconstruction in English Politics, 1832–1852* (Oxford, 1965) pp. 195–200.

43.　For example, Palmerston to William Temple, 30 April 1852, in Hon. E. Ashley, *Life of Lord Palmerston, 1846–65* (London, 1876) vol. 1, pp. 336–41; Russell to Lord Minto, 16 March 1858, in Spencer Walpole, *Life of Lord John Russell* (London, 1889) vol. 2, p. 296; Granville to Russell, 26 March 1866, in Lord Edmond Fitzmaurice, *Life of Lord Granville, 1815–1891* (London, 1905), vol. 1, pp. 501–2.

44.　Palmerston to William Temple, 20 June and 17 September 1852, in Ashley, *Palmerston*, vol. 1, pp. 347–50, 368–70; Clarendon to Granville, 14 December 1858, in Maxwell, *Clarendon*, vol. 2, pp. 171–2.

45.　Palmer to Edward Cardwell, 25 February 1852, in Lord Selborne, *Memorials: Family and Personal, 1766–1865* (London, 1896) vol. 2, pp. 133–5.

3 Lord Palmerston and Mid-Victorian Liberalism

Introduction

It has been seen that after the break-up of the Conservative Party in 1846, over the question of the repeal of the corn laws, a long period of political confusion followed, in which it proved impossible to establish a stable government of the 'left-centre' embracing all those elements, committed to the principle of Free Trade, who were collectively known as 'Liberals'. Lord John Russell's ministry of 1846–52, which never commanded a reliable majority in the House of Commons, was seriously weakened by its inability to come to terms with the leading Peelites, a problem that arose, all too clearly, out of mutual suspicions and rivalries. Even when a coalition government of Whigs and Peelites was formed, under the premiership of Lord Aberdeen, in December 1852, the experiment lasted for only a little more than two years, as the ministry was brought down on a motion of censure in the House of Commons, prompted by its inept handling of the military expedition to the Crimea. The acrimonious circumstances surrounding the fall of the Aberdeen coalition, and its eventual replacement by a more purely Whiggish administration, formed by Lord Palmerston,[1] presented major obstacles to co-operation between the various Liberal groups. Palmerston's first ministry, indeed, was confronted by the most formidable array of opponents in the House of Commons imaginable, for quite apart from the official Conservative opposition, under the occasionally brilliant generalship of Disraeli, there was a small band of alienated Peelites, including Gladstone, Herbert and Graham, a number of radicals openly hostile to Palmerston's leadership, notably Cobden and Bright, and, for most of the time, the ex-Whig premier, Russell. It was to be the combination of all these groups and individuals (along with another separate group, the so-called 'Irish Brigade' of MPs, estranged from the Liberals since Russell's anti-papal stand of 1850–1) that inflicted defeats on Palmerston over the China War, in March 1857, and over the Orsini affair, in February 1858. Not until June 1859, after the famous meeting at Willis's rooms, was a more truly 'Liberal' government formed, with Palmerston again as Prime Minister: thus reinstated in office, he retained his post until his death in October 1865, two days short of his eighty-first birthday, and having recently obtained a clear majority at a general election.

If it is extraordinary that Palmerston should have proved so successful and durable as a Liberal leader, dominating British politics in the way he did for the last decade of his life, it is more surprising still that he ever managed to become Prime Minister in the first place. His political origins were hardly auspicious, in this respect. Palmerston had begun his career as a Tory, serving in successive administrations for over twenty years, until 1828. Moreover, this Tory phase was remarkable only for its unremarkableness, as Palmerston spent most of his time in the low-profile office of Secretary at War (a quite distinct post from that of Secretary *for* War), without a seat in the Cabinet, and he acquired a reputation, shared with many of his colleagues of the 1810s and 1820s, as a feeble parliamentary debater. It is not an exaggeration, in fact, to describe Palmerston as a late-developer, in political terms. Even in 1827, though he was identified as being on the Canningite, or 'Liberal', wing of the Tory party, because of his consistent support for Catholic emancipation, he was certainly not regarded by George Canning as an indispensable ally. It was only after Canning's death, and the subsequent breach between Canning's followers and the Duke of Wellington, in 1828, that Palmerston, by now in his mid-forties, began to emerge as a politician of the front rank. Crucial to this political metamorphosis was Palmerston's adoption and espousal of the 'Canningite principles' of foreign policy, setting himself up – probably consciously – as the heir to Canning in an area of policy in which he had previously shown little interest. At the same time he was slowly gravitating, along with the other Canningites, towards the Whig position that some measure of parliamentary reform was a political necessity. In this way, it became possible for Palmerston to join Earl Grey's reform ministry, in November 1830, taking the post of Foreign Secretary, which he was to hold in every Whig government up until December 1851.

Palmerston underwent a very slow process of evolution, therefore, before emerging as a senior political figure, and the stigma of his Tory background always seemed likely to tell against him when it came to the question of the 'Liberal' leadership. Compared with Russell, who enjoyed the advantages of hereditary connection as well as a genuine personal attachment to 'Liberal' principles, Palmerston looked to be a poor reformer. His support for the Great Reform Act itself had been cautious and lukewarm (he was one of the ministers who would have been ready to seek a compromise with Tory 'waverers'), and he was strongly disinclined, thereafter, to any further constitutional change. In consequence, there was no natural constituency within the Liberal Party to which Palmerston could appeal, for in spite of his aristocratic pedigree he was not strictly a 'Whig', and his views on domestic policy were not likely to win him much support amongst the more radical sections of the party. On top of these political handicaps, Palmerston's future prospects were further endangered by the increasingly strained relations that existed between himself and the Crown. The Queen and Prince Albert deeply resented Palmerston's imperious behaviour as Foreign Secretary, in particular his unwillingness to consult them – or, for that matter, his Cabinet colleagues – before formulating policy. Indeed, it was a sign of how formidable still was the power of Royal disapproval that, in December 1851, Palmerston's characteristically high-handed conduct in unilaterally recognising the new regime in France, created by Louis Napoleon's coup d'état, led to his being dismissed from office.

The Domestic Uses of Palmerstonian Foreign Policy

It is to the style in which Palmerston conducted and publicised foreign policy that we must, nevertheless, look for the key to his ultimate success. The essence of the Canningite tradition of foreign policy, to which Palmerston had made himself the legatee, lay in the belief that Britain, the leading constitutional nation in Europe, should remain free from entangling engagements with other European powers, especially the reactionary, autocratic regimes of the 'Holy alliance', and use her freedom of action to promote the cause of 'liberty' abroad. Inevitably, perhaps, such a high-minded approach had to be suitably qualified by the need to make allowance for considerations of national self-interest, as Palmerston openly acknowledged in a speech to the House of Commons, in March 1848:

> I hold that the real policy of England – *apart from questions which involve her own particular interests, political or commercial* – is to be the champion of Justice and right, pursuing that course with moderation and pru-

dence, not becoming the Quixote of the world, but giving the weight
of her moral sanction and support wherever she thinks that Justice is,
and wherever she thinks that wrong has been done.[2]

Thus, the selective Liberalism of Palmerston's foreign policy did not
deem it to be in the interests of the European balance of power for
Austria to be weakened by the loss of Hungary, in 1848–9, although
this did not prevent Palmerston from gaining credit in the public mind
by subsequently applying pressure in order to save the 'heroes' of the
Hungarian revolt from arrest and execution. Indeed, the notion of
Britain as the exemplar of Liberal values, acting in defiance of the
forces of tyranny and repression, all too easily degenerated into a crude
form of national chauvinism, and even the bullying of weaker states, as
in the famous Don Pacifico affair of 1850. On this occasion, British
gunboats were sent to intimidate the Greek government into paying
compensation to a Portuguese merchant for the loss of his property, on
the grounds that the merchant's birth at Gibraltar made him a British
citizen, and that British citizens, like the citizens of the Roman Republic in ancient times, were entitled to protection wherever they went in
the world. Palmerston thus defended his action, to the House of
Commons, in his famous *civis romanus sum* speech.

While it is easy enough to point to the inconsistencies in the Palmerstonian stance, it is still important to recognise the potency of the image
of Britain as the champion of liberty in helping to shape a plausible
version of what the British Liberal Party was about. On the one hand,
Palmerstonianism was perfectly compatible with the ideals of Foxite
Whiggery, and indeed benefited from the gratifying sense that it was
now Britain herself, rather than France, as it had seemed to be in the
1790s, who was on the side of the angels. Equally, however, the policy
of opposing Continental tyrants had an immense appeal to radicals of a
certain kind, who continued to be inspired by the eighteenth century
tradition of 'patriotism'. Such sentiments were anathema, of course, to
other radicals, like Cobden and Bright, who had hoped that the
triumph of Free Trade, and pressure for retrenchment in government
expenditure, would put an end to British interference in the affairs of
other nations, but this simply goes to show how misleading it is to
equate the radicalism of the 'Manchester school' with radicalism as a
whole. For example, when Palmerston was faced with a motion of
censure, over his handling of the Don Pacifico affair, the amendment
to this motion *approving* of Palmerston's conduct was successfully carried

by the philosophic radical, John Arthur Roebuck. Shortly afterwards, a banquet was held at the Reform Club, in honour of Palmerston, with another prominent radical MP, Ralph Bernal Osborne, in the chair.[3]

The diaries of Charles Greville, clerk to the privy council and a close friend of Lord John Russell, convey the impression that the Whig leader's position was being subtly undermined by his Foreign Secretary's ability to appeal to those nationalistic instincts which so obviously formed a strand within Liberal thinking. In August 1849, Greville noted that Palmerston was 'evidently endeavouring to make for himself a great Radical interest in the House of Commons, and thus to increase his power, and render himself more indispensable to the Government by making them feel how dangerous he would be out of office'. Similarly, in February 1850, Greville wrote in disgust that Palmerston 'is the pet of the Radicals, to whom he pays continual court, giving them sops in the shape of Liberal speeches, Hungarian sympathies, and claptrap'. The Don Pacifico debate, in which Palmerston spoke for four and three-quarter hours, triumphantly defending his conduct, served to reinforce, as Greville admitted, Palmerston's indispensability to the government, such was his popularity in the country. Worst of all, in Greville's view, was the way that Palmerston accepted a memorial from the largely working-class constituency of Finsbury, in November 1851, praising him for the way he had helped to save the Hungarian nationalist leader, Lajos Kossuth, who was currently paying a visit of thanks to England. 'To receive an address in which the Emperors of Russia and Austria are called despots, tyrants and odious assassins, and to express great gratification at it, is an unparalleled outrage', stormed Greville:

The ostentatious bidding for Radical favour and the flattery of the democracy, of which his speeches were full, are disgusting in themselves and full of danger. It is evident that he has seized the opportunity of the Kossuth demonstrations to associate himself with them, and convert the popular excitement into political capital for himself. He thinks to make himself too formidable, by having the masses at his back, for his colleagues to dare quarrel with him, and by this audacious defiance of them he intends to make himself once for all master of the situation.[4]

Critical to the cultivation of this popular image was Palmerston's appreciation of the importance of gaining favourable publicity through contacts with the press. In this respect, he appears to be acting in a recognisably 'modern' way, exploiting his connections in order to secure sympathetic treatment for himself and the denigration of his rivals. Such methods were to prove beyond the ability, or imagination, of the more aloof Russell. A typical Palmerstonian device was to feed his favoured newspapers with titbits of exclusive information, thus providing a practical (but not financial) inducement for the newspapers to maintain a favourable coverage. By the 1850s, in consequence, two London daily papers, the *Morning Post* and the evening *Globe*, were reckoned to be in Palmerston's pocket, while he was able to exercise some influence even on papers of a different political persuasion, such as the Conservative *Standard* and the radical *Daily News*, which were appreciative of the value of Palmerston's assistance.[5]

It is one of the great ironies of nineteenth-century politics that the difficulties into which Palmerston finally ran, because of his handling of foreign policy, ultimately proved to be his political salvation. So infuriated were Queen Victoria and Prince Albert with Palmerston's behaviour that not only did they press Russell to dismiss him, in December 1851, but they also ensured that when the Aberdeen coalition was formed, a year later, although Palmerston was included, he was placed out of harm's way at the Home Office. The fortuitousness of this move became clear after the outbreak of the Crimean War, in March 1854. Britain's participation, along with France, in the war against Russia, certainly excited a great deal of popular enthusiasm initially, and indeed, the cause for which Britain had taken her stand fitted in well with 'Palmerstonian' principles of foreign policy, namely resistance to the expansionist aims of the autocratic Tsar of Russia, who was encroaching once again on the territory of the Ottoman Empire. The integrity of the Ottoman Empire was considered to be vital for the preservation of the European balance of power, as it served as a bulwark against Russia, although it was also possible, by the 1850s, to regard the Turks as a 'weak' nation, being bullied by the despotic Russian bear. These strong feelings in favour of war soon turned against the Aberdeen coalition, however, as a result of the gross mismanagement of the expeditionary force, whose appalling condition by the end of 1854, stuck in the Crimean winter without even basic supplies such as tents and boots (let alone adequate medical facilities), was brought home to the British public by the reports from independent war correspondents like W. H. Russell of *The Times*. Consequently, when parliament was summoned in January 1855, a motion of censure against the govern-

ment, moved, significantly enough, by the radical Roebuck, was carried
by the astonishing margin of 305 votes to 148, with 83 Liberal MPs
voting against the coalition and many others absenting themselves.[6]
Such a disastrous defeat left ministers with no choice but to resign.

While Palmerston of course shared in the collective responsibility for
the Crimean fiasco, he nevertheless benefited, as Home Secretary, from
his relative lack of direct complicity in what had happened. In fact he
was able to derive considerable personal advantage from the widespread public perception, encouraged naturally enough by the pro-Pal-
merston elements in the press, that having been in favour all along of a
much tougher line against Russia, during the diplomatic build-up to
war, he was now clearly the right man to take over at the helm and
run the war properly. By contrast, the reputation of the leading
Peelites, as superior administrators, had suffered a serious blow, as,
quite apart from Aberdeen's overall responsibility for what had gone
wrong, all the ministers in departments directly concerned with the
military arrangements were Peelites: the Duke of Newcastle was Secretary of State for War, and Sidney Herbert the Secretary at War, while
the parsimonious Chancellor of the Exchequer, W. E. Gladstone, was
not altogether without blame.

Another important casualty of the Crimean War was Palmerston's
old rival, Lord John Russell. The damage done to Russell's position,
though, related not to any personal culpability for the failings of the
Crimean expedition, but to his generally disruptive behaviour throughout the lifetime of the Aberdeen coalition. It was understandable
enough that he should have resented the way Aberdeen and the
Peelites had usurped the leading positions in a government which
rested predominantly on Whig–Liberal parliamentary support, and that
he was tormented by feelings of guilt towards Whig colleagues, like Sir
George Grey, who had been sacrificed in order to make room for Peelites. In other words, it was hardly surprising that Russell, the proud
heir to the Foxite Whig tradition, feared that he might have allowed it
to be destroyed forever as the dominant force within the leadership of
Liberalism. However, his subsequent restless conduct only served to discredit him still further, even with his own Whig brethren. Russell
quickly became disgruntled as a result of what he considered to be
Aberdeen's failure to keep a 'promise' to step down after a few months
and allow him to resume the premiership. He became even more
unhappy when the outbreak of the Crimean War obliged him to shelve
his cherished plan for a second Reform Bill, which was by now more

or less a badge of Russell's Foxite honour, even though his Whig and Peelite colleagues did not care for the measure. Furthermore, he became increasingly dissatisfied with the government's handling of the war effort, and pressed urgently for a re-organisation of the War Office. His decision finally to carry out his oft-repeated threat to resign, coming as it did on the very day in January 1855 that Roebuck's censure motion was announced, gave the unfortunate appearance of a rat deserting a sinking ship. Russell was later to complain that he had been abandoned by his Whig colleagues, who he thought would resign with him,[7] but the fact that they did not is a sign of the extent to which even they were becoming disgusted with their erstwhile chief's erratic and disloyal proceedings.

Thus it was that by February 1855 Palmerston appeared to be the man of the moment, the politician to whom the premiership must naturally fall after the collapse of the Aberdeen coalition.[8] His position was, if anything, strengthened rather than weakened by the subsequent conduct of the Peelites and Russell. When Palmerston formed his ministry, Aberdeen and Newcastle were necessarily omitted, as the scapegoats for the problems of the Crimean campaign, but Gladstone, Herbert and Graham initially joined, only to resign within weeks because of Palmerston's decision to allow a parliamentary commission of inquiry to look into the administration of the war. In doing so, however, the Peelites left behind two Cabinet colleagues, the Duke of Argyll and Lord Canning, along with several junior ministers, revealing the extent to which the independent Peelites were being reduced to a small parliamentary rump. At the same time as Palmerston was detaching a number of the remaining Peelites from their leaders, he was also able to consolidate his hold over the Whigs, when Russell, who had briefly served as British plenipotentiary to a peace conference held in Vienna, was forced to resign from Palmerston's government in the most humiliating circumstances, in July 1855, when it was revealed that during the conference he had been willing to agree to peace terms which were considered unacceptably generous to Russia.

Palmerston therefore found himself at the head of a predominantly Whig government, shorn of his most dangerous rivals, and buoyed up by improvements in the Crimean campaign during the course of 1855. Once established in power, his achievement, it could be argued, was simply that which might have been Russell's all along, but for the latter's defects of temperament. By taking up the reins of government when he did, Palmerston gave a new lease of life to the British aris-

tocracy at a time when its presumed right to rule was being called into
question, in the light of the poor organisation of the Crimean expedition. With the war effort apparently now in capable hands, the
demands articulated by the Administrative Reform Association for
changes in the system of recruitment to the civil service, and to the
higher ranks of the army – both still very much preserves of the aristocracy – were to make little further headway.[9] Cobden, who, along
with other members of the Manchester school of radicals, significantly
remained aloof from the Administrative Reform Association, was well
aware of the irony at the heart of the crisis surrounding the fall of the
Aberdeen coalition and its replacement by Palmerston's government: 'It
is a pity that our quarrel with the aristocracy does not spring from
some other cause than the complaint that they don't carry on *war* with
sufficient vigour.'[10] That the aristocracy itself was appreciative of the
value of Palmerston's leadership is perhaps indicated by the way that,
over the next few years, Brooks's Club, the social stronghold of metropolitan Whiggery, seemed to forget its previous attachment to Russell
and became largely Palmerstonian in its sympathies.[11]

The Formation of the Liberal Party?

The process by which the various Liberal groups and individuals were
reconciled to Palmerston's leadership was to be a slow one, punctuated
by a number of crises. It has been seen that Palmerston's reputation
was sustained by his public image as an effective wartime leader, but in
reality Britain's military operations in the Crimea could hardly be
described as glorious, and compared unfavourably with those of her
ally, France. The Peace of Paris, which brought the war to an end in
March 1856, was the product of Russian exhaustion rather than of a
decisive military victory by the allied forces. While the peace treaty
could, nevertheless, be presented as a triumph for Britain, securing
amongst other things the exclusion of Russia's fleet from the Black Sea,
even this had been somewhat marred by the surrender, shortly before
the cessation of hostilities, of the fortress at Kars (in Armenia), after a
long siege. This setback enabled the Conservatives to launch a motion
of censure against the government, in May 1856, on the grounds of the
failure of ministers to relieve the fortress in time. The significance of
the Kars debate lies partly in the fact that Palmerston achieved a more
decisive victory in parliament than the British army had ever managed

in the Crimea, rallying all his potential Liberal supporters in the division lobby and winning by 303 votes to 176, in what became a straight party contest; but it was also important for the manner of Palmerston's success, which exhibited the witty and sparkling style of debating which was to become so characteristic of his handling of the House of Commons in his later years.[12]

What is equally interesting is that, during the parliamentary recess, Palmerston should have embarked upon a speaking tour in the north of England, addressing large audiences in Liverpool, Salford and Manchester. As with his cultivation of the press, so too, his flattery of provincial public opinion marks Palmerston out as a pioneer in the arts of political persuasion. The main theme of these, and later speeches was a constant one: the importance of the collaboration of social classes under the freely accepted leadership of the aristocracy. He maintained that the aristocracy had to fulfil its duty to the country through good government and gradual reform – what he described to his Lancastrian listeners as 'progressive improvement':

> why should we not endeavour to be perpetually ameliorating those laws and institutions, which, being human, cannot be perfect, but which, according to the progress of society and the change of circumstances must be continually in need of emendation and extension.

Clearly, such language fitted in well with the notion of constant progress which had, by this time, become central to the creed of Liberalism. Palmerston was also able to relate this popular nostrum to the realm of foreign policy, by asserting that Britain's superiority over other States, in terms of the stability and flexibility of her internal institutions, provided an object lesson to the rest of the world, and thus served to enhance Britain's 'moral authority' in its dealings with militarily more powerful nations.[13]

It remains extremely difficult, all the same, to measure the true extent of Palmerston's popularity in the country as a whole, and there is reason to suppose, for instance, that the large overall Liberal majority of some 85 or 90 seats (excluding Peelites), achieved at the general election of April 1857, was not simply a vote of confidence in Palmerston personally. The election had been prompted by a vote of censure on the government, moved by Cobden and supported by all the dissident Liberal groupings, as well as by the Conservatives, following the bombardment of Canton by a British naval force. On the surface, the election appeared to be very much in the nature of a plebiscite on Palmerston's leadership, with radical critics like Cobden, Bright, Layard and Milner Gibson losing their seats in consequence, and the Peelites being reduced to a small rump of about 25 MPs. In reality, however, many contests were decided on local issues, as was usually the case in this period, and, in spite of the handful of notable radical casualties already mentioned, the vast majority of MPs who had voted against Palmerston on the censure motion survived the general election, many of them having made parliamentary reform an important plank in their individual electoral platforms.[14]

The most significant feature of the 1857 election was the Liberals' gain of 23 seats in the English counties (giving them a total of 52 out of 144), which marked a substantial recovery from the low point of the 1840s, when Liberal support for the repeal of the corn laws had alienated much of the agricultural interest. Considerable gains were also made in the smaller English boroughs (those having electorates of under 1000), with the Liberals achieving a clear majority of 120 out of 198 seats in this category. This recovery of the Liberals' position in the rural constituencies undoubtedly reflected the prosperity in these areas, thanks to the buoyancy of agricultural prices in spite of the removal of protective tariffs (there simply were not, at this time, large supplies of cheap foreign produce capable of undermining domestic prices). However, the personal popularity of Palmerston also played a role in the county elections, and, quite apart from the gains made by the Liberals, many Conservative candidates found it necessary to pledge their general support for Palmerston's conduct of foreign policy.[15] More generally, public confidence in the Palmerston government must have been inspired by the fact that, thanks to the ending of the Crimean War, the Chancellor of the Exchequer, Cornewall Lewis, had been able to halve the rate of income tax in his budget just prior to the general election.

The election in Manchester, where two of the heroes of the anti-corn law-league days, Bright and Milner Gibson, were defeated by the moderate Liberals, Sir John Potter and J. A. Turner, provides a useful perspective on the 'Palmerstonian ascendancy'. In this case, the rejection of the representatives of the 'Manchester school' of radicalism was the culmination of a process of growing disenchantment, on the part of the town's commercial elite, which can be traced back to the immediate aftermath of the triumph over the corn-law issue. Resentful of the dictatorial attitude of the anti-corn-law league's electoral machine, based in Newall's building, which sought to maintain control over parliamentary nominations both for Manchester itself and for a number of neighbouring county seats, leading commercial families such as the Potters, Neilds, Garnetts, Turners and Heywoods also disliked Bright's subsequent concentration on the question of parliamentary reform. At the 1852 general election, the defence of Free Trade provided a rallying-cry for all Liberals in Manchester, as in other parts of the country, but thereafter the underlying divisions became more openly apparent. Bright was bitterly attacked for his opposition to the Crimean War, causing him to suffer a nervous breakdown. The Mancunian commercial elite also responded favourably, in more general terms, to the aggressive style of foreign policy associated with Palmerston, which seemed to offer the prospect of new markets, in places like the Levant and China, for manufactured cotton goods. Not surprisingly, in the circumstances, Palmerston's visit to Manchester in November 1856 was a great success, and a few months later the MPs who had helped to censure his government for its policy in China were duly removed. It is important to remember, though, that what Derek Fraser has described as 'the assertion of authority by an urban aristocracy' was representative of the views of only a minority of the Liberal electors in Manchester, probably about 25 per cent, and that the victory of Potter and Turner was secured with the help of some 6000 Conservative voters (there being no Conservative candidate in the field).[16] Nevertheless, in a broadly-based coalition such as the mid-Victorian Liberal party, it only required a shift of opinion on the part of a minority to bring about the demise of the critics of Palmerstonianism.

Palmerston's nominal Liberal majority of 85 to 90 seats in the new parliament was not a stable one, and within a year of the general election he had been defeated again, and this time forced to resign. The occasion of this defeat was the so-called 'Orsini affair', when the government proposed to increase the penalty for conspiracy to murder, in response to French complaints after an assassination attempt on the Emperor Napoleon III, which, it emerged, had been organised by a group of Italian nationalists operating from Britain. A hostile combination of Conservatives, Peelites, radicals and Lord John Russell, similar to that of March 1857, effectively accused Palmerston of bowing to pressure from the French government and of proposing a measure that would undermine Britain's reputation as a haven for exiled nationalists. It was a case, ironically enough, of Palmerston being 'out-Palmerstoned' by his numerous political enemies, who were turning against him precisely the same sentiments of popular nationalism that he had hitherto succeeded in harnessing. This was one of the few occasions, in the later stage of his career, when Palmerston lost his temper during a parliamentary debate, and lost with it his usual ability to carry the House of Commons with him.[17]

An extraordinary fifteen-month period followed, with a minority Conservative government in power under Lord Derby, in which the rival Liberal leaders, Palmerston and Russell, engaged in a series of deft manoeuvres designed to prevent one another from emerging as the focus for Liberal reunification.[18] Within the ranks of Liberal MPs, too, in spite of their numerical majority in the House of Commons, serious differences existed as to the terms on which a new Liberal government ought to be formed. The consequence, as the former Chancellor of the Exchequer, Cornewall Lewis, complained, was that 'the Liberal party' was for a time 'extinct as a *party* . . . the only organisation which at present exists within it is for the purpose of keeping in the [Conservative] Government and preventing the formation of a Liberal Ministry'. Cornewall Lewis was referring to the existence of a group of 'independent Liberals', led by Roebuck, numbering perhaps as many as 120 MPs, who were determined to prevent the restoration of Palmerston to power because of his hostility to parliamentary reform.[19] This is a remarkable illustration of the point that the 1857 general election had by no means turned the Liberal party into a loyal body of Palmerstonians. In pursuit of their aims, the 'independent Liberals' were content to allow Derby to remain in office until a suitable moment arose for the construction of a more radically committed Liberal government.

The unification of all the elements of the Liberal coalition, which finally took place in June 1859 under Palmerston's leadership, was to be the product of a remarkably fortuitous set of circumstances. As in 1852, it was the conduct of a minority Conservative government, and suspicion about some of its intentions, which served to draw the Liberals closer together. First, the Conservatives attempted to pass a Parliamentary Reform Bill of their own, the provisions of which were so modest (principally a £10 household franchise for the counties, and some additional 'fancy franchises' for the boroughs), that it enabled nearly all Liberals to unite in contemptuous rejection of the proposal without having to agree upon an alternative measure. It was thus possible even for Palmerston to join in the attack upon the Conservatives' bill. Secondly, the general election called by the Conservatives, following the defeat of their Reform Bill, took place in the context of an international crisis arising from the outbreak of war between France and Austria over the Italian question. This had a double advantage for Palmerston in that not only did many people regard him as a preferable national leader to Derby in a time of emergency, but also, the Conservatives' failure to clarify their own position with regard to Italy meant that during the election campaign they were suspected of being sympathetic to the maintenance of Austrian control in northern Italy.[20] A classic 'Palmerstonian' issue, that of sympathy for the cause of Italian independence, therefore provided a basis for the reconciliation of all Liberals at the famous Willis's rooms meeting, of 6 June 1859, immediately after the general election. Only a handful of the 'independent Liberals', like Roebuck and Horsman, were still disposed to hold out against the formation of a Liberal ministry, but the progress of events had been so rapid that such a position was now untenable.[21] The meeting agreed to support a motion of no confidence in Derby's ministry, which was duly carried by 323 votes to 310, on 10 June. Queen Victoria and Prince Albert, as hostile as ever to Palmerston personally, attempted to set up Lord Granville as an alternative Liberal Prime Minister, but this proved to be a futile manoeuvre and they were forced to call upon Palmerston to form the new government. In retrospect, the events of June 1859 can be seen as marking an important triumph for the idea of 'party', over Royal favour, which became all the more decisive after the premature death of Prince Albert, in December 1861.

It is important to stress the ambiguity of Liberal attitudes, even in relation to the Italian question, which had brought them all together. Support for the creation of an independent state in northern Italy – no-one could have foreseen, in 1859, the events that would lead to the unification of virtually the whole of Italy the following year – created common ground between Palmerston, Russell (who insisted on becoming Foreign Secretary in the new government), and Peelites like Gladstone (who again became Chancellor of the Exchequer); but radicals of the 'Manchester school', such as Bright, who had spoken at the Willis's rooms meeting, were only prepared to support a Liberal government on condition that it did not involve Britain in the military conflict between France and Austria. Britain, and the Liberal Party, were to benefit, in the eyes of posterity, from their support for the Italian cause, which was to become as potent a part of the Liberals' ideological heritage as their support for Free Trade; but in reality, Liberal unity on the issue had only been possible so long as Britain did not actually do anything directly to assist the Italians. Clearly, Italy did far more for Liberal unity than the Liberals ever did for Italian unity.

The Second Palmerston Administration, 1859–65

Palmerston's second ministry, of 1859 to 1865, is often considered to have been the first truly 'Liberal' ministry, incorporating as it did all of the groups and individuals who had been committed to the cause of Free Trade since the 1840s. Not only were Palmerston and Russell finally reconciled – indeed, they were to work together well, in the realm of foreign affairs – but three of the remaining Peelites, Gladstone, Herbert and Newcastle, were included in the Cabinet, along with two representatives of the radicals, Thomas Milner Gibson and C. P. Villiers (Cobden having declined the offer of a post). However, it would be a mistake to assume that the Liberals were, thereafter, a more united body than they had been in the past. In fact, the stability of the government was to be seriously threatened, particularly in the early 1860s, by the titanic disputes between Palmerston and Gladstone over the related questions of military expenditure and fiscal policy. Potentially, at least, Russell's insistence that he should be allowed to bring in another Reform Bill, as a condition of his taking office at all, was another source of ministerial instability, given Palmerston's own well known aversion to such a measure. When we also bear in mind that Palmerston's government, contrary to what is usually stated by historians, could only rely on a small majority in the House of Commons, of about fifteen (the Conservatives having made significant gains in the 1859 general election), it can be seen that the position of the 'first Liberal government' was a rather precarious one.

It was precisely because of the delicate balancing act necessarily being performed by Palmerston that the Conservative leader, Lord Derby, sought to tempt him into leaning over too far, in the hope that he could thus be brought crashing to the ground. This was what lay behind the intriguing offers of support which Derby made to Palmerston secretly, using Lord Malmesbury as an intermediary, in the spring of 1860 and again early in 1861. Derby's immediate object was to encourage Palmerston to stand firm over the franchise question, in the event of Russell resigning if his bill failed to pass, but the offer of tacit Conservative assistance also extended to cover Palmerston's dispute with Gladstone over finance and defence. Whereas an aggressive Conservative stance would have been likely to drive Palmerston and the Liberals closer together, Derby perceived that in helping to buttress Palmerston's moderate position lay the best hope of driving in a wedge between the Prime Minister and the radical section of his party. So far from these secret Conservative overtures having any friendly intention behind them, therefore, they were believed to be the most effective way of prising apart the Liberal coalition formed at the Willis's rooms meeting.[22]

In the event, the collusion between Derby and Palmerston was both partial and short-lived. It soon became clear that such was Russell's absorption in foreign affairs, and so obvious the lack of enthusiasm for parliamentary reform in the House of Commons, that he was prepared to abandon his unloved franchise bill, honour having been satisfied by introducing it. Far more serious, for a time at least, was the battle between the Prime Minister and the Chancellor of the Exchequer. Gladstone's budget of 1860 had increased the income tax in order to cover major reductions in the range of import duties, but part of the package, a separate bill to abolish the duty on paper, was rejected by the House of Lords. Palmerston's reaction was to avoid turning the situation into a direct conflict between Lords and Commons, in spite of Gladstone's protests and the anger of radical MPs. Furthermore, Palmerston's determination to spend £9 million on coastal fortifications, as a precaution against a feared French invasion, placed in jeopardy Gladstone's whole financial strategy, which looked to the eventual abolition of the income tax. Relations between the Prime Minister and his Chancellor of the Exchequer became so strained that there was a distinct possibility that the latter might resign, although in the end the prospect of another long period in the political wilderness seems to have deterred Gladstone from taking this step. At this stage, in the summer of 1860, it appeared that Palmerston had swallowed the bait laid for him by Derby, and was exploiting the availability of Conservative support where necessary in order to keep in check Gladstone and his growing band of radical admirers.[23] During the early months of the 1861 session of parliament, there were indeed a number of instances where the opposition came to Palmerston's aid in order to help him beat off radical attacks on such issues as the pay of naval officers.[24] However, this cross-party co-operation came to an end when Gladstone, determined to force through his financial policy, succeeded in tacking on to his budget the repeal of the paper duties, which left the

House of Lords with the stark choice of either accepting the budget in its entirety or else rejecting it and provoking a constitutional crisis. The result was a personal triumph for Gladstone, as the Lords backed down. Ultimately, it was clear, Palmerston recognised the expediency of retaining the services of his Chancellor, and was not prepared to lose him by holding out on such an issue as the paper duties. Significantly, once Palmerston had opted to try to maintain Liberal unity rather than rely on Conservative support, the opposition abandoned their political truce and launched a general attack on the government's financial policy.[25] The period of collusion between Palmerston and Derby was thus only a temporary phase, rather than a permanent feature of the politics of the first half of the 1860s.

While Derby's strategy was to seek to open up the fissures in the Liberal Party, it can be argued that it was Palmerston who enjoyed far greater success in exploiting the dissensions among the Conservatives. Part of the difficulty for the Conservative leadership lay in the fact that Palmerston was so obviously moderate in his own views on domestic policy that it was virtually impossible to present his government as posing any threat to the traditional institutions of the Country. No-one could seriously argue that the Crown, or the aristocracy, or the Church of England, were endangered by a Palmerston ministry. As far as foreign policy was concerned, here too there was little scope for Conservative criticism of a Prime Minister who was perceived, in the public mind, as a man who stood up for British interests abroad, and it was noted earlier how, in 1857, many Conservative candidates were obliged to give pledges of general support for Palmerston. Deprived of any obvious targets for attack, Derby had therefore opted, in 1860–1, for the approach of trying to kill Palmerston's ministry with kindness.

A more specific problem for the opposition leaders was the continuing hostility exhibited by many of their back-bench followers towards Disraeli, the parvenu adventurer who had made himself indispensable to the party because of his skill in debate, but whose leadership in the House of Commons was still not agreeable to many of the landed squires. In particular, there was a group of about two dozen malcontents, led by G. W. Bentinck, who detested Disraeli's leadership of their party and ensured that his authority remained in serious doubt throughout the period of Palmerston's ascendancy. The practical result of Disraeli's difficulties with his own backbenchers was that the rare opposition attempts to launch major assaults on Palmerston's government, in May 1861 and June 1862, ended in humiliating failure through Disraeli's inability to carry the whole of his party with him.[26] Consequently, as the radical MP Alexander Kinglake gloomily noted, Disraeli's leadership in itself constituted a serious obstacle to the creation of a united opposition to Palmerston: 'It seems to me that Dizzy is the man who spoils all wholesome strife of politics, for that shiftiness of his prevents the proper play of party, and obliges the honest Conservatives to take "the old sinner" Palmerston for their real chief'.[27]

Palmerston's ability to exacerbate the rifts in the Conservative Party was of great value to him, for he could never take the support of the back-bench radicals for granted. Financial policy was one area in which tensions were openly apparent, and this serves to highlight why it was so important for Palmerston to keep Gladstone in his government. Prior to the opening of the 1861 session of parliament, for example, 51 Liberal MPs signed a circular, addressed to the Prime Minister, urging him to review the scale of government expenditure. According to the chief whip, Henry Brand, the inspiration behind the circular came from the nonconformist, Samuel Morley – 'the active spirit of the Administrative Reform Association' – but there was little doubt that two MPs whose names were conspicuous by their absence from the list, Cobden and Bright, were also implicated. The signatories argued that with the war in Italy now over, and relations with France improving, the country expected a substantial reduction in 'warlike Establishments from the extraordinary scale of the present year'. Government expenditure for civil purposes – 'which has for many years been in course of rapid and extraordinary increase' – also had to be curtailed.

> We are convinced that retrenchment will prove the truest policy of the Government as the only method of meeting the financial exigencies of the State, satisfying the expectations of Parliament, conciliating the good opinion of the commercial and monied interests, allaying the dissatisfaction of the taxpayers, and preventing the loud outcry which would inevitably arise in case of another unfavourable harvest or any check to the public prosperity.

Palmerston's reaction to the report that this circular was being prepared had been characteristically trenchant, and showed just how wide the rift was between the Prime Minister and a substantial group of his own back-benchers. The call for across-the-board reductions in government spending, according to Palmerston, was:

a leap in the dark at the bidding of that political fanatic Cobden . . .
the true meaning of the Memorial is that we should have no more
rifled muskets, rifled cannon, Iron ships, or defensive works, that we
should have no sufficient army or navy, that we should cease to be
an influential Power in the world . . . that our Commerce shall be
shut out from the Mediterranean, that we should hold our existence
as a nation at the good will of France and Russia, and that we
should sink down to be the object of contempt and derision to the
nations of the world.[28]

A more direct attack on Palmerston's government by the financial
reformers came in June 1862, when James Stansfeld put forward a
motion in the House of Commons calling for a reduction in national
expenditure. The effectiveness of Stansfeld's argument was marred by
his inability to specify the areas in which retrenchment should take
place, and indeed his speech revealed the differences of opinion that
existed amongst the radicals even on this issue, for Stansfeld was a
fervent advocate of Britain's supporting various nationalist causes
abroad, which was a rather Palmerstonian point of view and one that
was obviously incompatible with the policy of large cuts in expenditure
on armaments advocated by Cobden and Bright.[29] Nevertheless, the
fact that 65 MPs voted for this ambiguous motion was an important
warning signal to the government, and Palmerston heeded the advice
of his chief whip to proceed only with modest proposals for additional
expenditure on fortifications: 'we must not shut our eyes to the fact that
the cry for retrenchment is strong & growing, & that the H. of C.
requires humouring just now upon this point'. To do otherwise, Brand
warned, might lead to a fatal combination between the radicals and the
Conservatives.[30]

Parliamentary reform naturally remained another issue on which a
wide difference of opinion existed between Palmerston and the radical
section on the Liberal back-benches. It is true, of course, that Palmerston had allowed Russell to propose a bill, in 1860, which would have
created a £6 household franchise in the boroughs and redistributed 25
seats from the smaller boroughs, but, no doubt to Palmerston's satisfaction, this plan had met with an apathetic reception in the House of
Commons. There was no strong pressure for change from outside
Westminster at this time, and the quiescent public mood evidently
suited many MPs who were nervous of any change, especially one
involving the disfranchisement of certain small boroughs. One radical

MP, Sir John Trelawny, even suspected that many of his fellow radicals were insincere in their protestations of support for reform, which were often 'a mere pretence & stepping stone to seats'. Later on, Trelawny also felt that the outbreak of civil war in the United States had discredited the reformers' cause, as it seemed to suggest that the absolute power conferred on governments in a democracy was incompatible with respect for the rights of minorities, and that this had compelled the Confederate states to secede from the Union.[31] Democracy, in other words, was considered to be synonymous with the tyranny of the majority.

To what extent such views gained ground in Britain as a whole is difficult to tell, but in Bradford, for example, Liberal opinion seems to have been divided between those who sympathised with the Federal cause, and saw in the fight against slavery a parallel to the struggle for votes for the English working man, and others who deplored what they saw as the military despotism of the North and who favoured independence for the South.[32] In all probability the strongest feeling against parliamentary reform was to be found in London 'society', where it was certainly fashionable to be Palmerstonian in the early 1860s. Palmerston himself was confident, however, that the tide of public opinion was running in his favour throughout the Country. Thus, after the defeat of a Liberal candidate espousing radical opinions, at a by-election in Southampton in 1862, Palmerston had no doubt as to where the blame lay:

> The truth is that Radicalism is out of fashion at present, and if Government candidates *go the whole hog* they run the risk of being beat by disgusting many Liberals who ought to be their supporters. This foolish Mangles thought to recommend himself by adopting the Bright and Cobden creed and that was one of the causes of his failure.

Palmerston even went so far as to suggest to his chief whip that 'It would be useful that in future Government candidates should be warned that the wind has changed and that their course must be adapted to the present state of public feeling'.[33]

In many ways, Palmerston's approach to religious questions represented an extension of his broad political appeal to moderate Liberal – and indeed moderate Conservative – opinion. From 1855 onwards a deliberate policy was pursued of favouring evangelicals, or alternatively moderate broad-churchmen, rather than high churchmen, when it came to filling senior positions in the Anglican hierarchy, and Palmerston often sought the advice of his evangelical son-in-law, Lord Shaftesbury. Palmerston's ecclesiastical appointments thus won him the approval of a wide spectrum of evangelical opinion, including its main Anglican press organ, *The Record*, many Wesleyan Methodists who were still well disposed towards the Church of England, and even the group of Conservative MPs led by G. W. Bentinck (mostly evangelicals), who detested Disraeli's leadership. Once again, Palmerston's appeal tended to cut across political boundaries. Not the least of his achievements in the religious sphere was to cultivate an image as 'the man of God', which was ironic for someone with such a rakish private life!

Palmerston's attitude towards the claims of militant dissent, on the other hand, was much less encouraging, although his position was arguably made a great deal easier by the intransigence exhibited by organisations like the Liberation Society. This was particularly evident in the case of the most urgent issue on which the Society campaigned during the 1850s and early 1860s, namely the compulsory payment of Church rates. On several occasions, bills to abolish the rate were introduced to parliament on the Society's behalf by back-bench radicals, first Sir William Clay and later Sir John Trelawny, and in 1858, for the first time, an abolition bill was passed by the House of Commons, only to be lost in the Lords. This high-water mark subsequently receded, however, as a result of the Liberation Society's unwillingness to agree to any compromise measure that might have been acceptable to the Conservatives, as well as the explicit admission, by leaders such as Samuel Morley, that they regarded the abolition of Church rates not as an end in itself but merely as a step towards their ultimate objective, the disestablishment of the Church of England. Trelawny, himself an Anglican, therefore found his position becoming increasingly untenable (in much the same way as the Melbourne government's had been, in 1837), and after 1863 he abandoned his parliamentary leadership of the anti-Church-rates campaign. Ironically, after the 1859 general election the government had decided to make Church rates an open question, and Palmerston was one of the ministers who voted for the abolition bill, but to Trelawny's dismay he discovered that there was no intention of offering any practical government assistance to the bill. In fact, Trelawny was forced to the conclusion that ministers were simply using him as a convenient screen for their own inaction on the matter, and that they had no real desire to see a settlement reached, any more than the militants of the Liberation Society, who seemed content to keep the Church rates grievance alive as a useful weapon in their long-term battle for Church disestablishment.[34] Both sides, apparently, were willing to accept the temporary stalemate, or state of paralysis, which was the true essence of the mid-Victorian 'age of equipoise', in its religious dimension.

In Scotland, on the other hand, there appears to have been a more definite reaction in favour of the Whigs, owing to the disintegration of the alliance between the United Presbyterians and the Free Church. The attempts by successive governments, in 1854 and 1855, to deal with the question of Scottish elementary education, had brought out the latent tension between the Free Church, which was willing to see the parochial schools financed out of the rates, and the United Presbyterians, who adopted an uncompromising Voluntaryist stance. Consequently, at the 1857 general election, nearly all the seats held by the United Presbyterian–Free Church alliance were lost, including Glasgow, and the Whigs succeeded in recovering much of the political ground taken from them ten years earlier.[35]

Palmerston's efforts to conciliate evangelical feeling can be related to another feature of his style of leadership, which was based on a general hostility to Roman Catholicism. Of course, relations between the British Liberals and the Pope had been poor ever since Russell's Durham letter of 1850, and the main consequence of this, in parliamentary terms, had been the formation of an independent group of Irish Catholic MPs, some forty strong, known as the 'Irish Brigade'. The estrangement of what had always been the most uneasy element of the Reform coalition of the 1830s, was only intensified by the circumstances which helped to bring about greater unity among the British Liberals in 1859. As we have seen, sympathy for the cause of Italian nationalism created an important bond between the various Liberal groups, but, as one of the principal casualties of the 'Risorgimento' was the Pope, who lost most of his temporal power in Italy in 1860, the issue that united the British Liberals served to alienate still further the Irish Catholics. It therefore seemed to Palmerston that there was little point in even attempting to conciliate the Irish Brigade, as he explained to his chief whip, Brand, in 1864: 'until the Roman Question [i.e. the Pope's temporal authority in the city of Rome] is finally settled and hopelessly for the Pope, we shall have the Irish Catholics against us and they would be equally so against Derby's Government'. Brand was increasingly inclined to his chief's view that the dispensing of government patronage in Ireland, in so far as this could do any good, should be directed towards the Protestant minority: 'These are the men to whom we must look for support in Ireland; for they are upon principle true friends of Liberal Governments. The R. Catholics on the other hand are upon principle Ultra Tory, although they may occasionally, to serve their own or the Pope's purposes, join hands with a Liberal Government.' An anti-Catholic and anti-Irish stance may have been dictated by the circumstances of the time, but it also provided a serviceable means of playing up to the nationalistic strand of feeling amongst British, Protestant Liberals. As the radical, Trelawny, remarked, it often appeared as if 'Ministers hope to live by quarrelling with the whole Catholic world.'[36]

Conclusion

Although the Willis's rooms meeting of June 1859, and the subsequent formation of Palmerston's second ministry, are usually taken to mark the decisive point in the formation of the Victorian Liberal Party, the precise nature of Palmerston's contribution to this process is far from clear. It would perhaps be more accurate to describe the new Liberal unity achieved in 1859 as *front-bench* unity, involving as it did the reconciliation of Whigs and Peelites, together with the inclusion of a number of radicals (demonstrating that for ambitious young politicians radicalism had, for the first time, become a viable pathway to office). But Palmerston's greatest success in this respect – and there is no doubt that he would have regarded it as a success – lay in the rejuvenation of the Whig tradition of administrative leadership. By 1859 there was no longer any question of a Peelite takeover of a Liberal government, as had seemed to be a possibility during Russell's time as leader, and the few remaining Peelites were now effectively absorbed:[37] Herbert, Newcastle and Gladstone joined Palmerston's Cabinet (Aberdeen and Graham were too old to take office again), and the first two predeceased Palmerston, leaving only Gladstone to endeavour to keep alive Peelite maxims of government, through his financial policy. In the meantime, a generation of young Whig aristocrats were gaining experience of government under Palmerston's leadership, men who were to figure prominently in Gladstone's own ministries, like Hartington, Spencer, Wodehouse (later Earl of Kimberley), de Grey (later Marquess of Ripon), and Thomas Baring (later Earl of Northbrook).

There is certainly no reason to doubt the sincerity of the sentiments expressed in Palmerston's letter to Hartington's father, seeking the Duke of Devonshire's approval of the proposal that his son should take office:

> I feel very strongly that it is of great importance to the Country, and is highly conducive to the working of our Constitution, that young men in high aristocratical positions should take part in the administration of public affairs, and should not leave the working of our political machine to classes whose pursuits and interests are of a different kind.[38]

Palmerston, in truth, was almost as guilty as Russell of the crime for which the latter was always condemned – aristocratic exclusiveness. Indeed, the Liberal chief whip was later to observe that 'Palmerston's plan was to rest upon Whig support'. One sign of Palmerston's success in this respect is the confident assertion by the *Edinburgh Review*, the traditional organ of Whiggery, on the eve of the 1865 general election, that, while the British public expected improvement, they had no desire for violent change, and that it was to the Whigs, who were 'firmly attached to Liberal principles', that the Country looked for leadership: 'The policy of the Whig party is to guide that movement and to give effect by gradual and well-considered measures to the just desires of the Country at large'.[39]

The Liberal Party as a whole, however, continued to be a fragile entity. We have already seen, for example, that Liberal unity on the question of Italian independence was only sustainable so long as Britain did not become involved militarily. A similarly ironic situation surrounded the virtual unanimity of Liberals in defending Palmerston's ministry against a dangerous attack, in July 1864, when the Conservatives moved a vote of censure condemning the government for its mishandling of the Schleswig–Holstein affair. This had been a humiliating set-back for the foreign policy of Palmerston and Russell, who found themselves impotent in the face of Prussia's attack on Denmark, in spite of earlier bellicose statements which had seemed to imply British support for the Danes.[40] The censure motion was defeated by 313 votes to 295, but Palmerston had to endure speeches of 'support', from radicals like Cobden and Kinglake, congratulating him on having kept Britain out of the military conflict.

We must certainly be careful not to exaggerate the extent to which the radicals were absorbed by 'Palmerstonian Liberalism'. It is perfectly true, of course, that Palmerston succeeded in detaching a few prominent radicals, notably Villiers and Milner Gibson (both, it should be noted, from aristocratic or landed backgrounds), who were prepared to work for gradual reform from within Palmerston's government. Likewise, it is possible to point to evidence suggesting that other radicals, like Cobden and Bright, who remained outside the Palmerstonian regime, were nevertheless coming to despair of ever inducing the middle classes to engage in political warfare against the aristocracy.[11] But one might equally point to the fact that some of the radicals who had been attracted by Palmerston's style of foreign policy, during the late 1840s and early 1850s, subsequently became bitterly antagonistic towards him for a mixture of personal and political reasons: such was the case with Roebuck and Bernal Osborne. And the temporary bouts of despondency, which afflicted someone like Cobden, should not be taken as an accurate guide to his usual state of mind. It might be true, as Cobden acknowledged in a letter written a few months before his death in 1865, that '*at present* our comfortable middle classes have no idea of making war on feudalism. On the contrary they are busy at the herald's office hunting up coats of arms for Brown, Jones & Robinson!'[42] For the future, however, there was every expectation that radical views would prevail. In Bright's opinion, the key was to be found in a further extension of the franchise, against which only the ageing Palmerston blocked the way: 'The Land question is believed to be the whole question between a privileged order & a full equality – & nothing will be yielded on this point, except in the last extremity. The first thing to be done is to get another million men within the electoral boundary, & then we may say something serious with a chance of being listened to'. Cobden showed the greater prescience, though, by recognising that, in the long term, the impact of radical ideas in Britain would be aided by the weak link in the system of aristocratic government: 'both on the Land & the ecclesiastical questions, the initiatory movement will come from Ireland. In politics as in mechanics, the whole cannot be permanently stronger than the weakest part'.[43]

It is also important to note that the era of Palmerston's ascendancy had seen the emergence of a major new centre of provincial radicalism. Bradford, the capital of the West Riding worsted industry, was the boom-town *par excellence* of the mid-nineteenth century, and for a time at least it managed to eclipse the radicalism of rival manufacturing towns like Manchester and Birmingham. In 1861 the town elected as one of its MPs a local businessman, W. E. Forster, who was to rival Bright as the foremost advocate of a new Parliamentary Reform Bill. It is surely significant that when Palmerston paid a visit to Bradford, in 1864, he was greeted with a deliberate stony silence from the working men of the town.[44]

In fact, the parliamentary reform movement gained fresh momentum, after 1864, from the visit to England by the hero of the Italian Risorgimento, Giuseppe Garibaldi.[45] Attempts by the police to put down demonstrations organised by working men's groups, in the wake of Garibaldi's premature departure, resulted in the formation of the National Reform League, in March 1865, with a programme of universal manhood suffrage. The League was to work closely, for the time being, with John Bright and the Manchester-based National Reform Union, established in 1864, a mainly middle-class organisation with the more limited aim of household suffrage. At the same time, the victory of the Federals in the American Civil War, in the spring of 1865, provided further inspiration for British reformers, who were now able to claim that the cause of 'democracy', across the Atlantic, had finally been vindicated.

While it may be true, as E. D. Steele has recently argued, that Palmerston was not opposed in principle to a modest extension of the franchise, the fact remains that by 1864–5, when prominent Whig colleagues like Sir Charles Wood and Sir George Grey were supporting Edward Baines's annual motions for a £6 borough franchise, the Prime Minister continued to show no interest in acting on the issue. Even after the general election, in the summer of 1865, Palmerston remained adamant that there was no need for the government to settle on a policy, and he also rejected the suggestion that preparatory arrangements, like the gathering of information, should be taken. As he maintained in a letter to his chief whip:

> the dissolution had nothing whatever to do with Reform, and though many candidates mentioned Reform vaguely and generally that Question was by no means put forward by constituents as a Pledge to be given by candidates . . . At all events it is not for us to begin an agitation on a subject on which there are many different opinions even among men who on other subjects act cordially together.[46]

Palmerston's ability to survive as Liberal leader owed much to the ambiguity of his personal position. Indeed, there is a remarkable similarity here with the style of leadership later adopted by Gladstone: neither man was originally a Liberal, and neither restricted his political appeal exclusively to one section of the Liberal Party. Palmerston might be described as an 'honorary Whig', and he certainly led the Liberals from the 'right' with regard to domestic policy, but his foreign policy attracted sympathy and support from across the political spectrum, including some Conservatives and radicals, and this enormously strengthened his own authority, especially against pressure from radicals in the field of domestic reform. The Palmerstonian method of government, it therefore seems, was to cancel out the potentially hostile political forces surrounding him, through a skilful combination of a 'Liberal' foreign policy with a more conservative approach to domestic questions. If Palmerston created a sort of Liberal unity, he did so not by integrating more fully the various groups espousing Liberal principles, but by neutralising them – it was as if he kept them in a state of suspended animation.

It was always Palmerston's belief that the strength of his governments rested largely on what he called 'favourable public opinion'.[47] The nature of this 'Palmerstonian' public opinion, however, is not something that is easy to gauge. As Table 1[48] shows, the Palmerstonian Liberal Party represented a substantial minority in the English counties, after the 1865 general election, and a majority in English boroughs of all sizes, especially the largest ones. In Scotland and Wales, the Liberals were the dominant party, but the really striking point is that at this stage they were still the majority party in England as well.

Palmerston's personal appeal was undoubtedly a positive factor in the English counties, as we have already seen in relation to the 1857 general election. Further efforts by the Liberals to make incursions into these traditional Conservative strongholds were to follow, with the formation, in 1860, of the Liberal Registration Association, which aimed at assisting the process of electoral registration in areas where the Liberal Party was not well organised. Little is known about the achievements of the Association, other than the fact that its activities, coupled with a notable by-election success in East Kent in 1863, caused great alarm amongst the Conservatives, who began to take steps to establish a rival organisation.[49]

It seems highly likely that the positive attraction of Palmerston was also particularly strong among the business community in the towns. Indeed, the Palmerstonian regime could be presented, in various ways, as one that was good for business. A government not noted for its inter-

Table 1 *Distribution of Liberal Seats, 1865*

	Lib	*(total)*
English counties	52	(147)
Large English boroughs (2000+ electors)	49	(59)
Medium English boroughs (1000–2000 electors)	43	(63)
Small English boroughs (under 1000 electors)	104	(198)
English Universities	0	(4)
England Total	248	(471)
Wales	18	(29)
Scotland	41	(53)
Great Britain Total	307	(553)
Ireland	55	(105)
United Kingdom Total	362	(658)

est in major domestic changes, for instance, was nevertheless responsible for the legislation of 1856 and 1862 which permitted the setting up of joint stock companies with limited liability for shareholders. It is surely significant that Palmerston enjoyed the increasingly strong approbation of *The Economist* magazine, which welcomed the relief his leadership provided from the political instability of the 1850s, and detected in the ministry of 1859–65 a laudably non-partisan, 'national' approach to government.[50] Of course, *The Economist's* editor, Walter Bagehot, was later to write his famous study of *The English Constitution*, which, by the time of its second edition (1872), had become in many respects a lament for the departed Palmerstonian system. Palmerston's forceful conduct of foreign policy, too, was often directed towards furthering the interests of businessmen: the famous Don Pacifico affair was primarily about the protection of the rights of 'British' merchants operating in foreign countries, and the China War of 1857 arose from the determination to ensure British traders' access to Chinese markets. On the other hand, Palmerston was equally capable of selling peace rather than war to the electorate, and the series of public speeches made in 1864, following the Schleswig–Holstein fiasco, were a celebration of the blessings of prosperity enjoyed by a country that was at peace.

W. D. Rubinstein's argument that there were in fact two middle classes in mid-Victorian Britain, one based on manufacturing and centred mainly in the north of England, the other, larger and more prosperous, based on commerce and finance, and centred principally on London, may also be pertinent to an assessment of Palmerston's popular appeal.[51] It is at least plausible to suggest that the association of Palmerston with stability and business confidence was particularly attractive to the commercial and financial middle class. At the general elections of 1859 and 1865, for instance, the Conservatives were unable to win a single seat in London (the situation began to change from 1868). This raises the intriguing question of to what extent Palmerston's leadership may have forestalled the process whereby the trading and banking interests in the City, together with the expanding clerical and professional occupational groups, tended to move away from their attachment to a Liberal Party hitherto identified with the benefits of the mid-Victorian Free Trade system. The classic individual example of a Palmerstonian businessman who subsequently turned to the Conservatives was, of course, W. H. Smith, the owner of the railway-bookstall empire: he unsuccessfully contested the borough of Westminster for the Liberals, in 1865, before winning the seat as a Conservative in 1868. How many others there were of Smith's type is a subject that has yet to be fully investigated.

Whatever the true nature of Palmerston's popular appeal, it remains the case that his skill as a parliamentarian was equally critical to his political success. It was obviously a great advantage for him that, regardless of what the Liberal party represented in the country as a whole, in the House of Commons it was still a predominantly aristocratic and landed body. An analysis of the 358 Liberal MPs listed in *Dod's Parliamentary Companion* for 1859 produces the picture set out in Table 2.

A total of 108 MPs, or slightly more than 30 per cent of the parliamentary Liberal Party, were thus directly connected to the titled aristocracy of Britain and Ireland (in other words, they were the sons and

Table 2   *Social Background of Liberal MPs, 1859*

Peerage connections	59 (16.5%)
Baronets	35 (9.8%)
Baronets' sons	14 (3.9%)
Landed gentry	71 (19.8%)
Heirs of gentry	14 (3.9%)
'Gentlemen'	35 (9.8%)
Merchants/manufacturers	50 (14.0%)
Bankers	8 (2.2%)
Lawyers	41 (11.5%)
Miscellaneous	13 (3.6%)
No information	18 (5.0%)

brothers of peers, Irish peers, baronets or sons of baronets), and if to these are added the members listed in *Burke's Landed Gentry* (1858 and 1868 editions) and their heirs, we find that 53.9 per cent of the party can be classified as belonging to the aristocratic and landed classes. Even this is not quite the full story, as another 35 MPs can be described as 'gentlemen', in the sense that they were more distant connections of the aristocracy and gentry, or else were retired members of the armed forces, and none had any other discernible occupation. Taking all of these categories together, therefore, considerably more than 60 per cent of the parliamentary party were connected to the aristocratic and landed classes. By contrast, barely more than 16 per cent of Liberal MPs had been involved in business, either as merchants, manufacturers or bankers, and they did not greatly outnumber those who had pursued an active career in the legal profession.[52]

In the institutional, clubbable atmosphere of Westminster, it was possible for a leader who was as astute as he was genial to inspire personal loyalty, even through trite personal attentions to back bench MPs.[53] An invitation to one of Lady Palmerston's famous dinner parties was another useful device for securing the allegiance of otherwise nondescript back-benchers. There was, too, a widespread admiration for the resilience and good humour of the veteran Prime Minister, which even extended to a radical like Sir John Trelawny, who noted in his diary on one occasion:

> Lord P. outdid himself in gay and sparkling fancy – and skilful banter. He was radiant. In an enormous House, after one o'clock, his stentorian voice rang through the anterooms where many a far younger man was stretched at length and sound asleep. Cheers and laughter followed almost every sentence. I believe he was asleep during most of the debate – at least, he generally is – & I heard he was at Ascot all day.[54]

The contrast with his eventual successor as Liberal Prime Minister could hardly be greater: whereas Gladstone sought to appeal to men's higher nature, Palmerston relied on their good nature.

NOTES

1.   Palmerston's peerage was an Irish creation, which did not confer the right to sit in the House of Lords; he therefore sat in the Commons throughout his career.

2.   1 March 1848, in Kenneth Bourne (ed.), *The Foreign Policy of Victorian England* (London, 1970) pp. 291–3. My italics.

3.   P. H. Bagenal, *Ralph Bernal Osborne MP* (privately printed, 1884) pp. 110–16.

4.   Henry Reeve (ed.), *The Greville Memoirs* (8 vols, London, 1888): 8 August 1849; 10 February 1850; 1 July 1850; 22 November 1851.

5.   Stephen Koss, *The Rise and Fall of the Political Press in Britain*: vol. I, *The Nineteenth Century* (London, 1981) pp. 74–82.

6.   J. B. Conacher, *The Aberdeen Coalition, 1852–1855* (Cambridge, 1968) pp. 547–8.

7.   Russell to Sir George Grey, 9 February 1855, in G. P. Gooch (ed.), *The Later Correspondence of Lord John Russell, 1840–1878* (London, 1925) vol. 2, p. 182.

8.   In fact, the Queen first asked Derby to form a government, but he declined to do so; she then offered the task to Russell, who found that none of his former colleagues (except Palmerston!) were willing to serve under him.

9.   See G. R. Searle, *Entrepreneurial Politics in Mid-Victorian Britain* (Oxford, 1993) pp. 89–125.

10.   Cobden to Walmsley, n.d. [1855], in H. M. Walmsley, *The Life of Sir Josuah Walmsley* (London, 1879) p. 298.

11.　P.　M.　Gurowich,　'The　Continuation　of　War　by　Other　Means: Party and Politics, 1855–1865', *Historical Journal*, XXVII (1984) p. 609, note 42.

12.　William White, *The Inner Life of the House of Commons*, edited by Justin McCarthy (London, 1897) vol. 1, pp. 11–17 (entry for 10 May 1856). The size of the division, involving 479 MPs, was unusually large for the mid-nineteenth century.

13.　E. D. Steele, *Palmerston and Liberalism, 1855–1865* (Cambridge, 1991) pp. 23–42.

14.　Angus Hawkins, *Parliament, Party and the Art of Politics in Britain, 1855–9* (London, 1987) pp. 64–5.

15.　Robert Stewart, *The Foundation of the Conservative Party, 1830–1867* (London, 1978) pp. 340–4.

16.　Derek Fraser, *Urban Politics in Victorian England* (London, 1976) pp. 205–10.

17.　T. A. Jenkins (ed.), *The Parliamentary Diaries of Sir John Trelawny, 1858–1865* (Royal Historical Society, Camden Series, 1990) entry for 19 February 1858.

18.　Hawkins, *Art of Politics*, pp. 118–76.

19.　Cornewall Lewis to Henry Reeve, 7 September 1858, in Sir G. F. Lewis (ed.), *Letters of the Right Honourable Sir George Cornewall Lewis* (London, 1870) pp. 341–5; cf. Gurowich, 'Party and Politics', p. 609 and note 45.

20.　Derek Beales, *England and Italy, 1859–60* (London, 1961) pp. 62–92.

21.　Jenkins (ed.), *Trelawny Diaries*, 6 June 1859.

22.　See Gurowich, 'Party and Politics', pp. 621–7, for a penetrating analysis of Derby's motives.

23.　See the comments of the Saxon Ambassador to London, in Henry Reeve (ed.), *St. Petersburg and London in the Years 1852–1864: Reminiscences of Count Charles Frederick Vitzthum von Eckstaedt* (London, 1887) vol. 2, pp. 89–94 (9 July 1860).

24.　Jenkins (ed.), *Trelawny Diaries*, 11 and 19 March 1861.

25.　For the change in Conservative tactics, see Gurowich, 'Party and Politics', p. 629, note 166.

26.　J. R. Vincent (ed.), *Disraeli, Derby and the Conservative Party: The Political Journals of Lord Stanley, 1849–69* (Brighton, 1978): 30 May and 3 June 1861; 3 June 1862.

27.　Kinglake to Osborne, 3 January 1863, in Bagenal, *Bernal Osborne*, pp. 183–4.

28.　Brand to Palmerston, 7 January 1861, Broadlands MSS (Southampton University Library) GC/BR/7; printed memorial, 15 January 1861, and Palmerston to Brand, 18 January 1861, both in the Brand MSS (House of Lords Record Office).

29.　Jenkins (ed.), *Trelawny Diaries*, 3 June 1862, for an account of the Stansfeld debate.

30.　Brand to Palmerston, 7 June 1862, Broadlands MSS, GC/BR/13.

31.　Jenkins (ed.), *Trelawny Diaries*, 23 April 1860; 20 March 1862.

32.　D. G. Wright, 'Bradford and the American Civil War', *Journal of British Studies*, VIII (1969). In Leeds, on the other hand, the focus on slavery helped to mask divisions on the franchise question: idem., 'Leeds Politics and the American Civil War', *Northern History*, IX (1974).

33. Palmerston to Brand, 12 December 1862, Brand MSS.

34. Jenkins (ed.), *Trelawny Diaries*, pp. 10–14.

35. I. G. C. Hutchison, *A Political History of Scotland, 1832–1924* (Edinburgh, 1986) pp. 80–3.

36. Palmerston to Brand, 8 September 1864, Brand MSS; Brand to Palmerston, 24 August 1862, Broadlands MSS, GC/BR/14; Jenkins (ed.), *Trelawny Diaries*, 20 June 1863.

37. See Steele, *Palmerston and Liberalism*, pp. 108–17.

38. Palmerston to the seventh Duke of Devonshire, 7 February 1863, in Bernard Holland, *Life of Spencer Compton, Eighth Duke of Devonshire, 1833–1908* (London, 1911) vol. 1, p. 55.

39. Brand to Lord Halifax, 21 April 1866, in Sir Herbert Maxwell, *Life and Letters of the Fourth Earl of Clarendon* (London, 1913) vol. 2, p. 314; 'Dissolution of Parliament', *Edinburgh Review*, July 1865.

40. David F. Krein, *The Last Palmerston Government* (Iowa, 1978) pp. 119–73.

41. Steele, *Palmerston and Liberalism*, pp. 117–34.

42. Cobden to Thorold Rogers, 1 January 1865, Thorold Rogers MSS (Bodleian Library) Box 1/242.

43. Bright to Thorold Rogers, 28 August 1865, ibid., Box 1/84; Cobden to same, 5 January 1864, ibid., Box 1/228. See also Cobden's letter of 6 February 1865, regarding Free Trade in land, ibid., Box 1/245.

44. For Palmerston's relations with the northern towns generally, see Searle, *Entrepreneurial Politics*, pp. 134–40.

45. See Derek Beales, 'Garibaldi in England: the Politics of Italian Enthusiasm', in J. A. Davis and P. Ginsborg (eds), *Society and Politics in the Age of the Risorgimento* (Cambridge, 1991).

46. Palmerston to Brand, 3 August 1865, Brand MSS; cf. Steele, *Palmerston and Liberalism*, p. 221, for a different assessment.

47. Palmerston to Brand, 14 August 1863, Broadlands MSS, GC/BR/28.

48. Figures derived from Robert Blake, *The Conservative Party from Peel to Churchill* (London, 1970) p. 46.

49. Stewart, *Foundation of Conservative Party*, pp. 337–8. A printed circular relating to the Liberal Registration Association, dated 21 February 1860, is in BL Add MSS 44193, f. 12.

50. *The Economist*, 14 March 1857, pp. 277–8; 2 April 1864, pp. 413–14.

51. W. D. Rubinstein, 'Wealth, Elites and the Class Structure of Modern Britain', *Past and Present*, LXXVI (1977).

52. Inevitably, there are always difficulties involved in attempting to classify MPs in this way. A small number of the baronets and gentry for example, were men who had succeeded either in business or in law, and thus made their way into the aristocratic and landed classes. I have confined those listed as lawyers (barristers, solicitors, attorneys, Scottish advocates) to men who had evidently made a career in the profession, or for whom no other information was available than the fact that they had been 'called to the bar'. Members of the aristocracy and gentry often qualified as lawyers, but with no intention of practising the profession. The 'miscellaneous' category includes surgeons, pub-

lishers, an architect, an accountant, a landscape gardner and an ex-dissenting minister.

53. See White, *Inner Life*, 20 May 1868, making a comparison with Gladstone, unfavourable to the latter.

54. Jenkins (ed.), *Trelawny Diaries*, 7 June 1860.

4 The Rise and Fall of Gladstonian Liberalism

Gladstone and Liberalism

The history of the Liberal Party during the second half of the nineteenth century might have been a great deal simpler if W. E. Gladstone had been born a Liberal. As the son of a successful Liverpool merchant – the Gladstone family were among the *nouveaux riches* created by the 'industrial revolution' – he would seem to have been ideally suited to lead a party that derived much of its support from the rapidly expanding towns and cities: he might, in fact, have been the first 'businessman' to hold the Liberal premiership. In reality, matters were tremendously complicated by the nature of Gladstone's upbringing. So far from being a Liberal, Gladstone's early politics were shaped by the Canningite Tory principles of his father, and, rather than training in the family business, he received a classic, aristocratic education at Eton and Oxford. His early, evangelical, religious beliefs were also overlaid with the then fashionable High Church doctrines of Oxford. Identified as a young man of obvious promise, Gladstone's election to the House of Commons, at the age of only twenty-three, was facilitated by the patronage of one of the great Tory magnates, the Duke of Newcastle. The young Gladstone thus represented the antithesis of everything the Whig governments of the 1830s stood for, in terms of political reform and religious equality. His provocative book, *The State in its Relations with the Church*, published in 1838, through its uncompromising defence of the principle of Church Establishment, prompted Macaulay's celebrated description of him as 'the rising hope of those stern and unbending Tories'.

One consequence of these formative influences was that the process by which Gladstone's political career subsequently evolved towards Liberalism was tortuous, often tormented, and never wholly complete: what might, in different circumstances, have been the natural path to follow for a man of Gladstone's social origins, proved instead to be one that he had to discover gradually, and hesitantly, for himself. As an old man, indeed, he was to confess that he had been a learner all his life.[1] This fact also meant that the relationship which eventually developed between Gladstone and Liberalism was quite unique, and characterised as much by ambiguity as by a clear, mutual understanding.

It would be wrong to suppose, however, that the peculiarities of Gladstone's background were entirely disadvantageous from the point of view of the later course of his career. Indeed, it is doubtful whether Gladstone could have achieved the position he did when he did, but for the fact that he had shed his mercantile origins and been groomed for high office alongside members of the traditional ruling class. He may even have been better off starting out as a Tory, rather than trying to penetrate the social barriers erected by the often more exclusively aristocratic Whigs. At any rate, it was of critical importance that during the course of his political evolution, which involved reaching out to sections of society not hitherto fully represented at Westminster, Gladstone was always accepted as an insider, a highly respectable member of the 'establishment', rather than as an interloper stirring up popular forces in an effort to break his way into the system.

Appropriately enough, given what has been said in earlier chapters about the centrality of Free Trade to the mid-Victorian Liberal identity, it was Gladstone's experience in helping to implement this policy, as a young minister in Sir Robert Peel's Conservative government of 1841–6, that contributed more than anything to his maturing political perceptions, and thus enabled him to distance himself from his earlier, extreme opinions. Only in a mind with such a religious bent as Gladstone's could Free Trade have been perceived not merely as a policy that was good for the British economy, but as something that was beneficial for the moral improvement of society: all the same, the result was to establish a firm mental link between 'liberty' (the unshackling of human activity) and social progress.[2] In 1846 he followed Peel out of the Conservative Party, after the crisis over the repeal of the corn laws, and after Peel's death in 1850 he was clearly identified as the keeper of the Peelite fiscal conscience. Gladstone's first budget as Chancellor of the Exchequer, in the Aberdeen coalition government in 1853, was a bold affirmation of the superiority of the Free Trade strategy over the Disraelian approach, although his long-term plans were thwarted by the heavy expenditure necessitated by the Crimean War. More seriously still, there followed the breach between the leading Peelites and Lord Palmerston, and four years in the political wilderness, during which time Gladstone was still obviously attracted by the possibility of Conservative reunion. It was not until June 1859, therefore, that Gladstone finally threw in his lot with Palmerston and the Liberals, and his consequent return to the Exchequer marked the beginning of a more sustained experiment in fiscal policy.

The essence of Gladstonian finance lay in the endeavour to achieve an equitable balance between the burdens of direct and indirect taxation, and it is in the solution which Gladstone arrived at that Colin Matthew has discerned 'the social contract of the Victorian State'.[3] In 1853, and again in 1860, Gladstone renewed and extended the income tax, which bore only on those earning more than £100 per annum, and the revenue gained enabled him to reduce, and in 1860 to abolish altogether, many of the remaining duties on imported commodities. The burden of taxation on the better off – significantly, Gladstone equated the income-taxpayer with the £10 household voter – was thus increased, while a small number of valuable, revenue-raising duties remained on such items as tea, coffee, sugar, tobacco and alcohol, to ensure that the non-income-tax-paying – and largely non-voting – classes paid their share as well. So successful did Gladstone's tariff cutting policy appear to be in stimulating economic activity, and therefore boosting government revenue from the remaining indirect taxes, that by 1865 he had reduced the income tax to the rate of 4d. in the pound, and the prospect of its eventual abolition was held out to console those unfortunate enough to have to pay it. (His ultimate intention was to preserve the balance between direct and indirect taxation by introducing a new duty on houses, while retaining the succession duties which he had introduced in 1853.)

If Free Trade provided the essential link between Gladstone and Liberalism, its wider policy implications also assisted in his general political conversion. The removal of tariffs on raw materials for industry, the Reciprocity Treaty of 1860, between Britain and France, and the abolition of the paper duties in 1861, were naturally attractive to businessmen of all kinds, not least the proprietors of newspapers, and in this way valuable sources of support were secured for the future. Equally important, though, was the way that the pursuit of Free Trade influenced Gladstone's thinking on the question of parliamentary reform. Up until 1859, he had remained opposed to any further extension of the franchise, but during the early 1860s his perspective gradually changed as he came to be convinced that reform would strengthen his position in the quest for that retrenchment of government expenditure which was so vital if his financial strategy was to succeed. So far from seeing an expanded electorate as a force making for extravagance in government spending, therefore, Gladstone regarded it as a potential ally in his battle for financial rectitude.

Gladstone's altered perception of the political character of the working classes was evidently influenced by the enthusiastic reception which he received when he visited northern industrial towns such as Newcastle (where the first of these demonstrations took place, in October 1862), Manchester, Bradford and Middlesborough. He was stunned, and excited, that there should have been such remarkable public responses to the policies of someone who had hitherto considered himself as an 'executive' rather than a popular politician. Of course, it may not seem terribly surprising that Gladstone was received so well when we remember that the effect of his work as Chancellor of the Exchequer had been to reduce the incidence of indirect taxation, which bore especially on manufacturers and on working-class consumers, and that his policies were widely credited with the exceptionally buoyant state of the economy at that time. Material self-interest – more money in ordinary people's pockets, good trade, and high levels of employment – was an undeniable aspect of Gladstone's growing popularity in the country during the first half of the 1860s. For Gladstone himself, though, these manifestations of public approval were interpreted quite differently, as proof of the high moral worth of the working man, who was evidently appreciative of the need for low taxation, and therefore recognised the importance of economy in government expenditure. It was with this view in mind that, in June 1864, Gladstone made his dramatic declaration in the House of Commons that he considered every adult male 'who is not presumably incapacitated by some consideration of personal unfitness or of political danger', to be 'morally entitled to come within the pale of the Constitution'.[4] This was a wonderful specimen of Gladstonian ambiguity, as it did not commit him to any specific measure, but seemed to hold out the prospect of an almost limitless enfranchisement of working men, provided they were not personally unfit or politically dangerous (criteria which Gladstone never defined, of course).

In accepting the case for some modification of the franchise qualification, Gladstone's attitude towards working men reflected an increasingly widespread view, among the ruling elite, that they were no longer a force to be feared, and that they could, in reasonable numbers, be safely integrated into the existing political system. Gladstone was acknowledging that at least the 'respectable' section of the working classes, characterised by the virtues of sobriety, self-dignity, thrift and a desire for self-improvement, had shown themselves to be worthy of the franchise. – something that was still regarded, by most Liberals, as a trust and a duty, rather than as a 'right'. The popularity of the Post Office savings banks, established by Gladstone in 1861, was one example of the working men's desire for 'self-help' and 'respectability', which proved their entitlement to the full obligations of citizenship. No doubt historians have tended to exaggerate the distinction between working-class attitudes during the Chartist era and in the subsequent 'age of equipoise', and in reality there was much more continuity than is usually allowed.[5] Chartism was itself a spasmodic movement, the product of exceptional distress and desperation, and its political demands should be seen in the context of a long-established tradition of radical reform rather than as the manifestation of a new, independent, working-class movement. Aspirations for self-improvement, among working men, were not a purely mid-Victorian phenomenon, any more than was the instinctive hostility towards State interference in their lives. The essential point to be made, therefore, is that there is no reason to suppose that working-class voters and the Liberal Party were intrinsically incompatible, and it is not at all surprising to find that during the 1850s and 1860s Chartism usually fed into grass-roots Liberalism. To Gladstone and his fellow parliamentarians, all the same, the atmosphere of the mid-Victorian years must have seemed refreshingly different, and more reassuring, after the alarms of the, depressed and turbulent years of the late 1830s and 1840s.

Gladstone's developing conception of the critical importance of 'liberty' for the progress of human society was not confined to the fields of economic and electoral policy, either. By the early 1860s he was displaying a far deeper sensitivity to the grievances of nonconformists, and indeed was establishing personal links with a number of the more pragmatic nonconformist leaders, such as the Congregationalist minister, Christopher Newman Hall, with whom he discussed the possibility of a settlement of the long-standing question of Church rates.[6] In the House of Commons, during the session of 1863, his sympathetic speeches on the Qualification for Offices Bill, and on the abolition of University Tests, were tangible signs of the growing rapprochement between Gladstone and nonconformity. This marked the beginnings of a relationship that was to mature over the years, so that eventually even the more militant nonconformist leaders, like Samuel Morley, were to become personally devoted to Gladstone. There has always appeared to be a particular incongruity in the rapport that existed between Gladstone, a High Church Anglican, and the nonconformists, to whose claims he had originally been profoundly hostile, but the key to this surely lies in Gladstone's evangelical family upbringing, which produced distinctive traits of character that were never entirely concealed by his subsequent training at Oxford. In spite of their ostensibly opposite religious positions, therefore, a mutual attraction developed between Gladstone and nonconformity which was sustained by their shared sense of earnestness and high moral purpose in politics.

The Irish Roman Catholics, too, became an object for Gladstone's extended religious sympathies when, in May 1865, he made known to the House of Commons his belief that the disestablishment of the Irish Church would be the most pressing issue of the future. As well as giving encouragement to the Irish Liberal MPs, who had been largely alienated from the leaderships of Russell and Palmerston, Gladstone's declaration naturally delighted his growing band of nonconformist admirers, who regarded this as a useful first step in the direction of all-round disestablishment, while it also appealed to radicals of a more secular type, who welcomed any attack on a privileged Church establishment. Furthermore, Gladstone's pronouncement served to accelerate his political evolution because of the way it prompted his rejection by Oxford University, which he had represented since 1847, and his adoption instead by the industrialised county constituency of South Lancashire, where he 'came unmuzzled' at the general election in the summer of 1865.

J. R. Vincent, in his classic analysis of Gladstone's emergence as the leader of popular Liberalism, has stressed the uniqueness of his ability to appeal to different sections of society, so much so that for a time he appeared to be all things to (nearly) all men:

after 1859, Gladstone became associated, in the space of a few years, with the conflicting aims of half the great interests of the Country. He stood at once for the serious aristocracy, the High Churchmen, the industrialists, the cheap press and radical agitation, the provincial towns, Dissent and the working class. So quickly did he evolve, that differing impressions of him, mutually exclusive in the long run, but all favourable, were co-existent in the minds of great classes. . . . By the velocity of his evolution towards many-sidedness, he temporarily squared the political circle.[7]

It is virtually impossible to disentangle the momentum of events carrying Gladstone forward, from the element of political calculation, or
opportunism, that was undoubtedly present as well. Walter Bagehot, in
a famous essay published in 1860, had already identified the salient
characteristic of Gladstone's political personality as being that, as his
shift away from Toryism showed, 'he has a susceptible nature . . . he
will not live out of sympathy with his age. . . . Mr. Gladstone is essentially a man who cannot impose his creed *on* his time, but must learn
his creed *of* his time.'[8] No-one could have been unaware of the fact
that, by 1865, with the Prime Minister an octogenarian, and his likely
successor, Earl Russell (the former Lord John Russell), a septuagenar-
ian, there was an obvious political vacuum to be filled in the medium-
to-long-term, and that Gladstone, through his conduct as Chancellor of
the Exchequer, was building in a highly effective way a constituency for
himself both in parliament and in the country.

Gladstone and the Liberal Mind

Gladstone's political development was so distinctive, and his relationship with Liberalism in many ways so incongruous, that it is worth
exploring further the climate in which the phenomenon of 'Gladstonian
Liberalism' became possible. In particular, we need to consider whether
it is true that the emotional – perhaps even irrational – ties that bound
Gladstone and the Liberals together were more important than the
purely rational appeal of his policies. This also raises a more general
question about what motivated the supporters of the Liberal cause in
the country: what was it that made them tick?

The recent trend in historical research has certainly favoured the view
that the coalition of interests that came together around Gladstone in
the 1860s was inspired by the positive and rational attractions of his
policies. We have already seen that Gladstone's budgets offered tangible
benefits to businessmen of all sorts – whether they be large-scale manufacturers, merchant princes, newspaper proprietors, small shopkeepers,
or craftsmen – as well as to the ordinary consumer. Beyond this, there
was a more general political dimension to Gladstonian financial policy
which commended it to those members of the business classes who still
swore by the doctrines of the 'Manchester school', and also to an articulate minority of working men whose views have been identified as
forming part of a long-established tradition of plebeian radicalism.[9] To

groups such as these, Gladstonian finance, with its emphasis on government retrenchment and the minimalist State, represented an assault upon the corruption and extravagance that was deemed to be inherent in a political system still dominated by the aristocracy. Likewise, the repeal of the paper duties was welcomed not simply because it eliminated the last of the 'taxes on knowledge', but because it had been achieved after a struggle against the greatest of all bastions of aristocratic privilege, the House of Lords, which had originally rejected Gladstone's plan in 1860, only to be forced to give way the following year when the Chancellor of the Exchequer incorporated the measure into his budget.

Naturally, Gladstone's modified views on the franchise question, and his willingness to consider concessions to nonconformists and Roman Catholics at the expense of the Established Churches, provide further examples of the 'practical' side of Gladstonian Liberalism. There may still be something to be said, however, for the alternative view that, for many ordinary Liberal supporters in the country what the Liberal creed offered, above all else, was the 'visceral thrill' of being involved in a great moral cause.[10] It was the sense of superiority gained from their attachment to the side of 'right', against 'wrong', that mattered at least as much, and probably more, than the precise policy that happened to be at issue at any particular moment. Certainly, when we consider the periodic bouts of mass-enthusiasm for Gladstone, which manifested themselves from the 1860s onwards, the hyperbolic praise that was heaped upon him, and the almost mystical, superhuman qualities that were attributed to him, it is difficult to believe that this was the product of a purely rational assessment of the virtues of the policies with which he was associated. In an age when opportunities for leisure activity were in limited supply, politics itself became a form of entertainment for the masses (political meetings were often 'family' occasions), and political leaders, Gladstone above all others, became the heroes, the cult-figures of their day. (Indeed, a comparison can properly be made with certain cinema and pop-music stars of the twentieth century, who have provoked a similar hysterical excitement and suspension of rational belief amongst their admirers.) The phenomenon of popular 'Gladstonianism', in other words, reflected not so much the attitudes of an enlightened, responsible Victorian citizenry, as some historians have claimed,[11] as the unsophisticated passions and enthusiasms of a poorly educated populace at the dawn of the era of mass-participatory politics.

A popular poem, composed in 1868, conveys the sense of an almost mindless faith in Gladstone, shared by many working people who were convinced that he was one of them. But such beliefs belonged to the realm of fantasy rather than of reason:

> Who's the Liberal Leader? he
> Who for us has stood, Stood through triumph and defeat
> For the People's good;
> We the People have a mind
> Well, it shall be known,
> Gladstone, he shall lead us still,
> He and he alone.
> We have votes and let them need us
> Gladstone, he alone shall lead us.
> Why? Because our wrongs he feels
> And our right would win;
> Why? Because for us he fights
> Out of power and in . . .

The testimony of an artisan, some years later, illustrates the hypnotic effect which Gladstone's oratory clearly had on many people:

> Without an effort – so it seemed to me – the great orator held his audience for nearly two hours. I stood so far off that the features were indistinct, but was spellbound by the music and magnetism of the wonderful voice. . . . I was only conscious of the presence of a great human personality under whose spell I was, and from whom I could in no way escape. . . . *If the things he said were unintelligible to me, the voice brought with it something of an inspiration and of uplifting power.* . . . I felt lifted into a holy region of politics, where Tories cannot corrupt or Jingoes break through and yell.[12]

Gladstone's charismatic leadership may indeed offer an important insight into the essence of the Liberal mind, which was often concerned much more with the appeal to emotions than with the mundane details of legislation. It was a mark of Gladstone's political genius, of course, that he was able to inject a sense of strong moral imperative into rather prosaic questions such as financial policy. This leads us to a more general point, that 'Liberalism' was often much clearer about its methods than its objects, that is to say, much stronger on means than on ends. At one level, this tendency can be detected in the popular writings of the radical Liberal, Samuel Smiles, whose most famous book, *Self Help*, appeared in 1859. Smiles's message was the simple one, that it was possible for all men to improve their condition, through their own efforts and personal conduct. In fact, there was a potentially far-reaching implication here, with regard to ultimate social equality, but the point that registered most with contemporaries was the belief in the possibility of constant progress, rather than the final goal. Even at a more exalted level, such as in the work of the outstanding Liberal philosopher of the mid-Victorian age, John Stuart Mill, whose *On Liberty* was also published in 1859, this distinctive Liberal mentalité is apparent. In endeavouring to modify the crude Benthamite principle of utility, Mill came to see happiness as a by-product of the pursuit of some other, nobler end than mere personal gratification. Consequently, for Mill, the quest for 'truth' became crucial for the internal cultivation of one's individuality. Indeed, Mill was convinced that intellectual freedom was not simply a means towards social improvement, but was an integral part of that process.[13] The quest for 'truth' was thus itself a beneficial process, quite apart from the actual attainment of that goal. After all, it remained unclear what exactly the 'truth' consisted of, in its application to the practical issues of the day, beyond the search for an unprejudiced, disinterested approach to government. That other great Liberal sage, Matthew Arnold, whose *Culture and Anarchy* appeared in 1869, was no clearer in his objects, seeking 'sweetness and light', but prescribing nothing more precise than 'right reason' as the means towards this end. The one thing that Smiles, Mill and Arnold all agreed was critically important was that the provision of education must be expanded. All citizens should thus be able to participate in the quest for 'truth' or 'sweetness and light', which was a vital condition for the development of their own individuality; and while in one sense this was merely a means to an end, in another sense it was the end itself.

It is possible to detect certain tendencies in Gladstone's character which help us to understand why the notion of participation, for its own sake, had an instinctive attraction for him. As Boyd Hilton has argued, the evangelical influences on Gladstone's upbringing remained apparent throughout his life, and vitally informed his whole outlook on politics. For a man who believed, literally, in divine providence, that God was present in everything one did and experienced, it followed that politics itself was an arena in which the struggle between good and evil – darkness and light – was fought out. It was for this reason that Gladstone invested so much enthusiasm and passion in his political work, and was therefore capable of conceiving of an issue like Free

Trade in very much more than secular, economic terms. The Palmerstonian approach to domestic policy, that of quietly keeping the
machine of government ticking over, was simply an impossibility for
Gladstone. As he was to put it in a famous letter to Lord Granville,
written in 1877, 'My opinion is and has long been that the vital principle of the Liberal party, like that of Greek art, is action, and that
nothing but action will ever make it worthy of the name of a party.'[14]
'Action', then, was an indispensable condition of political life for Gladstone, and the doing of a thing could be as important as the thing itself
(perhaps more so). In Hilton's view, Gladstone sought political conflict
'gratuitously, not from the dictates of reason, but in the belief that
societies which are not in turmoil will stagnate'; and he 'preferred his
followers to run on the spot, as it were, in a flurry of mental and moral
activity, rather than to create a heaven on earth'.[15]

In spite of the tangible benefits of Gladstonian policy, therefore, one
is struck much more by the sense in which Gladstone was engaged in a
crusade for higher, and less clearly definable, goals. (A cynic might say
that Gladstonian Liberalism embodied a potent combination of material self-interest and high-minded morality.) The notion that many
ordinary Liberals were captivated by the 'visceral thrill' of their participation in the political battle, and that this was precisely what Gladstone
was seeking to encourage, is not one that can be easily dismissed.
Arguably, what held together the diverse coalition of interests that was
the Liberal Party, for so long, was the shared feeling of being engaged
in the pursuit of 'progress'. It was entirely appropriate, for the Victorian age, that the railway should frequently have been used in literature
as an image for 'progress', and fitting too that an analogy was so often
made between the Liberal Party and the train.[16] Moreover, such a
conception of the nature of Liberal activity could leave plenty of scope
for different points of view. Liberals might legitimately disagree over
the speed at which the train of progress ought to be moving, at what
points along the track it ought to pause, and even where the ultimate
destination should be; but at least there was a feeling that everyone on
board was moving – usually – in the same direction.

The Second Reform Crisis

The events of 1866–8 usefully illustrate what the essential vagueness
and ambiguity of Liberalism could mean in practice. In April 1866 the

Liberal ministry headed by Earl Russell (who had succeeded Palmerston in October 1865), with Gladstone as Chancellor of the Exchequer and leader of the House of Commons, introduced a modest Parliamentary Reform Bill. Adopting a cautious interpretation of the 'principles' of reform which Gladstone had enunciated in June 1864, the bill proposed to reduce the borough franchise qualification from £10 to £7, and to introduce a £14 household franchise for the counties, which together would have increased the size of the electorate in England and Wales from around 1,100,000 to 1,500,000. Forty-nine seats were to be taken from small boroughs for the purpose of redistribution. It was far from being a drastic measure of reform, and indeed it seemed to be aimed at little more than the reinforcement of the Liberals' existing domination of the boroughs. Working men's representation was to be modestly increased, but not to such an extent that they would be allowed a preponderant voice within the electoral system.

Nevertheless, the government's plan encountered vigorous opposition from a group of dissident Liberals, including Robert Lowe, Edward Horsman, Lord Elcho and Lord Grosvenor, who came to be known as the 'Adullamites'. To Liberals such as these – and it must be remembered that Russell's ministry was operating in a parliament elected while Palmerston was still Prime Minister – any further change in the electoral system was bound to undermine the enlightened, moderate Liberal regime of the mid-Victorian era, over which Palmerston had so successfully presided, because of the undue weight it would give to the working classes (who, as a result of rising prices and living standards, already accounted for about one-quarter of the borough electorate by the mid-1860s). Lowe especially, in a series of trenchant parliamentary speeches, which infuriated his opponents, stressed the peril to the existing order of society posed by the enfranchisement of working men, who, he argued, were characterised by their ignorance, venality and propensity for collective action (as evidenced by the recent growth of trade unions). The granting of greater political power to the working classes would therefore be inimical to the whole Liberal ideal of an electorate composed of individual, independently minded citizens, and would inevitably result in the abuse of the powers of the State by those who stood to gain from it. Lowe himself, it is interesting to note, had been brought up in the Benthamite faith, but he was in no doubt that, even judged by the criteria of utilitarianism, parliamentary reform could not be justified, as it would not be conducive to good government.[17] In the event, the Russell ministry was defeated, in June 1866, on a wrecking amendment to its Reform Bill moved by the Adullamite, Lord Dunkellin, which was supported by some 48 Liberal MPs as well as by the Conservatives. Rather than seeking another dissolution of parliament, less than a year after the last one, Russell decided to resign.

It is not necessary to discuss in detail the subsequent events which led to the minority Conservative government of Lord Derby carrying, in 1867, a much more far-reaching measure of reform, enacting the principle of household suffrage for the boroughs, and introducing a £12 household franchise for the counties. The overall effect was to almost double the size of the electorate in England and Wales, to just under 2,000,000. In Scotland, which was still dealt with by a separate Act, household suffrage for the burghs was also adopted, although the county franchise was more restricted than in England and Wales. Nevertheless, the Scottish electorate was more than doubled, to around 235,000. For the Liberals, the conduct of the Conservatives proved to be doubly divisive. Having first joined with the Adullamites in order to bring about the defeat of Russell's bill, the Conservatives had then proceeded to change tack by abandoning the Adullamites and introducing their own measure. Disraeli had then skilfully exploited the divisions between the Liberal leaders and their more radical back-bench followers by accepting a number of radical amendments to the Conservatives' bill. Indeed, it was precisely because the radicals became convinced that they could obtain a more extensive measure of reform from a minority Conservative government, which needed their votes, that they refused, in the famous 'tea room revolt' of April 1867, to support Gladstone's amendment designed to castrate the Conservatives' bill by inserting a £5 borough voting qualification. Some 45 radical MPs either voted or paired with the government against Gladstone's amendment. By thus driving in a wedge between Gladstone and the radicals, in the House of Commons, the Conservatives were able to secure the passage of their bill.

On an eminently practical question of reform, like that of the franchise in 1866–7, the Liberals could demonstrate a remarkable capacity for internal division. The contrast with the unifying effect of a relatively abstract issue, Irish Church disestablishment, is therefore all the more striking. It was through the resolutions on this subject, which he carried against the Conservative government in April 1868, that Gladstone (now the overall Liberal leader, following Russell's retirement) succeeded in rallying his party. Of course, the Irish Church was a matter of obvious concern for the Irish Roman Catholic MPs, but as regards the rest of the Liberal Party the perceived merits of disestablishment were, to say the least, indirect. Radicals and nonconformists could acclaim Gladstone's policy, but they did so rather from the point of view of its possible future implications for Britain than from any real solicitude for the grievances of the Irish people. In the meantime, though, Irish Church disestablishment served to push into the background other potentially awkward issues, such as elementary education. As for the Whigs, acceptance of Irish Church disestablishment was primarily a pragmatic step, a response to the pressure of events dictated by others, and it had little or nothing to do with any belief that it would do real good in Ireland. Still, the fact that Gladstone's policy had been endorsed by the veteran Russell, made the position of the Whigs that much easier. Such expediency was even more pronounced in the case of Lowe and his fellow Adullamites, who were clearly glad of an issue which permitted them to fall back into line after their unhappy dalliance with Derby and Disraeli. Towards the end of 1868, as the country prepared for a general election under the new electoral system, Gladstone had equipped the Liberals with a valuable rallying-cry, and the new voters with a suitably emotive and 'moral' cause for their own edification: justice to the Irish people. At the same time, Gladstone had finally established a firm grip – albeit temporarily – on his party.

It could even be argued that the Conservatives did the Liberals a favour, in 1867, by passing an extensive measure of parliamentary reform, which then enabled the Liberals to forget just how chronically divided they had been on the subject. After all, the Liberals' own bill, of 1866, had been a modest measure, falling a long way short of the demand for universal manhood suffrage being articulated by the National Reform League, a broadly-based working men's organisation, which had emerged in 1865 and was responsible for the Hyde Park demonstrations in 1866 and 1867. The League had only very reluctantly accepted John Bright's advice to support the Russell government's bill, but, if this measure had been implemented in 1866, it is by no means clear that it would have provided a satisfactory and lasting settlement. As it was, however, the government was seen to have been defeated as a result of the desertion by the traitorous Adullamites, and this enabled Liberal supporters to lose sight of the moderation of their own leaders' original intentions. Consequently, after the Conservatives had carried their more drastic measure, the Liberals were propelled further to the 'left', the only remaining political ground on which they could regroup, although they had not themselves been the cause of their movement. Eventually, Liberal mythology about the second reform episode would manage to obscure completely what the real views of Russell and Gladstone had been, to the extent that Liberals came to believe that it was Gladstone who had imposed the principle of household suffrage upon the Conservative government.[18] By the time of the 1868 general election, the Reform League seems to have had no difficulty in co-operating wholeheartedly with the Liberal Party, even accepting a secret financial subvention from the chief whip, and it soon ceased to operate in any meaningful way as a separate entity. A similar fate befell the Scottish National Reform League, which made little impact in 1868 in a country where the new voters apparently shared the same political proclivities as the established electorate.[19]

The Liberal Party in 1868

The Conservative governments of 1866–8 had survived because of the divisions amongst the Liberals, rather than through their command of a regular majority in the House of Commons, and the general election of November 1868 merely served to weaken the Conservatives' position still further (see Table 3). According to H. J. Hanham's estimate, the Liberal majority over the Conservatives in 1865 had been around 70, and this was now increased to 110. With the Liberals not only stronger but also united, thanks to the Irish Church question, Disraeli chose to break with convention by resigning immediately rather than waiting to face the new parliament. The way was therefore open for Gladstone to form his first administration.

Table 3   *The Liberal Victory in 1868*[20]

	Con.	Lib.	Lib. majority
England	217	243	26
Wales	10	23	13
Scotland	7	53	46
Ireland	40	65	25
UK TOTAL	274	384	110

In many respects, the election results simply repeated the familiar pattern whereby the Conservatives enjoyed a large preponderance in the English counties while the Liberals remained firmly entrenched in the boroughs, particularly the large ones. The main exceptions to this rule were the Conservative gains in Westminster and Middlesex – early portents of the movement away from the Liberals by the business and suburban middle classes, which was to be a much more significant feature of later elections – and in Lancashire and the industrial part of Cheshire, where they won 24 out of 36 borough seats, including notable triumphs in Manchester, Salford, Bolton and Stockport. The Conservatives also achieved a clean-sweep of the eight Lancashire county seats. Indeed, Lancashire, with its distinctive factory culture and strong Protestant sentiments (the product largely of hostility towards the large numbers of Irish migrant workers), was the one really disturbing blot on the Liberals' electoral landscape, and one of the Liberal victims was Gladstone himself, who was defeated in the newly created South West Lancashire constituency (he was elected, instead, for the London borough of Greenwich).

So far as Liberal gains are concerned, it is necessary to look beyond England to the Celtic fringe, Scotland, Wales and Ireland, where, again according to Hanham, the Liberals' total majority increased to 84, compared with 47 in 1865. Most striking of all was the Liberal advance in Wales, where the balance of forces had previously been fairly even – 18 Liberals to 14 Conservatives in 1865, for instance. This change reflected a growing militancy on the part of the overwhelmingly dominant nonconformist sects, whose political power had been greatly enhanced by the new borough and county franchise qualifications. In the Welsh counties, nonconformist feeling also became channelled into agrarian grievances, directed against the mainly Anglican landlords, the two forces combining to foster nationalist sentiments. The late 1860s thus witnessed the emergence of a natural Liberal hegemony in Wales, which was to survive for as long as the Liberals remained a party of government.[21]

The perpetuation of Liberal dominance in the larger English boroughs, with their often greatly increased electorates, combined with the similar ascendancy in Scotland and Wales, undoubtedly explains what appears to have been a significant rise in the number of non-conformist MPs. Unfortunately, there are no reliable estimates of the position in previous parliaments with which precise comparisons can be made, but it seems certain that the 62 back-bench Liberal MPs, identified in J. P. Parry's survey of the 1868 parliament, represented an important breakthrough for nonconformity.[22] Moreover, these MPs were drawn overwhelmingly from the older sects, which were usually the most radical in their attitudes both towards the Church of England and towards politics in general. No less than 17 were Unitarians, a figure that is out of all proportion to this tiny sect's numerical presence in British society as a whole, while a similar number were Baptists or Congregationalists, and 11 were Scottish Presbyterians. There were also handfuls of Quakers and Jews. By contrast, only three of the 62 MPs came from the numerically powerful, but politically moderate, Wesleyan Methodists. Parliamentary nonconformity, which accounted for rather more than one-sixth of all British Liberal MPs, was therefore aligned almost entirely with the 'radical' section of the party on many key areas of policy. Indeed, as Parry shows, in addition to the 50 nonconformist MPs whose voting behaviour demonstrates a clear support for Church disestablishment and/or secular education, some 65 MPs who were not nonconformists themselves (but often represented urban constituencies, with substantial nonconformist electorates) supported one or both of these measures. Altogether, then, there was a powerful bloc of some 115 MPs – nearly one-third of the parliamentary Liberal Party – who followed a 'radical' line, at least on religious questions.

An analysis of the social composition of the parliamentary party, based on the 386 MPs listed in *Dod's Parliamentary Companion* for 1869, confirms what one would naturally have expected, that the Second Reform Act had brought about significant changes in the type of men elected to the House of Commons, although it would be an exaggeration to describe these changes as dramatic. Table 4 can be compared with that relating to Liberal MPs in 1859 (Table 2), which appears in Chapter 3.

All of the categories relating to the aristocratic and landed classes thus registered a decline compared with 1859, the most notable victims being the landed gentry. Nevertheless, the aristocracy and gentry still accounted for nearly 45 per cent of Liberal MPs, and if to these are added the 'gentlemen' (men with more distant aristocratic and landed connections, and no discernible career other than in the armed forces), then the figure is over 50 per cent, which puts their decline in perspective. The main beneficiaries of change were those MPs engaged (or previously engaged) in business activities – manufacturing, trade and banking – who rose as a proportion of the party to over 24 per cent, while the lawyers enjoyed a slight increase.

Table 4 *Social Background of Liberal MPs, 1869*

		(1859)
Peerage connections	52 (13.5%)	(16.5%)
Baronets	30 (7.8%)	(9.8%)
Baronets' sons	13 (3.4%)	(3.9%)
Landed gentry	57 (14.8%)	(19.8%)
Heirs of gentry	12 (3.1%)	(3.9%)
'Gentlemen'	33 (8.5%)	(9.8%)
Merchants/manufacturers	86 (22.3%)	(14.0%)
Bankers	8 (2.1%)	(2.2%)
Lawyers	51 (13.2%)	(11.5%)
Miscellaneous	20 (5.2%)	(3.6%)
No information	24 (6.2%)	(5.0%)

At the level of Cabinet appointments, the preponderance of members of the aristocratic and landed classes was more marked than in the parliamentary party as a whole, but Gladstone's Cabinet of 1868 nevertheless included a significantly greater number of 'middle class' men than had been found in previous Liberal governments. Of the fourteen Cabinet members (excluding the Prime Minister himself), it seems reasonable to count eight as representatives of the 'Whig' tradition of aristocratic administration: namely, Clarendon, Granville, Hartington, Kimberley, Hatherley, Chichester Fortescue, Argyll and de Grey (although the last two were Peelites by origin). The proportion of Whigs would probably have been greater but for the fact that several former Cabinet ministers, notably Russell, Somerset, Sir George Grey and Halifax, declined offers from Gladstone (Halifax did join the Cabinet in 1870, however). Four of those who did accept high office can be regarded as representatives of the business and professional middle classes: Bright, Lowe, Cardwell and Goschen. The two remaining ministers, Childers and Bruce, are more difficult to categorise, for, while they were both connected to landed families, they also had significant business interests. In political terms, the outstanding feature of this government was the inclusion, as President of the Board of Trade, of the veteran radical campaigner, John Bright, a man who had always been *de rigueur* to the Palmerstonian regime. Bright's presence was a powerful symbol of Gladstone's success in integrating the different components of the Liberal coalition, to an extent never achieved – or probably desired – by his predecessors.

Liberal Reforms, 1868–74

Although the first Gladstone ministry could only properly claim an electoral mandate for the disestablishment and disendowment of the Church of Ireland, which was duly implemented in 1869, the current of reform clearly ran much deeper than this. For Gladstone personally, the desire to 'pacify Ireland' was a major preoccupation throughout the lifetime of his government, and he had never been in any doubt that a comprehensive settlement of the Irish problem required action on the questions of land and university education, as well as dealing with the Church. Accordingly, in 1870, an Irish Land Bill was introduced in an attempt to redress the grievances of the tenant farmers. This bill, in the preparation of which the Prime Minister had invested a great deal of his own time, offered greater security for the tenant by enabling him to claim compensation from his landlord for unfair eviction (though this did not cover eviction for non-payment of rent), as well as a right to compensation for improvements made by him, when he vacated the holding. There can be no doubt that, by the standards of the time, the Land Bill appeared to be a drastic step, interfering as it did in the contractual relations between landlord and tenant; and while there was no serious resistance to the bill, either by Conservatives or Whigs, and the Irish landlords themselves seemed resigned to the inevitability of some such measure, it was nevertheless thought to represent a dangerous departure from generally accepted notions of the legitimate role of government. One Liberal MP, a Cornish landowner, who supported the bill, confided to his diary that 'The naked fact stares us in the face – we have turned our backs upon Political economy. The science appears to have broken down.'[24] It would be quite unfair, then, to dismiss Gladstone's bill as a timid or half-hearted measure, but unfortunately this was still how it was viewed by many Irish Liberal MPs, notably Isaac Butt, who had wanted a much more far-reaching system of tenant right (the so-called '3 fs': fair rents, fixity of tenure and free sale). The consequences of Irish disappointment with the Land Bill were to become fully apparent in 1873 when, as we shall see, Gladstone made an abortive attempt to tackle the university dimension to the Irish Question.

In the field of domestic legislation, Gladstône's ministry is rightly considered to have been one of the most productive of the nineteenth century. Reform of the system of elementary education (1870), the introduction of competitive examinations for entrance to most areas of the civil service (1870, 1873), the abolition of the purchase of commissions in the army (1871), a major overhaul of the judicial system (1873), the abolition of the remaining religious tests in the universities (1871), and the introduction of a secret ballot for elections (1872): all of these important measures emanated from this remarkably fertile period of Liberal government.

Such a flurry of ministerial activity can be partly explained in general terms, as the product of a 'climate' of reforming opinion that had been building up over a number of years. Many of the measures implemented between 1868 and 1874 had long been subjects of public discussion, as in the case of civil service reform, which was based on the recommendations of the Northcote–Trevelyan Commission of 1853. One source of new ideas was undoubtedly the annual conferences of the Social Science Association, beginning in 1857, which provided a forum for debates involving politicians, academics and professionals, most of whom were committed Liberals.[25] The participation of academics was typical of the mid-Victorian age, which had witnessed the emergence of an increasingly influential lay intelligentsia, anxious to engage in discussions on the major public issues of the time. Two collections of essays, published in March and April 1867, during the midst of the parliamentary reform crisis, stand as testaments to the growing mood in favour of change that was spreading amongst the Oxbridge-educated intellectual elite: *Essays on Reform* and *Questions for a Reformed Parliament*. The contributors included A. V. Dicey, Leslie Stephen, Goldwin Smith, James Bryce, Frederic Harrison, Thorold Rogers and G. C. Brodrick, many of whom had become involved in the campaign against university tests, during the early 1860s, and had subsequently widened their political horizons, coming to admire the working classes for what seemed to be their principled stand against slavery, through their support for the Federal side in the American Civil War. Indeed, the University Liberals had believed that a moderately enlarged working-class electorate – along the lines of Russell's Reform Bill of

1866 – would provide the momentum for action on many other issues; and the essayists therefore put the case for reform in such areas as the legal system, the provision of elementary education, the land laws, and the laws affecting the status of trade unions. While the authors were motivated by the belief that it was right, and natural, for an educated elite to govern in the interests of the masses, there was at least a positive recognition of the need to reform laws and institutions in order to prevent the working classes from becoming alienated from them. It was in a review of the *Essays on Reform* volume that the young radical editor of the *Fortnightly Review*, John Morley, proudly boasted that 'The extreme advanced party is likely for the future to have on its side the most highly cultivated intellect in the nation, and the contest will lie between brains and numbers on one side, and wealth, rank, vested interest, possession in short, on the other.'[26]

Nevertheless, it seems plausible to suggest that the greatest impetus for reform came from the concerns felt by the political elite about how best to address the new electorate which had been so drastically, and abruptly, created as a result of the opportunism of the Conservatives in 1867. After all, many Liberals, including the intellectuals, had not intended the process of parliamentary reform to go quite as far as it did, and there had been some alarm at the manifestations of extra-parliamentary action by the predominantly working-class National Reform League. This situation raised serious questions as to what were likely to be the expectations of 'public opinion', now that it was obviously going to be more powerful than in the past, and a sense of urgency was thus created as politicians sought to find a suitable mode of government for the new, more 'democratic' era. During the 1868 general election, it is true, Irish Church disestablishment was so much the dominant issue that it obscured most other matters, but the subsequent course pursued by the Gladstone ministry made it clear that the floodgates against reform, so carefully maintained by Palmerston, were now open.

If a single thread is to be detected running through much of the government's legislation, this would be the need to modify the nation's institutions so as to promote the efficiency, and greater professionalisation, of the State. The principle was established, through the civil-service, army and university reforms, that henceforth, employment in the higher education system, and in the service of the State, should be determined by merit, rather than by religious affiliation or patronage. In the case of the Army Regulation Act, which re-organised the armed forces, creating a new reserve force, as well as abolishing the purchase of commissions, the impetus necessary for forcing through change was provided by the Prussian military victories over Austria and France, in 1866 and 1870, which had highlighted the need for a more professional system. Lord Chancellor Selborne's Judicature Act of 1873, which does not always receive the attention it deserves, was an impressive measure of rationalisation, incorporating several separate and sometimes conflicting law courts, operating different legal codes, into a single High Court of Justice, administering a more uniform system of law. At the same time, Selborne's act established a Court of Appeal.

Concern for the efficiency of the State was a reciprocal matter, however, in which the citizen, too, had a part to play, and it was therefore important that the large, new, working-class electorate should be an educated body. Once again, Prussia, which had had a system of compulsory elementary education since 1806, provided a model. W. E. Forster's Education Act did not go quite as far as the Prussian system (it was another ten years before school attendance was made compulsory), but it established a procedure whereby elected School Boards could be set up in order to provide additional school places in areas where the existing provision by the voluntary agencies was found to be inadequate. There was a similar logic, perhaps, behind the government's decision to implement the traditional radical demand for the secret ballot: at least, it was possible to contend that a measure designed to put an end to bribery and intimidation at elections was a necessary corollary of education reform, ensuring that the votes cast by the newly enfranchised working electors – the educated, and, it was hoped, responsible citizenry of the future – were given freely.

It would be a mistake to suppose that the legislation passed by Gladstone's government was all part of a programme inspired and masterminded by the Prime Minister. On the contrary, Gladstone's own strong sympathies with the Church of England meant that he was not at all enthusiastic about the non-denominational School Boards provided for in the Education Act, and he was therefore disposed to leave the responsibility for this measure largely in the hands of the relevant minister, Forster. The Act, indeed, was framed along lines that were far more congenial to the Whigs, with their traditional preference for a conciliatory religious policy designed to bring Anglicans and nonconformists closer together. Gladstone's Churchmanship also explains why he was somewhat reluctant to act on the question of university tests, although in the end the Abolition Bill, which had been pressed for several years by private members, was adopted as a government

measure in 1870 and carried the following year. In the case of the
Ballot Act, political expediency had an important part to play, and
Gladstone, who had no strong personal commitment to the principle of
the secret ballot, adopted the policy in 1868 simply because he was
anxious to secure the adhesion of Bright and the radicals to his new
ministry.[27]

With regard to civil-service reform, it is interesting to note that the
initiative was taken not by Gladstone (although he approved of the
policy), but by his Chancellor of the Exchequer, Robert Lowe, who, in
spite of his reputation as a 'reactionary' because of his stand in 1866–7,
was in reality a Benthamite radical with a keen interest in administrative reform. Lowe's views are instructive, moreover, for what they
show us about the anticipations which lay behind many of the Liberal
reforms. The purpose of competitive examinations was to inject the
criterion of merit into the selection procedure, certainly, but the way
the examinations were designed was meant to ensure that they were
suited for Oxbridge-educated candidates. There was no question, in
Lowe's scheme of things, of using civil-service reform as a means of
promoting greater upward social mobility by making entry more acces-
sible to young men from less privileged backgrounds.[28] In practice, too,
the working of Cardwell's army reforms indicates that there was no
dramatic change in the social origins of commissioned officers, in spite
of the abolition of purchase. Meritocracy within the existing elite,
rather than a more general equality of opportunity, was the keynote of
the Liberal reforms.

The Political Costs of Liberal Reform

Great credit is due to Gladstone and his colleagues for the substantial
legislative achievements of the Liberal ministry of 1868–74. The enact-
ment of so many measures of first-rate importance required not only
energy, but much determination as well: the Ballot Bill, for instance,
was blocked by the Conservative majority in the House of Lords, in
1871, and had to be reintroduced the following year; while the Army
Regulation Bill was subjected to obstructionist tactics by Conservative
MPs, and was only agreed to by the House of Lords after the government had resorted to the use of a Royal Warrant in order to force
through the bill's main provision, the abolition of the purchase of commissions. A great deal of political courage was also shown, particularly

in the way the government resolved to tackle the question of elementary education, one that was so beset by sectarian rivalries that previous governments had preferred to leave it well alone. Unfortunately for the Gladstone ministry, its efforts in relation to education marked the beginning of a process by which many important components of what was still very much a 'Liberal coalition' became disenchanted with their own government and rebellious in their attitudes towards it.

The difficulty over education arose from the fact that the solution devised by Forster left intact the existing system of Voluntary schools, run predominantly by the Church of England, which were to continue to receive State grants. Only in those areas where the voluntary sector was failing to make sufficient provision of school places, were Board schools to be established, in which religious instruction was to be provided on a non-denominational basis. Forster's pragmatic measure, through its unwillingness to attack the entrenched position of the Established Church within the education system, infuriated many non-conformists, and it was denounced by a new pressure group, the National Education League, which had been founded in Birmingham in 1869. To men such as the president of the League, Joseph Chamberlain, a unitarian businessman, and parliamentary spokesmen for nonconformity, like George Dixon and Henry Richard, a purely secular system of elementary education, compulsory and free, was preferable to any arrangement which perpetuated Anglican domination. The outcome of a conference of radical nonconformists, held in Manchester in January 1872, indicated that this extreme solution was now gaining majority support. A formidable extra-parliamentary agitation against Forster's Act was organised by the National Education League, during the early 1870s, with nonconformist hostility being particularly directed against Clause 25, which permitted the payment of Church school fees for pauper children out of the local rates.

Licensing reform was another invidious subject which brought the government nothing but trouble, as it succeeded in offending both of the interest groups involved. H. A. Bruce, the Home Secretary, brought in a complex bill in 1871 which would, among other things, have prevented any increase in the number of public houses, as well as leaving the long-term security of publicans' licences in doubt. The bill provoked a series of angry meetings in the country, and in the end made little progress in the House of Commons. As the *Annual Register* observed, 'It proved unnecessary to discuss a Bill for which no borough member could have voted without forfeiting his seat.' Even so, the unpopularity of Bruce's bill was probably a contributory factor to the loss of Liberal seats in by-elections at East Surrey and Plymouth, during the summer of 1871, which marked the beginning of a definite adverse trend against the government in the constituencies.[29] Having alienated the drink interest, however, Bruce proceeded in 1872 to disappoint the temperance movement by bringing in a much milder bill, which only regulated the granting of *new* licences, and restricted the opening hours of public houses. Consequently, the United Kingdom Alliance, a nonconformist-dominated pressure group campaigning for temperance reform, was provoked into condemnation of the Gladstone ministry, and even went so far as to intervene against official Liberal candidates at certain by-elections, such as that at Bath in June 1873.

Militant nonconformists were also dismayed by the clear evidence that, in spite of the disestablishment of the Irish Church in 1869, the government had no intention of applying this policy to the Established Churches of England, Wales and Scotland. In May 1871 Edward Miall, acting on behalf of the Liberation Society, introduced in the House of Commons a motion for the disestablishment of the Church of England, which received 89 votes in spite of strong opposition from Gladstone. Motions were also brought forward in 1872 and 1873, with similar results. Disappointed by the government's unwillingness to extend the precedent of the 1869 Act, the Liberation Society, like the National Education League and the United Kingdom Alliance, became openly hostile to the Liberal leadership and threatened to withhold electoral support from Liberal candidates who refused to endorse the Society's programme.

This 'revolt of the nonconformists', which characterised the politics of the early 1870s, raises interesting and important questions about the very nature and meaning of high-Victorian Liberalism. Indeed, it reveals the tensions and ambiguities that were probably inevitable, in such a diverse coalition of interests as the Liberal Party, at a time of great legislative endeavour. For instance, all Liberals could agree that the principle of 'religious liberty' was a fundamental part of their political creed, but this left considerable scope for dissension as to what precisely this principle meant in practical terms. To many Liberals, including of course Gladstone himself, the Church of England was deemed to be a socially valuable institution, which deserved to be maintained as the Established Church of the nation, and religious reform was therefore conceived in terms of piecemeal, ameliorative measures, like the abolition of university tests, designed to remove any remaining irritants in the relationship between Church and dissent. However, for the more extreme nonconformist sects (and these were the ones most likely to be committed to the Liberal cause), as well as to many secular-minded radicals, 'religious liberty' necessarily involved the dismantling of all Established Churches, and also the ending of Church domination over the education system. What to many radicals and nonconformists seemed to be measures designed to promote full equality between the religious denominations, appeared to other Liberals to betray an underlying class hatred, and even a desire for the spoliation of property. A fundamental difference of opinion among Liberals was thus possible as to what exactly were the policy prescriptions of 'Liberalism'.

Similar problems arose from the United Kingdom Alliance's agitation for temperance reform. The demand embodied in the 'permissive bill', introduced annually by Sir Wilfrid Lawson, that local ratepayers should be given control over the issuing of licences to publicans, raised serious questions about individual liberties, that were capable of being argued in different ways. To temperance campaigners, for whom drunkenness was the single greatest cause of human misery, degradation and impoverishment, the suppression of public houses and the consequent spread of sober habits was seen as a means by which individuals could better themselves, morally and materially. Furthermore, the 'permissive bill' could be presented as a democratic measure, in that it gave power to the people in their localities. Conversely, Lawson's bill could still be regarded, as it was by the majority of Liberal MPs in the early 1870s, as a serious infringement of the right of individuals to purchase alcoholic beverages if they so wished. The withdrawing of publicans' licences, *without financial compensation*, as advocated by Lawson and his friends, was also seen as an oppressive measure, with all sorts of dangerous implications for other areas of policy. Equally objectionable was the fact that ratepayers usually constituted only a minority of any local community, which made it all the more iniquitous that a minority of – mostly better-off – inhabitants of a district should be allowed to exercise coercive powers over the majority. It is hardly surprising to find one radical MP, Bernal Osborne, expressing the opinion that he 'would rather see England free than sober'.[30]

Many other issues, which exemplify the practical dilemmas of Liberalism, served to inflict further political damage on the Gladstone ministry. A series of Contagious Diseases Acts, passed by Liberal governments during the 1860s, had given powers to magistrates in certain towns, with large army or naval bases, to order that prostitutes should undergo medical examinations, and that those women found to be infected with venereal disease should be detained in 'lock hospitals' while they received treatment. These Acts, which had widespread support from the medical profession, were also accepted by many Liberal MPs as sensible public-health measures, intended to prevent the spread of disease among the nation's armed forces. However, during the early 1870s a major agitation against the Acts was launched, involving campaigners for womens' rights such as Josephine Butler, which received the usual infusion of nonconformist moral indignation – represented in this case by the parliamentary spokesman for the campaigners, Jacob Bright. To such people it was outrageous that the State should be tacitly condoning prostitution, but worse still that the stigma of illegality was attached to the female prostitutes rather than to their male clients. The government, under attack from these 'moral purity' campaigners at by-elections, such as that at Colchester in 1870, finally, but half-heartedly, proposed in 1872 to repeal the Contagious Diseases Acts. But the existence of a powerful, organised cross-party group in the House of Commons, dedicated to the maintenance of the Acts, deterred the government from proceeding with its Repeal Bill. In the end, typically, the government gained no credit from either side in the controversy.[31]

It has often been assumed that the question of trade union reform also posed a serious dilemma for Liberals, as it is certainly true that the Gladstone ministry proved a disappointment to the trade union movement in this respect. Ostensibly, the existence of combinations of workmen for the purpose of distorting the labour market for their own advantage would seem to be inimical to the individualist philosophy that underlay Liberalism. In reality, however, the government was much less hostile to trade unionism than might have been expected, a fact that was no doubt due in large part to the 'respectable' image cultivated by leaders of craft unions, such as Robert Applegarth, a key witness before the Royal Commission on Trades Unions in 1867. The Gladstone ministry was prepared, through its Trades Union Act of 1871, to accede to the demand that unions be accorded full legal status, and thus enjoy protection for their funds. The Criminal Law Amendment Act, of the same year, intended to resolve the unions' concern about the right of peaceful picketing, by removing the possibility of prosecution under the law of conspiracy. However, the inadequate drafting of this act meant that in a court judgment relating to the case of the Gas Stokers, in December 1872, the old legal position was restored. If a criticism is to be made of Gladstone's ministry, therefore, it is not that it exhibited any ideological antagonism to the claims of trade unions to be allowed to operate effectively, but that it was not prepared to give urgent priority to new legislation to clarify the right to picket, following the Gas Stokers case.[32] The immediate consequence of this failure of Liberal policy was that the Labour Representation League, founded in 1869, ran 16 of its own candidates at the 1874 general election and captured two Liberal seats.

The government's abortive Irish University Bill, of 1873, exhibits more clearly the ideological difficulties which often constrained Liberal policy. While the demand of the Roman Catholic Church in Ireland was for the creation of a separate Catholic University, with State funding, the strength of protestant feeling within British Liberalism, especially the nonconformist element, made any such measure politically impossible for the Gladstone ministry. The unsatisfactory 'compromise' solution which finally emerged, was for the establishment of a non-denominational Irish University, to which the existing Protestant Colleges would be affiliated, along with any Catholic institutions that desired to join. Controversial subjects such as theology, philosophy and modern history were to be excluded from the curriculum. This ludicrous measure not only failed to satisfy the Roman Catholic Church, and therefore the Irish Liberal MPs, but it also provoked the wrath of the Conservative Party because of the proposal to reduce the endowments of Trinity College Dublin. A small number of secular radicals, like Henry Fawcett, also objected to the bill because they wanted to see an end to all religious tests, and the creation of a mixed-education system. It was this unlikely combination of political groups which succeeded in defeating the bill, in March 1873, prompting Gladstone to tender his government's resignation. Disraeli's unwillingness to form a minority administration forced the Liberals to resume office, but an important component of the Liberal coalition had now been lost. The majority of Irish Liberal MPs, aware of the fury in their country at the University Bill, on top of the failure of the Land Act to give adequate security to tenant farmers, felt compelled to throw in their lot with Issac Butt's Home Rule League, which campaigned independently of the Liberal party at the 1874 general election. After that election, only 10 Liberal MPs survived in Ireland, compared with some 59 'Home Rulers'.

Parliamentary Decline

A picture thus emerges of a highly complex, and often contradictory, 'Liberal Party', which by 1873 was in a state of rapid disintegration. This process, painfully evident in the activities of various pressure groups in the constituencies, was mirrored in the House of Commons, where the Gladstone ministry, nominally in command of a substantial majority, found its authority diminishing to such an extent that it was liable to suffer humiliating defeats, on issues great and small. Obviously the government's weakness was to some degree simply a consequence of its difficulties in the country, but we must also take into account the effects of laxity in parliamentary procedure, and the personal shortcomings of certain ministers, including the Prime Minister himself.

Concerns had been expressed about the efficiency of parliament as an instrument for legislation even during the relatively quiet days of the Palmerstonian ascendancy, and the problem became far more acute when a ministry committed to introducing ambitious legislative programmes, session after session, was installed in power. The cumbersome nature of parliamentary procedure, and in particular the limited amount of time available, in any case, for debating government bills (only two days per week were set aside for government business, such was the jealousy still felt for the rights of back-benchers, and a great deal of time was still required for private legislation), put a tremendous strain on both ministers and MPs, as sittings of the House of Commons regularly extended well into the early hours of the morning.[33] This may have been one of the reasons why the Liberal chief whip, George Glyn, was constantly complaining to the Prime Minister about the difficulties he experienced in securing the attendance of ministers during debates, and about the way that the absence of many ministers often set a bad example to back-benchers. Thus, on one occasion, when the Commons was 'counted out' (in other words, the sitting was suspended because less than 40 members were present), just before the navy estimates were due to be debated, Glyn reported immediately to his chief that 'I cannot complain of *private* members when neither of the Admiralty representatives are here!'[34] Furthermore, once it became clear that the force of public opinion, which had propelled the government through the sessions of 1869 and 1870, was petering out, the Conservative opposition were encouraged to exploit the rules of parliamentary procedure in order to obstruct legislation they found distasteful. The Army

Regulation Bill of 1871, for instance, and the Ballot Bills in 1871 and 1872, became the objects of deliberate delaying tactics, such as repeated adjournment motions. In this way, Liberal ministers and their back-bench followers were being physically worn down, compounding the demoralisation caused by the government's growing unpopularity in the constituencies, evidenced in particular by the nonconformist backlash against the Education Act. At a Cabinet meeting, held towards the end of the 1873 session, one minister recorded that 'Mr. G. . . . spoke of the present position of the Govt. in the House as "deplorable". Constant difficulty & danger − opposition active to damage − enemies on our own side − or members thinking only of their electioneering interests − (how unlike '69 and '70!).'[35]

In May 1871 the Liberal chief whip warned Gladstone of the danger posed to his government by 'the *apathy* & *political discontent*, which is now so prevalent in our majority'.[36] One particular episode, a couple of weeks earlier, nicely illustrates the strains that were being placed on relations between Liberal ministers and back-benchers, and the way that this could lead to eruptions and misunderstandings over a relatively minor matter. As Glyn reported to Gladstone:

> We have had an unpleasant scene in the House & Govt have been beaten upon the Charities Exemption Bill or rather on Stansfeld's [President of the Poor Law Board] motion to adjourn the debate. . . . Stansfeld got up *to protest agst a division being taken without discussion* − the House thought he got up to talk out the Bill & got furious. . . . Many men, who would have voted for us, taking up the idea that it had been an attempt on the part of the Government to talk out the Bill voted agt us & the motion for the adjournment was carried against us 117 to 84 [thus gaining more time for the bill].
>
> The House behaved really *very ill* for they would not listen either to Hibbert or to Stansfeld.
>
> I am very much annoyed & much blamed, in fact I may say all but insulted in the Lobby. It seems really impossible to get the men to see anything in its proper light.[37]

It is fair to observe that the government's waning prestige in the House of Commons was partly attributable to bad luck, and that the state of apathy and discontent on the back-benches described by Glyn in 1871, for example, had obviously been exacerbated by the unfortunate fiasco surrounding Robert Lowe's budget, earlier in the year.

Lowe had acquired a formidable reputation as an innovative financier, since his appointment to the Exchequer in 1868, but things went badly wrong for him when an anticipated budget deficit for 1871 prompted him to propose controversial additional taxes. The first irony in this situation was that the projected deficit stemmed largely from the antici- pated cost of one of the government's celebrated reforms, the abolition of the purchase of army commissions, and there was in fact consider- able resentment amongst radical MPs (even though they approved of the principle of the measure) at the generous scale of compensation being offered to current commissioned officers. Undeterred, Lowe pro- posed to raise the extra money by putting 1d. on income tax, doubling the succession duty payable in cases where the heir was also the next of kin, and imposing a new tax on matches. Lowe was forced to back down, however, in the face of protest demonstrations by the match girls (orchestrated by Bryant and May, the matchmakers), together with hos- tility from the landed interest, including many Liberal MPs, at the planned increase in the succession duties. In consequence, the unpopu- lar tax changes were dropped, and income tax raised by 2d. instead. The second irony in the situation, however, was that Lowe had ser- iously underestimated the buoyancy of the economy, and therefore the likely yield from existing taxes, and it eventually turned out that he need never have proposed any additional taxation at all.[38]

Lowe exemplified a further weakness of Gladstone's government in its relations with the House of Commons, namely the deep personal unpopularity of a number of prominent ministers. In Lowe's case, the problem stemmed from the pungency and biting sarcasm of his oratorical style, something that made him feared and admired initially, but which also caused unnecessary offence and ensured that there was no fund of sympathy on which he could draw when he encountered political difficulties. Even more notorious was the First Commissioner of Works and Buildings, A. S. Ayrton, who habitually savaged his back- bench interrogators, and was known to set his sights on other targets, such as the House of Lords, and, just before his removal to another post in 1873, some of his own ministerial colleagues. Other difficulties arose from the perceived weakness of certain ministers, of whom the most notable example was the Home Secretary, Bruce, whose reputa- tion had been shattered by his inept handling of the licensing question. As early as September 1871, Glyn was advising Gladstone that Bruce's position appeared to be irretrievably damaged, and eventually, in 1873, he was sent to the House of Lords.[39]

Above all, there was a growing feeling that Gladstone himself was losing his grip on the House of Commons. The Prime Minister who had been so effective in piloting the Irish Church and Land Bills, of 1869–70, when he still had the momentum of the great election victory of 1868 behind him, seemed to be less well equipped to handle matters in the more adverse political circumstances that prevailed from 1871 onwards. Too often, Gladstone's parliamentary performances were marred by the prolixity of his oratory, and more seriously still by the signs of impatience and even outright irritability that became increasingly apparent. Thus, on one occasion, in May 1873, a Liberal minister records that 'Gladstone lost his temper & walked out after the first division', when the Commons was considering an inquiry into alleged abuses in the Irish elementary-education system.[40] As another Cabinet colleague, Lord Kimberley, reflected in his journal, in the aftermath of the debacle over the Irish University Bill of 1873, the dilemma facing the government was that 'Our old programme is completely exhausted: and Gladstone is not the man to govern without 'measures', nor is he at all suited to lead a party in difficulties. He must have a strong current of opinion in his favour.' This view was shared by Lord Chancellor Selborne, writing after the fall of Gladstone's government, who thought that:

with respect to the business of legislation and government, his mind seems to me to be too one-sided and vehement, and to want accuracy, equability, the sense of proportion, and breadth. He can hardly be brought to interest himself at all in matters (even when they are really great matters) in which he is not carried away by some too strong attraction; and, when he is carried away, he does not sympathise, or take counsel with, those whose point of view is at all different from his own. This makes it hardly possible for him to be [Prime] Minister, except when it is time for some 'heroic' measures for which he can excite public enthusiasm; at other times his mind is not a centre, round which other minds can revolve, or which so associates itself with the thoughts and interests of other men as to harmonise and regulate their action in the manner necessary for ordinary good government.[41]

In the eyes of some Liberals, clearly, Gladstone's obsession with the need for 'action' in politics did not always seem appropriate to the situation.

The General Election of 1874

The parliamentary session of 1873 was a disastrous one for the Gladstone ministry. Little was achieved in terms of constructive legislation, and the Irish University Bill was lost. Further humiliations had followed as a result of revelations of administrative irregularities involving Lowe and Ayrton. Once the session was over, it became essential for Gladstone to regain the political initiative if his government was to avoid disintegration into total chaos. A lengthy process of ministerial reshuffling, during the summer and autumn, included the elevation of Bruce to the upper House, the removal of Lowe and Ayrton to other departments, and the admission to the junior ranks of a number of backbench critics hitherto aligned with the radicals, William Harcourt, Henry James and Lyon Playfair. Most important of all was the return of John Bright to the Cabinet (he had previously resigned, in 1870, owing to ill health), in an effort to deflect the continuing nonconformist hostility caused by the Education Act. Gladstone himself, meantime, decided to combine the premiership with his old post of Chancellor of the Exchequer. Characteristically, Gladstone was beginning to explore the possibilities for a new initiative on financial policy, hitherto his strongest point, in the hope that this would enable him to rally the discordant elements of the Liberal Party. The direction in which his thinking was moving was indicated in a letter to Bright, in August:

> What we want at present is a *positive* force to carry us onward as a body. . . . It may possibly, I think, be had out of finance. . . . If it can be worked into certain shapes, it may greatly help to mould the rest, at least for the time. . . . We must, I think, have a good bill of fare, or none. If we differ on the things to be done, this may end us in a way at least not dishonourable. If we agree on a good plan, it must come to good, *whether* we succeed or fail with it.[42]

The strategy that evolved in Gladstone's mind was to be a bold budgetary policy through which, taking advantage of the large surplus available thanks to the continued prosperity of the economy, he would fulfil the original Peelite objective of dispensing altogether with the income tax, and abolish the duty on sugar as well. Additional revenue would be raised through higher succession duties and spirit duties, but even so it was necessary, for this plan to be viable, to achieve further reductions of around £1 million on military expenditure. Gladstone's hope seems to have been that he would be able to secure the agreement of the army and navy ministers for these reductions, and then proceed to carry his financial plan through parliament, during the 1874 session, before calling a general election. In this way, the government might seek renewed approval from the people, in circumstances more favourable than could otherwise have been conceived, given the dismal state of affairs at the end of 1873. Unfortunately for Gladstone, resistance from the army and navy ministers to his request for further economies in expenditure created an obstacle to his overall plan, which could only be overcome, or so it seemed to him, by appealing over the heads of his colleagues to the country, for an electoral endorsement of his proposed budget *before* it was submitted to parliament. It was for this reason that, on 24 January 1874, Gladstone announced, to the astonishment of his party and most Cabinet ministers, that parliament was to be dissolved immediately.

Since 1871 there had been a strong trend against the Liberals, in by-elections, with the Conservatives making a net gain of 31 seats, of which an extraordinary 10 occurred between May 1873 and the dissolution in January 1874. Many Liberals nevertheless seem to have expected that their party would cling on to power after the general election, albeit with a greatly reduced majority. The outcome at the polls, however, was a shattering defeat for the Liberals, in spite of Gladstone's bold and dramatic new declaration of policy.[43] On balance, the Conservatives made a further gain of 82 seats, which ensured that they would be able to take office with a comfortable majority of some 50 seats over the Liberals and Irish Home Rulers combined. Following the precedent set by Disraeli in 1868, Gladstone chose to resign immediately rather than waiting to meet the new parliament.

The main features of the Conservative triumph were the substantial gains made in the traditional Liberal stronghold of London (the Conservatives winning 10 of the 22 seats, compared with just 3 in 1868), and the virtual clean-sweep achieved in the 'home counties' surrounding London, where the spread of the suburban middle classes was becoming apparent. More generally, the Conservatives had reinforced their existing domination of the English counties, where they now carried all but 27 of the 170 seats, and they also made valuable gains in the lowland counties of Scotland. The borough and county constituencies of Lancashire, meantime, confirmed their marked preference for Conservatism, already demonstrated in 1868.

Disraeli's achievement in 1874 was to exploit the full electoral potential of fears, evidently widespread among the voters, for the security of the country's traditional institutions under continued Liberal rule. By presenting the Conservatives as the party dedicated to the defence of the Crown, the Church and the Empire, and of property in general, Disraeli finally ended a generation of Liberal electoral hegemony. A temporary wave of republican feeling, during the early 1870s, for instance, with which a few Liberal MPs like Sir Charles Dilke became associated, enabled the Conservatives to depict the Liberal Party as a whole as a menace to the existence of the monarchy. Likewise, pressure from nonconformist groups like the Liberation Society and the National Education League made it easy for the Conservatives to raise their familiar old cry of 'the Church in danger'. Gladstone's offer to abolish the income tax became a target for attack, on the – not implausible – grounds that his sums simply did not add up, and that his policy would necessitate much heavier impositions on property owners through increased succession duties. The drink interest, though by no means as unanimous in its support for the Conservatives as used to be claimed, was naturally alarmed by the threat to its property interests implied in the prohibitionist campaign of the United Kingdom Alliance, and this concern could be usefully allied with a more populist appeal to the working man's right to his beer, which was being threatened by interfering, middle-class, Liberal 'do-gooders'.

In addition to all these charges in the domestic sphere, was added the serious indictment that Gladstone and the Liberals had failed to maintain Britain's international prestige and imperial strength. The Geneva arbitration of 1872, for instance, which had ended in Britain paying $15.5 million in compensation to the United States for the damage inflicted by a British-built ship, the Alabama, supplied to the confederates during the Civil War, was pointed to as proof that Gladstone's ministry was unwilling to stand up for Britain's international interests. Similarly, Liberal attempts to make economies in expenditure by requiring colonies like New Zealand to bear the cost of their own defence, could be presented as part of a sinister design to weaken Britain's imperial links. Disraeli thus sought to depict the Liberals as the party of national weakness and imperial disintegration. He was, in fact, attempting to wrest from the Liberals their 'Palmerstonian' mantle, and his criticisms may well have succeeded in capturing some moderate Liberal voters.

Furthermore, there was the problem of Ireland, where the Liberals were again accused of showing weakness in the face of the movement for Home Rule, and, even worse, of being in tacit sympathy with these Irish 'disintegrationists'. Gladstone himself was still accused by some of being a crypto-Catholic, and the fact that his election address had hinted at the possibility of some extension of local self-government to Ireland, simply heightened people's suspicions as to his real objectives. The overall message to come out of the Conservative critique of Liberal policy, therefore, was that the Gladstone government, through its constant, meddlesome legislative activity, had had an unsettling effect upon the country, and that for the future it was likely to be dependent on an alliance with various destructive forces in society, which it would be incapable of resisting. Demoralised and ill-prepared for Gladstone's sudden election, as the Liberals were, they appeared to be on the defensive throughout the campaign.

It is important to note, however, that the loss of support suffered by the Liberals was probably due more to defections by moderate supporters than to desertions by radical nonconformists. In fact, as J. P. Parry has shown, the agitations by the Liberation Society and the National Education League had become more muted by the time of the general election, thanks partly to the greater confidence in Gladstone's government inspired by the readmission of Bright, and also to the advice of veterans like Edward Miall that the way forward lay in nonconformist infiltration of the Liberal Party at the local level, rather than in open conflict. An analysis of the geographical distribution of Liberal seats in the boroughs confirms that the party fared far worse in southern England, particularly in the larger constituencies where Whig landlord influence was not a determining factor, than in the rest of England north of the Severn–Wash line, plus Scotland and Wales (listed collec-

Table 5 *The 1874 General Election in the British Boroughs*[44]

	Lib	Con	Con gain on 1868
Small boroughs, under 2000 voters	51	51	12
Southern boroughs, 2000–5000 voters	14	22	15
Northern boroughs, 2000–5000 voters	33	19	9
Southern boroughs, 5000+ voters	22	24	17
Northern boroughs, 5000+ voters	60	27	3

tively as 'Northern boroughs'). The implication is that it was moderate Liberal voters, especially in southern England, sharing fully in the fears about the tendencies of Liberal policy being articulated by the Conservatives, who were the most likely to rebel, or else abstain.

This pattern of moderate alienation from the Liberals, and the concentration of Liberal support in northern England and the Celtic fringe, may well help to explain the further significant shift in the social composition of the party at Westminster. It appears as if the changes prompted by the Second Reform Act came in two stages, at the general elections of 1868 and 1874, rather than at once. An analysis of the 243 Liberal MPs listed in *Dod's Parliamentary Companion* for 1874, compared with the figures for 1869 listed earlier in this chapter, reveals the picture shown in Table 6.

For the first time, members of the aristocratic and landed classes constituted less than half of all Liberal MPs, although they were still the largest social group by quite a long way, accounting for over 46 per cent of the party if we include the 'Gentlemen' (men with more distant aristocratic and landed connections, and no discernible career other than in the armed forces). The really striking change, of course, was in

Table 6 *Social Background of Liberal MPs, 1874*

			(1869)
Peerage connections	25	(10.3%)	(13.5%)
Baronets	20	(8.2%)	(7.8%)
Baronets' sons	8	(3.3%)	(3.4%)
Landed gentry	40	(16.5%)	(14.8%)
Heirs of gentry	3	(1.2%)	(3.1%)
'Gentlemen'	16	(6.6%)	(8.5%)
Merchants/manufacturers	72	(29.6%)	(22.3%)
Bankers	5	(2.1%)	(2.1%)
Lawyers	31	(12.8%)	(13.2%)
Miscellaneous	12	(5.0%)	(5.2%)
No information	9	(3.7%)	(6.2%)

the numbers of businessmen elected to the House of Commons, who now amounted to nearly 32 per cent, if bankers are included.[45]

Gladstone's First Retirement

For Gladstone himself, the sense of disappointment at the outcome of the elections was naturally acute, and this was exacerbated by the frequent criticisms, during the campaign, of his own style of leadership, which fostered a feeling of personal rejection. Gladstone's alleged unpredictability, and the feeling that he was too apt to plunge into uncharted political waters, appeared to have been endorsed by the electorate's verdict. What made Gladstone's position more uncomfortable still was the fact that he felt profoundly out of sympathy with important sections of the Liberal Party, especially on the question of denominational versus secular education. Future co-operation between the Liberal leader and his erstwhile followers therefore seemed to be extremely problematical. As for the leadership of the Liberal opposition in the new House of Commons, Gladstone made no attempt to conceal his irritation with what he considered to be the ungrateful way in which his party had behaved towards him in recent years, and in March 1874 he announced that he would take no part in parliamentary affairs during that session, and would reserve until a later date his decision as to whether he would agree to lead the party again. His belief was that the Liberals needed to rediscover party cohesion through their own efforts, and that until this was done attempts to impose leadership from above would be futile.[46] In any case, Gladstone was morbidly conscious of his advancing years (he was by now sixty-four), he could see no obvious reason why the Conservatives should not remain in office for several years to come, and he was anxious for a period of rest and contemplation before he went to the grave.

Gladstone's sense of isolation from his party, and from politics in general, was intensified during the course of the year, first by his vehement opposition to the Public Worship Regulation Bill, a measure designed to stamp out ritualism in the Church of England, which was supported by most Liberals as well as the Conservatives, and secondly by his immersion in a theological controversy with leading Roman Catholics, regarding the Vatican decrees of 1870 and the question of Catholic allegiance to a Protestant State. If, to the majority of Liberals, Gladstone's behaviour confirmed his reputation for inscrutable eccentricity, their bemusement provided yet further confirmation for Gladstone that there was no longer any place for him in ordinary political life. In January 1875, therefore, he wrote a public letter to the leader of the Liberal peers, Lord Granville, informing him of his retirement from the leadership of the party. Thus ended, or so it seemed, the era of 'Gladstonian Liberalism'.

NOTES

1.   John Morley, *The Life of William Ewart Gladstone* (London, 1903), vol. 1, pp. 195–208.

2.   H. C. G. Matthew, *Gladstone, 1809–74* (Oxford, 1986) pp. 66–8, 75–8.

3.   Ibid., pp. 109–28 (quotation at p. 123).

4.   Ibid., p. 139.

5.   See Eugenio F. Biagini, *Liberty, Retrenchment and Reform: Popular Liberalism in the Age of Gladstone, 1860–1880* (Cambridge, 1992) pp. 1–20.

6.   G. I. T. Machin, 'Gladstone and Nonconformity: The Formation of a Political Alliance in the 1860s', *Historical Journal*, XVII (1974).

7.   J. R. Vincent, *The Formation of the British Liberal Party, 1857–68* (2nd edn, Brighton, 1976) pp. 227–8.

8.   Walter Bagehot, *Biographical Studies*, ed., R. H. Hutton (London, 1881).

9.   Biagini, *Liberty, Retrenchment and Reform*, pp. 1–20.

10.   J. R. Vincent, *Pollbooks: How Victorians Voted* (Cambridge, 1967) pp. 43–50.

11.   H. C. G. Matthew (ed.), *The Gladstone Diaries*, vol. IX (Oxford, 1986) p. lxix.

12.   Biagini, *Liberty, Retrenchment and Reform*, pp. 384, 390–1, my italics. Biagini's book contains many other fascinating illustrations of popular attitudes to Gladstone.

13.   See Geraint L. Williams's introduction to *John Stuart Mill: On Politics and Society* (London, 1976).

14.   Gladstone to Granville, 19 May 1877, in Agatha Ramm (ed.), *The Political Correspondence of Mr Gladstone and Lord Granville, 1876–1886* (Oxford, 1962) vol. 1, p. 40.

15.   Boyd Hilton, 'Gladstone's Theological Politics', in Michael Bentley and John Stevenson (eds), *High and Low Politics in Modern Britain* (Oxford, 1983) pp. 45, 51. A recent student of the Irish Home Rule Bill of 1886 has drawn similar conclusions, that Gladstone was more interested in men's political participation than in the improvement of their material conditions: James Loughlin, *Gladstone, Home Rule and the Ulster Question, 1882–93* (Dublin, 1986) p. 288.

16.   For example, D. A. Hamer, *Liberal Politics in the Age of Gladstone and Rosebery* (Oxford, 1972) pp. 127–8.

17.   James Winter, *Robert Lowe* (Toronto, 1976) pp. 195–226.

18.   Matthew, *Gladstone*, p. 142.

19. H. J. Hanham, *Elections and Party Management: Politics in the Time of Disraeli and Gladstone* (2nd edn, Brighton, 1978) pp. 333–43; I. G. C. Hutchison, *A Political History of Scotland, 1832–1924* (Edinburgh, 1986) pp. 132–3.

20. Hanham, *Elections and Party Management*, p. 217.

21. Ibid., pp. 170–9.

22. J. P. Parry, *Democracy and Religion: Gladstone and the Liberal Party, 1867–1875* (Cambridge, 1986) pp. 212–29 and note 189.

23. Ibid., pp. 229–31. There was also an intermediate group of twelve MPs.

24. T. A. Jenkins (ed.), *The Parliamentary Diaries of Sir John Trelawny, 1868–1873* (Royal Historical Society, Camden Series, forthcoming 1994) entry for 5 April 1870.

25. Lawrence Goldman, 'The Social Science Association, 1857–1886: A Context for Mid-Victorian Liberalism', *English Historical Review*, CI (1986).

26. Christopher Harvie, *The Lights of Liberalism: University Liberals and the Challenge of Reform, 1860–86* (London, 1976) passim (quotation at p. 12).

27. Parry, *Democracy and Religion*, pp. 297–309; Bruce Kinzer, *The Ballot Question in Nineteenth-Century English Politics* (New York, 1982) pp. 98–103.

28. Winter, *Robert Lowe*, pp. 262–8.

29. *Annual Register*, 1871, pp. 61, 100–1.

30. P. H. Bagenal, *Ralph Bernal Osborne MP* (privately printed, 1884) p. 325.

31. Paul McHugh, *Prostitution and Victorian Social Reform* (London, 1980).

32. Matthew, *Gladstone*, pp. 213–15.

33. See Agatha Ramm, 'The Parliamentary Context of Cabinet Government, 1868–1874', *English Historical Review*, XCIX (1984).

34. Glyn to Gladstone, 4 April [1873], BL Add MSS 44348, f. 229. Several similar instances may be found in this volume of correspondence.

35. Chichester Fortescue's diary, 15 June 1873 (recording a Cabinet held the previous day), BL Add MSS 63682.

36. Glyn to Gladstone, 27 May 1871, BL Add MSS 44348, f. 100.

37. Glyn to Gladstone, 10 May 1871, ibid., f. 94.

38. Winter, *Robert Lowe*, pp. 272–8.

39. Glyn to Gladstone, 5 September 1871, BL Add MSS 44348, f. 123.

40. Chichester Fortescue's diary, 22 May 1873, BL Add MSS 63682.

41. Ethel Drus (ed.), *A Journal of Events During the Gladstone Ministry, 1868–74, by John, First Earl of Kimberley* (Royal Historical Society, Camden Miscellany, 1958) entry for 18 March 1873; Selborne to Arthur Gordon, 6 September 1874, in Selborne, *Memorials: Personal and Political, 1865–1895* (London, 1898) vol. 1, p. 334.

42. Gladstone to Bright, 14 August 1873, in Morley, *Life of Gladstone*, vol. 2, pp. 478–9.

43. The following account is based on Hanham, *Elections and Party Management*, pp. 218–27; Parry, *Democracy and Religion*, pp. 381–410; Richard Shannon, *The Age of Disraeli, 1868–1881* (London, 1992) pp. 172–81.

44. Figures from Parry, *Democracy and Religion*, p. 394.

45. This analysis represents a refinement of the figures given in my *Gladstone, Whiggery and the Liberal Party, 1874–1886* (Oxford, 1988) pp. 5–6. I have tried to resolve the problem of individuals who overlap between one category

and another. Some of those listed as 'Gentlemen' are those who, while not listed in *Burke's Landed Gentry* (1875 and 1879 edns), nevertheless appear in John Bateman's survey of *The Great Landowners of Great Britain and Ireland* (4th edn, London, 1883), meaning that they owned estates of at least 3000 acres.

46.   Ibid., pp. 30–2.

5 Whigs, Radicals and Gladstonians

The Whig Duumvirate

The greatest danger for those seeking to understand the history of the Liberal Party between 1875 and 1880 lies in the natural temptation to allow one's perceptions of the period to be shaped by the retrospective knowledge of what eventually happened in April 1880. Gladstone's return to the premiership at that time, after a general election had completely reversed the Liberal defeat of 1874, together with the fact that he then remained as Liberal leader until his final retirement in 1894, have tended to obscure certain interesting features of the party's position during the second half of the 1870s. In particular, the joint leadership of the party by the Whigs, Granville and Hartington, which survived until after the general election of 1880, has often been overlooked on the assumption that it was a relatively unimportant interlude in a much greater story, that of 'Gladstonian Liberalism'. Consequently, historians have tended to focus almost entirely on Gladstone's involvement in the Bulgarian atrocities agitation of 1876, and the dramatic Midlothian campaigns of 1879–80.

And yet the Granville–Hartington leadership had seemed the most appropriate arrangement, in 1875, given the weakened and divided state of the Liberals, and what was widely felt to be Gladstone's 'desertion' of his party. The reversion to Whig control indicated the need for a period of stability in Liberal politics, and indeed there was a strong sense that a reaction had set in against the more tempestuous style of leadership associated with Gladstone. Granville and Hartington's leadership also reflected the belief that the Liberal Party had been seriously damaged by the activities of members of various radical pressure groups, the 'faddists' or 'crotchet-mongers', belonging to organisations like the National Education League and the United Kingdom Alliance, and that if the Liberals were to regain power it was essential to recover the support of moderate voters who had been frightened away from the party at the time of the 1874 general election. All in all, people were inclined to look upon 'Gladstonian Liberalism' as a spent force, a thing of the past, the product of a special set of circumstances not likely soon to be repeated.[1]

Although Granville and Hartington were cousins, significant differences did exist between them in terms of age and temperament. Granville, who was sixty in 1875, had been a prominent figure on the Liberal front-bench in the House of Lords since the early 1850s, and he had succeeded Clarendon as Foreign Secretary and leader of the upper House in 1870. By nature Granville was a diplomat, genial, suave and courteous – one of his nicknames was 'puss' – and in his early days he had appeared to be more of a courtier than a party politician, becoming a favourite of Queen Victoria and Prince Albert. During the Liberal ministry of 1868–74, however, he had developed a close friendship with Gladstone, and they worked together harmoniously in the conduct of foreign policy after 1870. Granville's powers of conciliation were thereafter devoted consistently to the object of maintaining Liberal unity.

The contrast with cousin Hartington could hardly have been greater, in certain respects. Hartington, the heir of the Duke of Devonshire, was only in his forty-second year when he succeeded Gladstone as Liberal leader in the House of Commons (an arrangement that was approved by a meeting of Liberal MPs at the Reform Club, there being no other candidate for the position once W. E. Forster had made it clear that he would not stand). His exterior personality was not a particularly attractive one, as he appeared to be gruff and aloof – many who encountered him socially thought him rude – and he gave off an air of languor and indolence which often created the misleading impression that he was not really interested in politics. In political terms, the significant point to be made about Hartington is that he was self-consciously an heir to the 'Palmerstonian' tradition (he had first been given junior office by Palmerston in 1863), believing in the need for a strong foreign policy and for caution in dealing with domestic reform issues. Hartington's firm political views meant that he was instinctively less sympathetic to Gladstone than was Granville, and his term as Irish Chief Secretary (1870–4) had brought out serious differences of opinion with the Liberal Prime Minister, notably over the question of coercion.

In spite of the fact that Granville and Hartington were temperamentally different, and did not always share identical political views, what they did have in common was a firm belief in the role of the aris-

tocracy as the country's natural leaders. A description of the House of
Lords in 1877, by Lord Coleridge, a future Lord Chief Justice, conveys
some sense of the character of the Whig tradition. Coleridge was struck
by:

> The intense 'feudalism' of our great Liberal chiefs . . . combined
> with very free opinions on all things which don't touch them-
> selves. . . . Granville, who represents them very well, is, I think, very
> careless about *what* is done, so long as *they*, the great nobles, have the
> doing of it; and he is firmly resolved, I think, that they *shall* have the
> doing of it from that proud yet perfectly natural and unaffected
> belief in themselves and their power, as a fact in the Country.[2]

Even within the Liberal Party of the mid-1870s, apparently, the principles that had inspired Earl Grey and the Whigs of 1832 were still
alive and flourishing.

The Liberal Party and the Eastern Question

The diversity of the Liberal Party meant that the task of leadership was
rarely an easy or congenial one, and the problems of maintaining unity
were often exacerbated by the experience of being thrown into opposition, as Gladstone's difficulties in 1866–7 testify very clearly. In 1875
the outlook for the Liberals was exceptionally dismal, as for the first
time since 1841 they found themselves in opposition as a result of a
decisive electoral defeat rather than of temporary divisions in their own
ranks. There seemed little likelihood, therefore, of a return to power, at
least until the next general election, which was several years away, and
the fact that people at this time were not accustomed to thinking in
terms of a natural 'swing of the pendulum', at elections, meant that
there was little real optimism amongst Liberals that one general election would be enough to erode the Conservatives' large parliamentary
majority. Hartington's position as the new Liberal leader in the House
of Commons was inevitably a delicate one, in these circumstances, and
there were occasions during the 1875 session when he found it better to
stay away from the House rather than attempt to provide leadership to
which certain sections of his party were unlikely to respond. His unen-
viable task was made even more awkward, though, because of the continued presence in the Commons of the former Liberal Prime Minister

(while Gladstone had resigned the leadership, he had not given up his parliamentary seat), who now felt free to take his own line on such issues as finance, the government's purchase of shares in the Suez Canal, and the Royal Titles Bill of 1876. To be fair to Gladstone, his actions did not always conflict with the course adopted by the official opposition leader, but even so, Hartington, trying to assert his own authority in the House of Commons, cannot have welcomed his former leader's interventions.

It was over the 'Eastern Question', which came to the forefront of British politics after the end of the 1876 parliamentary session, that differences of approach between Gladstone and the Whig leaders became fully apparent. For some time, news had been filtering back to Britain of the atrocities committed against the Bulgarians as their revolt against Turkish rule was brutally suppressed. The fact that the Bulgarians were Christians, and their oppressors Muslims, made the terrible accounts of rape, slaughter, and even infanticide, seem all the more harrowing to the Victorian conscience. Initially, the work of organising a campaign to protest against the Bulgarian atrocities fell to a number of journalists, academics, working men's groups and radical MPs, but the really significant breakthrough, in terms of public consciousness, occurred as a result of Gladstone's decision to align himself with the movement. His pamphlet, *The Bulgarian Horrors and the Question of the East*, published in early September, caught the mood of the moment and sold 200,000 copies in a month. Subsequently, Gladstone agreed to appear at a National Conference on the Eastern Question, held at St James's Hall, Piccadilly, in December.

As Richard Shannon demonstrated, in his classic account of Gladstone's involvement in the Bulgarian agitation, the outburst of 'public feeling' against the Turks, and also against the flippant way in which Disraeli (recently ennobled as the Earl of Beaconsfield) initially responded to events in the Balkans, was important for Gladstone precisely because he saw it as a spontaneous movement, and not as something that he had created himself. In a famous letter to Granville, written late in August, Gladstone had excitedly expressed his belief that 'Good ends can rarely be attained in politics without passion: and there is now, the first time for a good many years, a virtuous passion'.[3] For Gladstone, his ability to identify with the manifestations of popular outrage against the barbarity of the Turks, and against the callous indifference of the Conservative government, served to restore, in his own mind, his sense of a special affinity between himself and 'the people'.

Ann Saab's recent analysis of the geographical distribution of protest meetings, and of petitions to the foreign office, confirms Shannon's finding that the movement was strongest in the South West of England, Wales and the North of England, all areas in which nonconformists were numerous. The agitation was also primarily a phenomenon of the towns and not of the countryside. Interestingly, however, there is some doubt as to whether the protest campaign was numerically very spectacular, given the usually large scale of political gatherings of both parties at this time. 'Apparently the Bulgarian agitation in 1876 appealed to a hard core of dedicated supporters, expanded by Nonconformist and working class groups who tended to associate themselves with Radical causes. It was not, at this point, either a mass concern or a mass threat.'[4] Nevertheless, for Gladstone personally, the campaign was subjectively important, as he sensed that he was beginning to repair his emotional links with 'the people', and especially with nonconformity, which had been subject to severe strain during his period in government.

Despite the subsequent mythology surrounding the public agitation over the Eastern Question, from 1876 to 1878, and Gladstone's involvement in it, it is more accurate to see this movement as one that passed through several phases, and experienced a number of ups and downs. The initial protests, during the autumn and winter of 1876, were dramatic and well publicised by sympathetic sections of the press, but, as we have noted, the numbers involved were probably not very large. At the St James's Hall meeting, it was resolved to form an organisation, the Eastern Question Association, dedicated to maintaining the campaign's momentum, and during 1877–8 it did a great deal of work, notably in distributing propaganda. However, the Eastern Question Association lacked an effective network of organisations in the country as a whole, and it was heavily dependent upon the efforts of existing bodies such as the Labour Representation League in London. Another organisation, the National Liberal Federation, founded by Joseph Chamberlain in Birmingham at the end of May 1877, was indeed a deliberate attempt to harness the popular movement over the Eastern Question for the purposes of developing a more general radical campaign. Thus, as Ann Saab has shown, 'In 1877, Liberal associations and other Liberal organisations (rather than spontaneous public meetings) dominated.' But the numbers of people involved were still comparatively small: in May 1877, for instance, taking into account those who had signed petitions to parliament, or communicated directly with

Gladstone, or attended meetings of Liberal associations, 'it seems unlikely that the group exceeded ten thousand'.[5] One reason for this was that the five resolutions, which Gladstone brought before parliament early in May 1877, calling for united action by the European Powers in order to force the Turks to make concessions to their subject peoples in the Balkans, provoked serious divisions amongst those who had supported the agitation in 1876. The problem here was that prominent peace campaigners, such as Henry Richard and John Bright, committed as they were to the principle of non-intervention in *all* cases, were not prepared to endorse resolutions which might have implied a readiness to undertake military action against the Turks. Furthermore, the public agitation had been put somewhat on the defensive by the fact that in April, Russia, claiming to act on behalf of the oppressed peoples of the Balkans, unilaterally declared war on Turkey, raising the spectre of fresh Russian aggrandisement at the expense of the Ottoman Empire.

By far the greatest manifestations of support for the agitation came in the early months of 1878, when it seemed possible that the Conservative government might draw Britain into a war against Russia in order to force the latter to revise the terms of the peace treaty (San Stefano) which she had imposed after defeating Turkey. On such a clear-cut issue of peace or war, it was possible to secure united action from a wide range of organisations, including the National Liberal Federation, the Manchester-based National Reform Union, the Labour Representation League, Henry Richard's Peace Society, the Workmen's Peace Association, and Joseph Arch's National Agricultural Labourers Union. Public meetings were not held as frequently as in 1876, largely because of the fear of violence from 'jingo' mobs, but those that did take place regularly secured attendances running into the low thousands, considerably more than had usually been the case in the previous two years. Petitioning also took place on a large scale, and it seems, for example, that '124,657 people eventually signed one or another of the petitions' opposing the government's proposal that parliament should grant a vote of credit for military preparations against Russia.[6]

However it is important to remember that, in the short term at least, it was the policy pursued by the Conservatives that was triumphant. The bellicose stance adopted by Britain against Russia evidently had a widespread public appeal, and demonstrations in favour of the government often outnumbered those calling for peace. And Beaconsfield's policy of bluffing the Russians, by making preparations for war, paid off in that the Russians finally agreed to submit the Treaty of San Stefano to a Congress of the European Powers at Berlin. The outcome was that a small, independent Bulgarian state was created, but Turkey retained some of her territory in South-Eastern Europe, while Britain acquired Cyprus as part of a separate convention with Turkey. Beaconsfield was therefore able to return from Berlin, in July 1878, claiming 'peace with honour'.

The Whig Leaders and the Liberal Party

The political ascendancy of Beaconsfield, in the summer of 1878, and the strength of 'jingoistic' passions in the country, merely confirmed the Whig leaders' suspicions that Gladstone's conduct, throughout the period since the autumn of 1876, had been damaging to the Liberal Party. Gladstone's stance on the Eastern Question, which was all too easily construed by his opponents as pro-Russian in its intent, had apparently now been proved to be unpopular with the public, as well as divisive for the Liberals themselves. In December 1876, after Gladstone's appearance at the St James's Hall conference, Hartington had warned Granville that 'the Whigs and moderate Liberals in the House [of Commons] are a good deal disgusted', and that, if Gladstone went much further, 'nothing can prevent a break-up of the party'.[7] Later, when Gladstone brought forward his five resolutions, the Whig leadership applied strong pressure behind the scenes to dissuade Liberal MPs from supporting him, and in the end Gladstone was obliged to back down and withdraw the substantive parts of the resolutions. His subsequent decision to attend the inaugural meeting of Chamberlain's National Liberal Federation, at Birmingham, appalled the Whigs, and when, in April 1878, Gladstone joined with Bright and some sixty other Liberal MPs to oppose the government's decision to call out the reserves, even Granville, who was still personally close to Gladstone, found it hard to conceal his disgust.

Hartington's position is of particular interest, for, as we have already noted, he was strongly imbued with the 'Palmerstonian' principle of assertiveness in the handling of foreign policy, as a means of protecting Britain's vital interests. Deplorable as the oppressive policy of the Turks may have been, therefore, Hartington's primary concern during the Eastern crisis of 1876–8 was with the security of Britain's trading routes to India and the East, and it was the prospect of Russian expansion towards the Eastern Mediterranean that seemed to present the greatest danger in the situation. While Gladstone was joining in the denunciations of Turkish misrule, Hartington was expressing to his Whig colleague, Lord Spencer, the fact that

> I have the worst possible opinion of Russian policy; and though I agree with you in thinking that Russia has no immediate designs on Constantinople, I believe that her politicians have their thoughts constantly fixed upon it, as an object of the future, and that they are now bent on extending Russian influence as far and as directly as may be possible at the moment.[8]

The subsequent Russo-Turkish War, of 1877–8, naturally raised the fear that Constantinople might be an immediate Russian objective after all, and, while this did not materialise, the large Bulgarian client state established by the Treaty of San Stefano was as unacceptable to Hartington as it was to Beaconsfield.

The great difficulty for Hartington, throughout the period 1876–8, was that he was anxious to preserve for the Liberal Party the 'Palmerstonian' tradition of foreign policy, which Gladstone seemed to wish to cast off, and which Beaconsfield was all too eager to claim for the Conservative Party. Hartington therefore found himself substantially in agreement with the policy being pursued by the Beaconsfield administration, and he was unwilling to engage in a factious opposition for purposes of partisan advantage. It is true to say that, in adopting this view, Hartington was reflecting the opinions of a substantial portion of the Liberal Party, in the House of Commons, who were horrified by what they regarded as Gladstone's erratic and irresponsible behaviour. Indeed, the eminent parliamentary journalist, Henry Lucy, commenting on the situation at the end of the 1877 session, reckoned that Gladstone's conduct, particularly over the five resolutions, had harmed his reputation, whereas Hartington's authority had been enhanced. According to Lucy, Gladstone's 'present position may be defined by the fact that whilst three years ago his retirement from the leadership of the Liberal party appeared to be a calamity never to be recovered from, a proposition for his return at the present time would, if submitted for the approval of members who sit on the opposition benches, be voted down by a majority of three to one'. Such was the strength of moderate Liberal feeling that when, in April 1878, John Bright and other radicals put pressure on the Whig leaders to vote against the government's policy of calling out the reserves, at least 100 back-bench MPs pledged themselves to go into the division lobby with the Conservatives if Granville and Hartington acceded to the radicals' demand. As was so often the case during the Eastern crisis, the Whig leaders found that the only possible course open to them, without breaking up the Liberal Party, was to abstain, but on this occasion 25 Liberals were still not satisfied and voted for the government.[9]

The simple fact is that the Liberal Party, deprived of the customary restraining influence of office and responsibility, was incapable of united action over the Eastern Question. During the parliamentary session of 1878, a total of 37 Liberal MPs (over 15 per cent of the party) rebelled against the Whig leaders and supported the government on one or more of the main divisions relating to Beaconsfield's foreign policy; while on the other hand 74 MPs (31 per cent of the party) rebelled against the Whig leaders by voting for one or other of the radical motions, in April–May, condemning the government. Furthermore, there was a definite social basis to these Liberal divisions. Of the 37 'moderate' rebels, over 60 per cent were members of the aristocratic and landowning classes, and most represented either county constituencies or small boroughs; whereas, of the 74 'radical' rebels, over 40 per cent had business backgrounds and 20 per cent were lawyers, and an overwhelming majority of them sat for borough constituencies.[10] In the circumstances, Hartington could do little more than offer the lowest common denominator form of leadership – deliberate abstention – in order to keep the bulk of the party with him. What is equally certain, however, is that Gladstone would have achieved no greater success in holding the Liberal Party together had he faced the responsibilities of leadership, rather than enjoying the luxury of being able to pursue an independent course.

Any assessment of the quality of the Granville–Hartington leadership must clearly take account of the fact that the Whigs were operating in an exceptionally difficult situation, up to the summer of 1878. In the more favourable political climate of late 1878 and 1879 the endeavours of the Whig leaders were more fully rewarded, as the Liberals achieved a far greater degree of cohesion. With the economic depression – already making itself felt in 1878 – worsening appreciably during the following year, the problem of financial policy came to the fore as the Conservatives were running a budget deficit (which prompted unflattering comparisons with the large surplus bequeathed by the outgoing

Liberal government in 1874). Furthermore, the 'forward' policies being pursued by the Viceroy of India, Lord Lytton, and the South African High Commissioner, Sir Bartle Frere, had implicated the government in questionable military campaigns against the Afghans and Zulus respectively. Worse still, these campaigns suffered serious reverses when a British force commanded by Lord Chelmsford was wiped out by the Zulus at Isandhlwana, in January 1879, and when the British mission imposed upon the Emir of Afghanistan was massacred at Kabul, in September. In both cases, further military operations became necessary in order to retrieve Britain's position. It was even possible for the Liberals to suggest that there was a link between the problems of the budget deficit and the fiascos in the government's imperial policy, and that it was in fact the Conservatives' habit of meddling in the affairs of distant countries which caused the excessive expenditure, and therefore high taxation, which was placing a crippling burden on the economy.

The parliamentary debate on Afghanistan, in December 1878, marked a turning point in Hartington's leadership of the Liberals in the Commons. To the delight of his back-benchers, Hartington launched a vigorous onslaught on the Conservatives, who had tried to pin the blame for the situation in Afghanistan on previous Liberal administrations. As one radical MP, A. J. Mundella, put it, 'Hartington made an entirely new departure. . . . He smote the Government *hip and thigh*', and Hartington's private secretary observed that the speech had 'pleased our extreme left amazingly'. Thereafter, Hartington frequently adopted a more decisive tone in his leadership, so that, by 1880, Thomas Wemyss Reid, the editor of the *Leeds Mercury*, in a collection of essays entitled *Politicians of Today*, could describe him as 'the man who has gained most in personal reputation during the existence of the present Parliament'.[11] Hartington's enhanced political stature was reflected in his public speeches to mass gatherings at Liverpool, Newcastle and Manchester, during the course of 1879. Interestingly, by the time of the 1880 general election Hartington had developed a specifically Whig critique of Beaconsfield's style of government, alleging that unconstitutional practices were being used, and even hinting at a sinister attempt to subvert the authority of parliament.[12]

We should also bear in mind that even when the Whig leaders had been placed on the defensive, during the dark days of the Eastern crisis, they had never been entirely negative in their approach to domestic reform. Indeed, it was Hartington who, in June 1877, gave official backing to G. O. Trevelyan's annual motion for the extension of household suffrage to the counties, a move that secured almost unanimous Liberal support for the proposal (only four MPs, including Robert Lowe, persisted in opposing it). By 1880, county franchise reform, together with the reform of local government (there were still no elective local authorities for the counties, or for London), formed the main planks of a political programme which was pretty much agreed by all Liberals. There was also a more vague commitment to some measure of land reform – relating to the laws of primogeniture and entail, which were deemed to produce an artificial concentration of land in large estates – although no clearly defined official plan was produced.

Hartington had also addressed the problem of the relationship between the Liberal Party and its more extreme nonconformist supporters. In his speeches in Scotland, during the autumn of 1877, Hartington's message had been that organisations like the Liberation Society and the United Kingdom Alliance must recognise that their views did not represent those of the majority in the country, but that they were nevertheless free to campaign for what they believed in within the framework of the Liberal Party, and should strive to convince the majority that their policies were right. Of course, Hartington had no intention of doing anything positively to promote such causes as Church disestablishment or temperance reform, and he probably hoped to be able to unobtrusively stifle these potentially divisive issues, but it must have seemed that a policy of holding the various elements of the Liberal Party on a loose rein offered the only prospect of keeping them all moving in the same direction. Hartington's invitation to the nonconformist pressure groups to infiltrate the Liberal Party, if they could, was evidently accepted by the United Kingdom Alliance, which was extremely successful at inducing Liberal candidates to endorse at least a modified measure of temperance reform, so that after 1880 there was a clear majority, among Liberal MPs, in support of what had come euphemistically to be described as 'local option'.[13]

Within the parliamentary Liberal Party, at least, it was undoubtedly the case that many of the leading radicals were becoming increasingly well disposed towards the Whig leadership. In part, this was simply a matter of political pragmatism, as it made sense for ambitious radicals to keep in with those who were still, after all, the official leaders of the party. It was also seen to be imperative that cordial relations be maintained between the various sections of the party if there was to be any chance of victory at the next general election. Beyond this, however, there was a more positive appreciation that a Whig leadership could work to the advantage of individual radicals, on the grounds that when a Liberal government came to be formed a Whig premier would find it necessary to give the radicals a generous share of posts in order to secure the allegiance of the whole of the parliamentary party to the government. Such considerations clearly influenced the attitude of men like Sir Charles Dilke, widely tipped as the young radical most likely to receive high office in the next Liberal ministry, and Henry Fawcett. Even Dilke's abrasive and controversial ally, Joseph Chamberlain, who had entered the House of Commons in 1876, seems to have come to the conclusion, by 1879–80, that it was better for him to work with the Whig leaders rather than attempting to topple them.[14]

The Liberal Revival, 1879–80

By the autumn of 1879, the general expectation in Liberal circles was that the party could look forward to significant gains at the next general election, particularly in the boroughs, but that the existence of an independent Irish Home Rule party, some 60 in number, would make it unlikely that the Liberals could achieve an overall parliamentary majority. A new dimension to the situation was added in November–December, however, with the dramatic reception accorded to Gladstone when he embarked upon a speaking tour in the Scottish county constituency of Midlothian. Encouraged by the Liberal chief whip, W. P. Adam, and the leading Liberal landowner in the constituency, Lord Rosebery, to believe that this Conservative-held seat was winnable for the Liberals, Gladstone had agreed to put himself forward in what was clearly conceived as a symbolic assault upon the very heart of Conservatism. The significance of the Midlothian campaign, indeed, lay not so much in the contest for what was a relatively small constituency, in which traditional landlord influence was still a dominant feature, but in the way that Gladstone was able to use the occasion to address the nation as a whole. Improvements in telegraphic communications meant that the speeches delivered on one day could be reported extensively in newspapers all over the country the next day. The Midlothian campaign thus marked an important step in the development of a new form of mass political communication.[15]

Gladstone's speeches are best remembered for their indictment of a 'system' of governmental policy, 'Beaconsfieldism', which had sullied

Britain's reputation in the eyes of the world, led to the massacre of innocent tribal peoples in Afghanistan and South Africa, imposed a heavy burden of taxation on the British public, and, worst of all, was totally unnecessary from the point of view of the nation's own interests. He therefore laid down 'six right principles', which he believed should inspire and guide the conduct of foreign and colonial policy. It should be stressed that Gladstone was not a pacifist, nor an insular-minded 'Little Englander', of the John Bright school, believing that war could only be justified for purposes of self-defence. In some respects there was a 'Palmerstonian' strain in Gladstone's thinking, detectable in his sixth principle, that 'the foreign policy of England should always be inspired by the love of freedom'. And, while the second, fourth and fifth principles – 'to preserve peace', 'to avoid needless and entangling engagements', and 'to acknowledge the equal rights of all nations' – were obviously not formulated with the Palmerstonian tradition in mind, where Gladstone's ideals fundamentally differed from those of the former Liberal premier was in the emphasis, embodied in the third principle, on the need to maintain co-operation between the Great Powers – 'the concert of Europe'. Gladstone, then, was no isolationist, but rather an internationalist, believing in the desirability of promoting a greater understanding between the European Powers in order to achieve rational and fair solutions to points of potential conflict. Nevertheless, he recognised that there might still be occasions when Britain ought to take decisive military or diplomatic action overseas, and, as the first of his principles stated, it was essential to ensure that there was good government at home so that Britain's moral standing in the eyes of the world was elevated, making its interventions 'for great and worthy occasions abroad' all the more effective.[16]

It is doubtless the case, as Richard Shannon has suggested, that the Midlothian campaign was of special significance for Gladstone, personally, in that for the first time he found it possible to use the conduct of foreign and colonial policy as the basis for a moral crusade. Hitherto, this area of policy had seemed to be a source of political weakness and unpopularity, rather than of strength, as such episodes as the Alabama affair, during the first Gladstone ministry, had indicated. Now, however, it finally appeared to Gladstone as if 'the people' had been weaned off their preference for the worst aspects of the 'Palmerstonian' style of policy, and above all that they had repudiated the perverted form of this policy which was 'Beaconsfieldism'.[17]

There is much more difficulty in trying to assess, in an objective

way, the nature and extent of 'Gladstonianism' as a popular phenomenon. A letter by A. J. Mundella, Liberal MP for Sheffield and a
prominent figure in the Eastern Question Association of 1877–8,
describing the response in London and elsewhere to the first Midlothian campaign, is highly suggestive:

> The reaction for *Gladstone* is very remarkable. As I passed a
> Stationer's shop in Queen Victoria Street, in the city (this morning)
> the window was crowded with Gladstone's photographs, and there
> was printed up in large letters 'The Man for England'. *This would
> have been impossible a year and a half ago.* In Portsmouth people went
> almost mad at the mention of his name. I have some capital Liberal
> songs sung in the Portsmouth demonstration. The effect was almost
> inspirating.[18]

Clearly, Gladstone had succeeded in arousing public passions in a way
that eclipsed the efforts of Hartington and other leading Liberals. The
question remains whether this was yet another manifestation of a
popular fervour for Gladstone that was a permanent feature of the
political landscape, or rather, a temporary outburst of excitement of a
kind that Gladstone was capable of tapping into only at certain
moments. Mundella, who had experienced the wrath of the jingo mobs
in 1877–8, was in no doubt that the success of the Midlothian campaign represented an important change in popular perceptions of Gladstone. Nor is it very surprising that Gladstone's message should have
struck a chord with the British public at a time when the economy was
moving deeper into depression, the government was running a large
budget deficit (£8 millions by 1880), and its jingoistic policies had gone
badly wrong in Afghanistan and South Africa. Gladstone, in fact, was
interpreting the adverse conditions of 1879 in his own distinctive way,
as a vindication of his stand against Beaconsfield's policies since 1876,
and it was possible to lose sight of the fact that this stand had not
originally been a universally popular one. As for the revivalist, almost
hysterical tone of much of the response to Gladstone's speeches, and to
his name, it must be remembered that this was a characteristic of the
high-Victorian temperament. The 1870s, which saw the Bulgarian
atrocities agitation and the first Midlothian campaign, had also witnessed the remarkable tours by the American evangelists, Moody and
Sankey, and the formation of the Salvation Army.
Certainly, the official Liberal leaders were unconvinced that the

demonstrations in Midlothian were indicative of a decisive shift of public opinion which might necessitate a reopening of the question of Gladstone's relationship with the party. On the contrary, a meeting at Devonshire House on 16 December, involving Granville, Hartington, Harcourt and Cardwell, concluded that it would be unwise to make any approach to Gladstone in order to clarify the situation. The over-riding consideration here was the fear that Gladstone's return as leader would immediately break up the Liberal Party, depriving it of the support of many moderates who had been reassured by the 'responsible' style of leadership associated with Granville and Hartington. It was by no means obvious, in other words, that on balance Gladstone's proceedings in Scotland were helping rather than harming the Liberal Party's prospects. In any case, even if Gladstone's campaigning was beneficial to the Liberal cause, it was doubtful whether the political momentum gained at Midlothian could be sustained until the general election, which might not take place until late in 1880 or even the beginning of 1881. Two disappointing by-election defeats for the Liberals, at Liverpool and Southwark in February 1880, appeared to confirm the wisdom of the official leaders' decision, suggesting that the political storm clouds conjured up by Gladstone the previous December had already dispersed. It was precisely because this seemed to be the case that Beaconsfield was emboldened to announce a sudden dissolution of parliament, on 8 March.[19]

It may very well be true that, in the event, the Liberal Party managed to get the best of all worlds during the 1880 general election. On the one hand, the continued presence of the Whig leaders, Granville and Hartington, helped the Liberals to maximise their potential support among influential territorial magnates, like the Duke of Bedford and Earl Fitzwilliam, while also securing the allegiance of moderate voters of the kind that had been alienated from Gladstone's government in 1874. Equally, however, the prominent role in the elections played by Gladstone, who launched a second campaign at Midlothian and triumphantly carried the seat, may have served to maintain the commitment and enthusiasm of some of the more zealous radical and nonconformist Liberals. It is interesting to note, for example, that the Labour Representation League appears to have become fully reintegrated into the Liberal Party by 1880, and the emphasis during the general election on foreign and colonial issues certainly had the effect of obscuring any specifically labour concerns.

In spite of Conservative hopes, and Liberal suspicions, that the general election would produce a small majority for Beaconsfield's government, the outcome was an astonishing turnaround of the result in 1874, with the Liberals securing a clear overall majority, winning 353 seats to the Conservatives' 238 and the Irish Home Rulers' 61. The main features of the general election were the complete wiping-out of the gains made by the Conservatives in 1874 in the largest English boroughs, and the significant recovery by the Liberals in Lancashire, where they gained 8 borough and 4 county seats. Hartington, in an often forgotten campaign which at least partially emulated Gladstone's, led the way by capturing the Conservative seat at North East Lancashire. Only the home counties, and to a lesser extent London itself, proved impervious to the Liberal tide. Perhaps the most disturbing aspect of the elections, from the Conservatives' point of view, was the fact that the Liberals had begun to make inroads into the traditionally Conservative-dominated English counties (the Liberals made a net gain of 28 seats in this category), something that was partly the consequence of a greater assertiveness by Liberal landowners, who were more heartily committed to the Liberal cause in 1880 than they had been in 1874. It was also attributable, though, to the efforts of the 'Farmers' Alliance', a pressure group campaigning for changes in the system of land tenure, which was symptomatic of the growing tensions between landlords and tenants arising from the severity of the depression affecting the agricultural sector.[20]

At the same time, the Liberals had strengthened their already firm grip in Scotland (50 seats to the Conservatives' 7) and Wales (28 seats to the Conservatives' 2). In the case of Wales, the strength of radical-nonconformity had a considerable influence on the social complexion of the principality's representatives, and few Whigs were therefore elected, although it appears that the contribution made by landowners to the Liberal cause was not insignificant. The Liberal triumph in Scotland has understandably been linked to Gladstone's intervention at Midlothian, but we should also recognise that the general election results were a considerable triumph for the Scottish Whigs. It is true that since 1874 there had been a resurgence of pressure for Church disestablishment in Scotland, orchestrated by a reconstituted alliance between the United Presbyterians and the Free Church. However, the impact of this alliance was largely contained, as a result of the Whigs' ability to dominate the local and regional party organisations, together with the fact that in some areas the Whigs acted in alliance with working-class Liberals – who were far more hostile towards the radical-nonconformists, many of whom were businessmen, unsympathetic to trade unionism and committed to a policy of financial retrenchment in municipal affairs. The result was that the radical-nonconformists found themselves outflanked, and in 1880 only eight Scottish Liberal candidates were unequivocal supporters of disestablishment.[21]

If the Liberal Party as a whole benefited from the leadership arrangements at the time of the general election, it is also the case that Gladstone's personal prestige was boosted by the outcome of events. The seemingly miraculous triumph for the Liberal Party could all too easily be attributed to the superhuman efforts of Gladstone alone, and even many Whig and moderate Liberals, who had limited sympathy for him, were so astonished by the size of the party's majority that they assumed that it *must* have been due to him. For Gladstone, personally, the transformation brought about by the elections was also crucial, as it enabled him to find a justification for reclaiming the premiership. Prior to the election, he had still refused to acknowledge that his active participation in politics had any implications for the question of the Liberal leadership: he maintained that he was merely doing all he could for the good of the Liberal cause, and that he remained loyal to Granville and Hartington. In truth, Gladstone must have been rather embarrassed by the awareness that, to many observers, his conduct appeared dishonourable, given that it was he who had 'abandoned' the Liberal Party in 1875, leaving the Whig leaders to pick up the pieces; and there was the added concern that Queen Victoria, who had become virtually infatuated with Beaconsfield, was virulently hostile to any suggestion of Gladstone's return to office. However, the fact that most Liberals, Gladstone included, had been so cautious about the party's election prospects, even in December 1879 after the first Midlothian campaign, made Gladstone's position a great deal easier as it was possible for him to acquiesce in the Whigs' view that the leadership question ought not to be reopened. On the other hand, once the general election had produced a decisive Liberal majority, Gladstone was able to point to this as a remarkable demonstration of the will of the people, and to persuade himself that he was called upon to take up the reins of government and devote his energies, for the little time that remained to him, to rectifying the damage inflicted on the country and on the world by 'Beaconsfieldism'.

Two obstacles remained in Gladstone's path, the first being the hostility of the Queen, who still exercised the prerogative power of appointing the Prime Minister, the second being the attitude of Hartington, who had led the Liberal Party through the elections and made notable contributions of his own to the campaign. In the event, the Queen's response was to commission Hartington to form the new government, a responsibility that Hartington could not brush off lightly given his role as the official leader in the House of Commons, and the view pressed on him, by his supporters behind the scenes, that it would be a betrayal of those moderate Liberal voters who had supported the party in the belief that he was the leader, if he gave way now. Accordingly, Hartington took steps towards the formation of a government by approaching Gladstone to see if he would be willing to serve in a subordinate capacity. Only when Gladstone made it clear that he would take no office but the premiership, and that he could not undertake to give full support to a Hartington ministry from the back-benches, was Hartington able to convince the Queen that his task was hopeless and that she would have to summon Gladstone instead. It was obvious to Hartington that a government formed by him could not survive with Gladstone roaming around on the back-benches, and all too likely to become the focus for discontented radicals, and, while he clearly felt that Gladstone had not behaved well towards him since the supposed 'retirement' of 1875, it nevertheless seemed expedient for Hartington to stand aside and look to the future succession.[22]

The Whigs may have felt aggrieved at the way Gladstone had forced his way back to the front, in April 1880, but it remains the case that they fared extremely well out of the subsequent distribution of government posts. Of the thirteen Cabinet ministers, excluding Gladstone himself, six were peers (including Granville as Foreign Secretary), four commoners were connected to aristocratic or landed families (including Hartington, who became Indian Secretary), while Bright, Forster and Chamberlain represented varying shades of middle-class radicalism. No doubt this selection reflected Gladstone's personal preference for aristocratic ministers, as well as the need to compensate the Whigs for the way he had forced Hartington to relinquish the leadership. Several important changes of personnel took place during the years that followed, including the resignations of Argyll, Forster and Bright, and the admission to the Cabinet of Chamberlain's closest radical ally, Sir Charles Dilke, but the overall social balance was not very different when the Fifteenth Earl of Derby, a recruit from the Conservatives, agreed to join Gladstone's ministry in December 1882. As Derby noted at that time, most members of the Cabinet were 'connected with the

Whig aristocracy, or with the landowning class', and only Chamberlain and Dilke were 'of the middle or trading class. . . . And of these two . . . one is a baronet, and the other they say not far from a millionaire. It would be difficult to find a Cabinet with less admixture of anything that in France would be called democracy in its composition.'[23]

Gladstone's Second Ministry and the Empire

Although the Liberal Party had been able to unite, by 1879–80, in condemnation of the abortive policies of Beaconsfield's government, the earlier differences over the Eastern Question suggested that the second Gladstone ministry would not necessarily find agreement easy to come by in the sphere of foreign and colonial policy. Within the parliamentary party as a whole, it is certainly possible to detect a division of opinion between those Liberals who preferred a 'Palmerstonian' approach, and were imperially minded, and others who advocated a 'Little Englander' policy of non-intervention abroad. At the Cabinet level, it would be an exaggeration to draw a similar clear-cut distinction, but we might reasonably analyse events in terms of the differences of approach represented, on the one hand, by the 'Palmerstonians', who were anxious to assert Britain's power abroad and maintain the nation's 'prestige' in the eyes of the world, and on the other by the 'Gladstonians', inspired by the Prime Minister's more idealistic notions of how policy should be conducted. As will become clear, though, such a distinction did not always correspond to the familiar political division between 'Whigs' and 'radicals'.

In one area the situation inherited from the Conservatives was cleared up in a manner that proved satisfactory to all Liberal ministers. True to his stated principles, Gladstone was able to secure Britain's military withdrawal from Afghanistan, in the autumn of 1880, but this was possible because of the presence of a new, and more co-operative Emir, who was willing to accept a virtual British protectorate over his country in order to keep out the Russians. This arrangement serves to emphasise the point that Gladstone was never a 'Little Englander', and that he was alive to the need to protect Britain's vital interests, in this case the security of India.

Events in the Transvaal, however, brought out the latent tensions within the Gladstone ministry. The Transvaal had been annexed by the Beaconsfield government in 1877, with the ultimate object of establishing a federal system for the whole of South Africa which would secure Britain's commercial and strategic interests. Initially, the new Liberal ministry of 1880 was also inclined to pursue this course, but the Boers of the Transvaal, determined to regain their independence, rebelled against British rule and in February 1881 inflicted a devastating defeat on General Colley's force at Majuba Hill. The Colonial Secretary, Lord Kimberley, backed strongly by Hartington, argued that further military operations, to avenge Majuba, were essential if Britain's authority was not to be seriously undermined; but Gladstone favoured a conciliatory approach towards the Boers, as did two of the radical Ministers, Bright and Chamberlain. Sir Charles Dilke, Chamberlain's closest ally, still a junior minister at this stage, also supported Gladstone's line, but, as his diary suggests, the course taken by himself and Chamberlain during the ensuing ministerial crisis was dictated by other political considerations:

> After a long interview between me and Chamberlain on the state of affairs – Chamberlain had an honest and holy [i.e. a straight talk] with Bright, and got him to write a strong letter to Gladstone about the Transvaal, which is put forward as our ground for proposed resignation, although of course the strength of the [Irish] coercion measures, the weakness of the [Irish] land measures, and the predominance of the Whigs in the Cabinet are the real reasons. On this Transvaal matter Bright and Courtney must go with us, and Lefevre might do so. If the Whigs yield, and we stay, Kimberley may go.[24]

On this occasion, the policy advocated by the radicals, and backed crucially by the premier himself, was the one that prevailed (though Kimberley did not resign). Rather than taking military reprisals, which would inevitably have created more bitterness, Britain conceded independence to the Transvaal, subject to a vague claim of overall 'suzerainty'. This alignment between Gladstone and the younger radical representatives, Chamberlain and Dilke, was a temporary one, however, specific to the circumstances of 1881, as is demonstrated by the fact that in 1884–5 these radicals were acting alongside 'Palmerstonians' like Hartington in forcing upon a reluctant Gladstone the need for a 'forward' policy in South Africa, including the annexation of Bechuanaland, in order to prevent German encroachment into the region.[25]

Chamberlain and Dilke's attitude is illustrative of the important point that a fault line existed within radicalism itself when it came to the question of colonial expansion. Whereas John Bright, at the Cabinet level, junior ministers like Leonard Courtney, and back-benchers like Sir Wilfrid Lawson and Henry Labouchere, advocated a 'Little Englander' line, believing that it was both unjust and wasteful for Britain to commit money and men to colonial ventures, Chamberlain and Dilke were the leading radical exponents of the 'imperial idea'. Dilke, indeed, had first made his mark as a very young man with the publication of a book, *Greater Britain* (1868), recounting his travels in the areas of white colonial settlement. Thus on one occasion, in 1884, we find Dilke recording in his diary: 'Chamberlain and I both very angry at the loss of the Cameroons, both of us in turn having thought we had annexed them – only now to find through Foreign Office and Colonial Office dawdling they have gone to Germany.'[26] The political significance of this 'Radical Imperialist' outlook is that it opened up potential common ground for united action with Hartington and other 'Palmerstonians', and this was precisely what happened in the case of Britain's military intervention in Egypt in 1882. With the Khedival regime having been overthrown by a nationalist revolt, led by Arabi Pasha, Hartington, Northbrook and Kimberley were the leading Whig ministers who pressed the case for military action in order to protect Britain's commercial and financial interests in the Near East, and at the vital moment they were supported by Chamberlain (and, from outside the Cabinet, Dilke), compelling a reluctant Gladstone to acquiesce in an interventionist policy, and leaving the 'Little Englander', Bright, to resign in protest.[27]

In one vital area of policy, then, the Liberal government did not always divide along simple Whig–radical lines, and there were times when some Whigs and radicals combined to force their views upon the Prime Minister. There is no doubt that Chamberlain and Dilke's position was often influenced by calculations of electoral advantage – the belief that a forward policy was popular in the country – and that they were apt to be less reliable in their support of the 'Palmerstonian' views of Hartington and others when they thought these would be electorally unpopular, as in the case of the proposed British guarantee for the raising of a large international loan by the Egyptian government, in 1885.[28] Nevertheless, the similarity in instinctive outlook between the radical, Chamberlain, and the Whig, Hartington, is indicated by the correspondence between Chamberlain and his close friend and radical

ally, John Morley, a 'Little Englander', shortly after the death of
General Gordon at the hands of the Dervishes, at Khartoum. Chamberlain dismissed Morley's view that Britain should evacuate the Sudan
as utopian: 'It may be right but it can't be carried out. To leave the
country in face of the Mahdi's success might be very noble and very
Christian, but it would be misunderstood by everyone else and in my
opinion would be very dangerous.' Consequently, Chamberlain
believed that 'We must show these fierce fanatics that we are strong as
they respect nothing but physical force. We must therefore retake
Khartoum, even if we leave it again immediately.'[29] This serious dis-
agreement between Chamberlain and Morley resulted in a personal
rift, lasting for several months, which was probably never fully healed.

Radical differences over imperial policy, which were fundamental
and not simply the product of a 'generation gap' – Bright, it is true,
was an old man, but Morley, Lawson, Labouchere, Courtney and other
Little Englanders were of much the same age as the radical imperialists,
Chamberlain and Dilke – helps to explain why Chamberlain was to be
unsuccessful in his ambition to establish himself as the leader of a
united radicalism. Ominously for Chamberlain's future political prospects, a total of 69 Liberal MPs voted for John Morley's motion, in
February 1885, which effectively called for British evacuation of Egypt
and the Sudan. But equally ominously, from the point of view of Gladstone and his colleagues, was the fact that the Conservatives' motion of
censure on the government, for failing to take more decisive action to
save General Gordon, was supported by 6 Liberal MPs while a further
36 abstained. With 31 Irish Home Rulers also voting for the censure
motion, the government only survived by a margin of 14 votes. The
shadows cast by the spirits of Cobden and Palmerston were long
indeed.

Gladstone's Second Ministry and Ireland

An even more divisive issue in Liberal politics, during the first half of
the 1880s, was the perennial 'Irish Question'. To a considerable
degree, this represented an extension of the fundamental ideological
differences which had underpinned Cabinet disputes over Irish policy
in the period of Gladstone's first ministry. Whereas Whigs like Hartington (Irish Chief Secretary, 1870–4) believed there was an overriding
need for strong government, combined with ameliorative economic and

religious concessions designed to help integrate Irish society more fully into the United Kingdom, Gladstone had always abhorred the use of coercive legislation, while his High Church, anti-erastian opinions had led him to adopt a policy on matters like university reform which tended towards recognition of the distinctness of the Irish people.[30] These inherent tensions between Gladstone and the Whigs were to become much more apparent after 1880, as the second Gladstone ministry struggled to cope with the challenge posed by the so-called 'new departure' in strategy by the Irish Nationalists, which included exploiting agrarian grievances, exacerbated by the severe agricultural depression, in order to fuel the political campaign for some form of 'Home Rule'. By 1880, Charles Stuart Parnell had established himself as the dominant figure, both in the Nationalist Party at Westminster, and within the movement for agrarian reform in Ireland.

Liberal concerns about the increasing militancy of Irish Nationalism had indeed played an important part in the Whig leadership's political calculations just prior to the 1880 general election. Believing as they did that the best result that the Liberals could realistically hope to achieve was a small majority over the Conservatives alone, many Whigs had felt that a further spell in opposition was preferable to coming into power dependent on the support of the Home Rule Party. The likely difficulties in devising a policy adequate to meeting the mounting crisis in Ireland, which could at the same time be supported by the more radical elements in the Liberal Party, was something of which Hartington and Granville were obviously well aware.[31] However, it was still possible, at this stage, to believe that the extremism of Parnell and the Land League would prove to be a temporary phenomenon, and that the Liberals might yet hope to come into power in more auspicious circumstances in the not-too-distant future. With the benefit of hindsight, of course, the long-term developments in Irish Nationalism which the 'new departure' initiated, suggest that if the Whig leaders had formed a Liberal government in the early 1880s, it would surely have encountered formidable problems in dealing with the situation in Ireland, and a split in the Liberal Party might have been difficult to avoid.

In the event, it fell to Gladstone, who had given little attention to Irish affairs during his Midlothian campaigns, to take responsibility for the handling of the rapidly deteriorating condition of Ireland in the months immediately following the 1880 general election. The initial response by the Irish Chief Secretary, W. E. Forster, was to bring forward a rather hastily conceived Compensation for Disturbance Bill, which was intended to penalise Irish landlords who ejected their tenants – even if this was for non-payment of rent – in order to put a stop to the growing number of evictions. Forster's bill horrified many of the Whig members of the government, and it was resented by landlords in general as imposing an unfair burden on them. While the measure passed through the House of Commons, it was overwhelmingly defeated in the Lords, where even a majority of the Liberal peers present voted against the bill. As the situation in Ireland continued to worsen, during the autumn of 1880, Forster, supported by Hartington and other Whigs, demanded that the Cabinet agree to an early recall of parliament in order to pass new coercive legislation, but this was strongly resisted by the radical ministers, Bright and Chamberlain, who enjoyed the Prime Minister's backing. A break-up of the government seemed a distinct possibility until Forster backed down and agreed to delay any coercive measures until a Land Bill was drawn up to accompany them.

Hartington nevertheless wrote to the Prime Minister, shortly before Christmas 1880, warning him of his dissatisfaction with the tendency of the government's Irish policy, and pointing out that, for those who thought like himself, 'the time must come when further concession becomes impossible'. He also advised Gladstone that 'it is only fair . . . that I should say that I hold that our Coercion measure will have to be strong in proportion to the delay in introducing it', and he was dismissive of the 'sentimental and illogical objections' to the use of force by the authorities. As for the question of land reform, Hartington accepted that something had to be done, but he also confessed that 'I have no confidence in the good effect at this time of any proposals which we may be able to make. I think that we have throughout been too sanguine in our estimate of the fairness and sense of justice of the Irish people.'[32]

Such language from the acknowledged leader of the Whigs, uncompromising and pessimistic as it was, accurately reflected widespread Whig alarm at the dangers posed by the Irish problem. The unstable social condition of Ireland raised fears about the security both of the United Kingdom and of the Empire as a whole, and Hartington was of the view that firm and consistent government was therefore as necessary in the case of Ireland as it might be in any of Britain's colonies. As far as Hartington was concerned, British rule had to be seen to be strong, if the processes making for national and imperial disintegration were to be stemmed, yet Gladstone appeared to favour the same sort of idealistic policies for Ireland as made him an unsuitable leader – in Hartington's eyes – in the realm of foreign and colonial affairs. At the same time, the prospect of further land legislation prompted Whig fears that Irish policy might become the vehicle for radical-inspired attacks upon the sanctity of landed property, which could have serious long-term implications for the position of landowners in Britain as well (fulfilling the prophesy made by Cobden, in the 1860s, that Ireland would be the weak link in the British aristocracy's chain). The fact that Chamberlain – as his opposition to coercion, in the winter of 1880, showed – favoured a more sympathetic treatment of Irish grievances, and indeed saw the Irish Nationalists as the natural allies of the British radicals, and himself as the natural conduit between the two, confirmed the feeling of many Whigs that they were involved in a fundamental struggle for control of the future character of British Liberalism.

Liberal legislation for Ireland in 1881 conformed to the usual pattern of coercion combined with conciliation. An Arms Bill was carried, designed to stop the spread of weapons in Ireland, and habeas corpus was suspended, resulting later in the year in the detention without trial of Parnell and a number of other Nationalist leaders. This coercive legislation was passed quickly, although there was some resistance from radical MPs: a hard-core of about 15 to 20, many of them representatives of northern constituencies with significant Irish migrant populations, seem to have voted with the Nationalists, on matters relating to Ireland, fairly regularly during the early 1880s, and on 15 February 1881 as many as 46 voted for James Stansfeld's amendment seeking to impose restrictions on the use of arrest warrants. The accompanying Land Bill, which sought to provide greater security for Irish tenant farmers by effectively granting them the 'three fs' ('fair rents', to be set by a land court, 'fixity of tenure' for fifteen years, so long as the rent was paid, and the 'free sale' of an outgoing tenant's 'interest' in the holding to the next tenant) was in fact a triumph for Forster, whose views had eventually prevailed over those of a reluctant Prime Minister.[33] There was no Liberal opposition to the second reading of the Land Bill, but during the committee stage there was a concerted and partially successful effort by a group of back-benchers, including a number of 'young Whigs', like Lord Edmond Fitzmaurice, Albert Grey, H. R. Brand and Arthur Elliot, to secure amendments designed to remove from the bill any provisions which might conceivably be used in future as precedents for land legislation applying to Britain.[34]

The battle for control of the direction of government policy towards Ireland continued through the 1882 session of parliament, and although the course favoured by Chamberlain achieved initial success, it was the Whigs' view that ultimately prevailed. Anxious to find a way out of the situation in which Parnell's imprisonment had made the Irish leader a martyr in the eyes of his own people, Gladstone encouraged Chamberlain to negotiate with Parnell, using another Irish MP, W. H. O'Shea, as an intermediary. The outcome was the so-called 'Kilmainham Treaty', whereby the government promised to release Parnell and pass an Arrears Bill (providing State money to pay off tenants' arrears of rent so that they could make use of the Land Courts established by the Act of 1881), and in return the Irish leader undertook to use his influence to promote peace in Ireland, and hinted at future co-operation with the Liberal government. Forster resigned in protest at these proceedings, but the crucial turning point came a few days later, when his replacement, Lord Frederick Cavendish (Hartington's younger brother), was murdered in Phoenix Park, along with the Permanent Under-Secretary, T. H. Burke. Although the terms of the 'Kilmainham Treaty' were still complied with, the government now proceeded to introduce rigorous new coercive legislation, and all subsequent efforts by Gladstone and Chamberlain to modify the provisions of the measure were blocked by the Whigs, either in Cabinet or in parliament. On one dramatic occasion in the House of Commons, in July 1882, Gladstone lost his temper and threatened to resign when a number of back-bench Whigs combined with the Conservatives to defeat an amendment proposed by the government to moderate its own Prevention of Crime Bill.[35]

Conditions in Ireland were relatively quiet during 1883–4, but in the last weeks of the Gladstone ministry's life, in the spring of 1885, the question of Irish policy was reopened in Cabinet. Chamberlain, again seeking to promote closer links between British radicals and Irish Nationalists, under his auspices, proposed to the Cabinet that they should adopt his plan for the creation of an elective 'Central Board' in Dublin, with responsibility for such matters as education and roads, and with limited tax-raising powers. He did so in the mistaken belief that such a measure would be accepted by Parnell as a final settlement of the Home Rule question; but, while Gladstone was supportive, it was strongly opposed by Hartington and a majority of Cabinet ministers, who were unwilling to see the government committed in this way to a policy that could not be implemented until after the next general election. Chamberlain was obliged to withdraw his scheme, but he and Dilke then retaliated by raising objections to the renewal of the Prevention of Crime Act (shortly due to expire), which was being strongly urged by the Lord Lieutenant, Spencer, backed by Hartington and other Whigs. An impasse over Irish policy was thus reached, which had not been resolved when an unexpected defeat in the House of Commons, on a detail of the budget, on 8 June, provided ministers with a welcome opportunity to tender their resignations.

Gladstone and Liberal Unity

It is probably true that during the early 1880s, at least, Gladstone's leadership was of great value from the point of view of maintaining Liberal unity. The inevitable tensions created by the need to deal with the seemingly intractable 'Irish Question' could conceivably have been far worse under another leader, and Gladstone's presence may therefore have helped to contain the scale of the revolts that did take place. As it was, the government carried several measures of coercion, including the imprisonment of suspects without trial, which were bound to be repugnant to many Liberals, and yet the Cabinet remained intact and resistance from back-bench radicals was muted; equally, a far-reaching measure of land reform was passed, involving serious infringements of the legal rights of Irish landlords, but only one Cabinet minister (Argyll) resigned, and no Liberal MPs were prepared to go so far as to vote against the principle of the Land Bill on its second reading.

Gladstone's undoubted unifying influence, in certain circumstances, has prompted a general analysis of his relationship with the Liberal Party which sees his leadership as absolutely indispensable for the purpose of delaying an impending schism. According to this view, Gladstone was truly the 'eagle's head' of Liberalism – the phrase was used in 1881 by the historian, Lord Acton, a sycophantic admirer of the Liberal leader – able to hold the party together because he was above it, rather than of it. In other words, the Liberal Party possessed two distinct and irreconcilable 'wings', the Whigs and the radicals, but the separation, that was bound to take place eventually, was forestalled thanks to the unique position occupied by Gladstone. The Liberal leader, so the argument goes, was associated with neither the Whigs nor the radicals, and drew his independent authority instead from another source, 'the people', who had responded to his moral appeal at the time of the 1880 general election. Such was the power exercised by the remarkable 'Grand Old Man', as he came to be known in the early 1880s, that the Whigs and radicals were deterred from breaking away from the main body of the Liberal Party, as both sections were afraid that by rebelling against Gladstone they would be playing into the other's hands, leaving them to inherit the rich political legacy that Gladstone would eventually leave behind. With neither 'wing' of the party willing to take the first step in breaking up the concern, while Gladstone was still around, a precarious unity was thus preserved.[36]

There is absolutely no doubt that political calculations, of the sort just described, genuinely were being made in the early 1880s. Whig frustration at the failure of Gladstone's ministry to take determined action over Irish coercion in the winter of 1880, for example, clearly was prevented from erupting into something far more serious by the fear that a large-scale revolt would simply drive Gladstone into the arms of the radicals. However, there is another side to the argument about Gladstone's unifying role that has not always been recognised by its proponents. For if it is true that the Whigs and the radicals were each afraid of playing into the other's hands, then this surely suggests that neither side really wished to abandon the Liberal Party at all. If there were serious Liberal divisions, these could just as well be interpreted as evidence of the competition for control of the party after Gladstone's final departure, than as symptoms of a great schism that was inevitably going to come.

Indeed, in some respects, it may be argued, Gladstone's style of leadership had a destabilising effect, especially at the Cabinet level. The fact that Gladstone continued to lead the Liberal Party until 1894, when he was in his eighty-fifth year, must not be allowed to obscure the point that in the early 1880s his position was thought to be a temporary one. Gladstone had only been able to justify to himself his resumption of the premiership, in 1880, on the grounds that he was being called back for the urgent and specific purpose of putting right the state of affairs created by Beaconsfield's pernicious policies. His return was therefore assumed to be for a brief period of time only, and the short-term outlook which this encouraged became a recurring theme throughout the duration of the second ministry. Gladstone was never willing to look very far ahead, and as time went on he attributed the fact that he had not retired to the emergence of a number of unexpected problems, such as those of Ireland, the reform of parliamentary procedure, and the Russian threat to Afghanistan, each of which required a further extension of his leadership. From the point of view of the Liberal Crown Prince, Hartington, who believed in 1880 that he was only temporarily stepping aside to make way for Gladstone, the continuing uncertainty about when exactly Gladstone would retire created a situation in which he found it necessary to fight hard to prevent the government's policy from drifting too far in the radicals' direction. Whereas Hartington consequently appeared to behave as a sectionalist leader, in an effort to protect his inheritance, at the same time the leading Cabinet representative of the radicals, Chamberlain (after Bright's resignation in July 1882), was naturally pressing for the adoption of his preferred policies. An impression of irreconcilable antagonism between Whigs and radicals was thus very easily created, and matters were made worse by Gladstone's reluctance to commit himself to the leadership for any long period of time. In the winter of 1883, for example, the fact that Gladstone was only prepared to lead the government for long enough to pass a County Franchise Bill, and would not consider staying to deal with the associated question of redistribution, resulted in a public dispute between Hartington and Chamberlain, as each man sought to put forward his own view of what form a Redistribution Bill should take. The end result was that Gladstone was induced to agree to stay for long enough to settle both bills. Similarly, in May 1885, the possibility that Gladstone might retire literally at any moment ensured that there was no chance of the Cabinet agreeing to a long-term policy for Ireland, and after the government had fallen, in June, it seems that Gladstone found in the disputes among his colleagues a reason for extending his leadership yet again. It would perhaps be slightly unfair, but not absurdly cynical, to suspect that Gladstone's mode of proceeding served to create precisely the conditions of disunity which then justified him, in his own eyes, in postponing his retirement.[37]

Certainly there is evidence to suggest that, in Gladstone's absence, a working relationship between Whigs and radicals could have been established. As we have already seen, there was a certain amount of common ground between 'Palmerstonian' Whigs like Hartington, on the one hand, and radicals of the ilk of Chamberlain and Dilke on the other, over matters of imperial policy. In the summer of 1882 this meant that Gladstone was being pressed to agree to military intervention in Egypt; and it was at the same time that a government defeat on a detail of its Irish Prevention of Crime Bill provoked Gladstone into losing his temper in the House of Commons and threatening to resign.

Dilke noted in his diary that 'Egypt is at the bottom of this outburst about Ireland. Mr. Bright and Ld. G[ranville] have been his supporters in a let alone policy, and he doesn't like sitting still while others that he looks upon as clerks and boys – clerks like Northbrook and Childers, and naughty boys like Hartington, Chamberlain and myself get our way.' More interestingly still, Dilke's account shows the way in which he and Chamberlain calculated their own position in view of Gladstone's apparently imminent departure. Evidently, the main contingency that had to be considered related to what course Gladstone would take if he did resign and make way for an alternative government, formed, presumably, by Hartington: 'we agreed that we could not join a new government if Mr. G. were outside it in the House of Commons, but that the case might be different if he quitted political life, or went to the Lords – and if we were satisfied with the new bill of fare'.[38]

The diary of Edward Hamilton, one of Gladstone's private secretaries, is also of considerable interest for the appreciation it reveals of many of Hartington's personal qualities, which fitted him for the future Liberal leadership. One particularly interesting point is that Hartington performed well in the House of Commons on those occasions when he was required to fill in for the indisposed Prime Minister: indeed he seemed to be more comfortable in the position of leader than as a subordinate minister. Thus, after the final month of the 1880 session of parliament, which Gladstone had missed due to a serious illness, Hamilton noted that 'I hear from all sides universal praise bestowed upon Lord Hartington's leading powers; everyone admires his sound judgment, his good sense, his sterling ability and unruffled temper.' Similarly, in the spring of 1884, Hamilton wrote that 'It is universally admitted that during Mr. Gladstone's recent absence from the House Lord Hartington has come out very strong as a leader.' In a general political assessment, made at the end of the 1881 session, Hamilton considered that Hartington was the man who had stood out:

> Lord Hartington has done whatever he had to do wonderfully well and has commanded more than ever respect from both sides of the House. His best performance was undoubtedly his speech in the Kandahar debate; but his exposition of the Indian Budget shows that he has an excellent aptitude for business, including figures.

During the debate on the motion of censure over the government's handling of the Egyptian difficulty, in May 1884, Hamilton thought that it was Hartington who had made the outstanding contribution to the debate. In sum, it seemed to Hamilton that Hartington was the only possible successor to Gladstone.[39]

A brief study of the Liberal Party in the House of Commons also suggests that it could be a mistake to assume that continued unity was impossible without Gladstone's presence. While it is, of course, true that the Liberals covered a broad spectrum of opinions, and often exhibited quite serious divisions, it is misleading to conceive of these *solely* in terms of two regularly organised blocs, or 'wings', the Whigs and the radicals. The belief that there was such a straightforward division stems largely from the subsequent mythology that came to surround Gladstone's leadership. In 1928, for example, Gladstone's youngest son, Herbert, published a book in which he depicted the Liberal Party in the parliament of 1880–5 as having distinct Whig and radical wings, each numbering about 70 MPs, and taking direct instructions from Hartington and Chamberlain respectively. Party unity was only achieved, according to Herbert, thanks to his father's personal prestige and authority, coupled with the fact that the vast majority of Liberal MPs were neither Whigs nor radicals, but simply loyal Gladstonians.[40] In reality, the so-called Whig section on the back-benches did not exist as a coherent group throughout the 1880–5 parliament, and there is no evidence at all that Hartington was issuing orders to any such group. The organisation which did develop, in 1881–2, related specifically to the question of Irish policy, and ceased to operate after the end of 1882 when two of its leading members, Fitzmaurice and Brand, were recruited to the government. As for the composition of this Whig group, it can best be likened to a series of concentric rings: a small group of activists, no more than about 15 in number, who were indeed mostly members of aristocratic families; a larger ring of some 30 to 40 MPs who were occasionally prepared to vote against the Gladstone ministry, but only with reluctance; and a still larger ring, probably numbering as many as the other two combined, of members who sympathised with the Whigs' views, but were unwilling to vote against their own government, and at the very most might be prepared to abstain.[41]

Estimates of the numerical dimensions of the back-bench 'radicals' are even more difficult to make, for although a sophisticated attempt has been made to measure them, using a computer analysis of parliamentary division lists,[42] what ultimately emerges is the conclusion that 'radicalism' cannot be reduced to a coherent set of principles, reflected in MPs' voting behaviour. In fact, it is not at all easy to select division lists that might be suitable for such an exercise: the outcome of such motions as Sir Wilfrid Lawson's, for 'local option' with regard to the licensing question, Henry Broadhurst's, for leaseholder enfranchisement (i.e. the right to convert leaseholds on small properties into freeholds), William Willis's for the removal of bishops from the House of Lords, and Henry Labouchere's, for some (unspecified) reform of the House of Lords, was always powerfully influenced by the precise wording of the motion, and by the precise circumstances in which the division took place, with the result that they were all supported by a broad spectrum of Liberals (even, in the case of Broadhurst's motion, by 12 Conservatives), and opposed by few if any on the Liberal side of the House.[43] By far the most serious revolts against the government, by MPs who could meaningfully be described as 'radicals', related to matters of imperial policy, and the most notable of these, John Morley's motion on the Sudan, in February 1885, has already been mentioned: but one final point to be made here is that these 'radicals' were hardly likely to be taking orders from the imperially-minded Chamberlain, in the way that Herbert Gladstone claimed. Clearly, then, we need to be sceptical of studies which seek to depict radicalism as a coherent and inexorably growing force, in the early 1880s, which was about to drive Whigs like Hartington out of the Liberal Party altogether.

Returning to the level of Cabinet politics, while there were undoubtedly major differences between rival ministers, the most enduring impression that emerges is one of a government that was all too often paralysed because of the style of leadership adopted by Gladstone. While the premier was still capable of impressive feats of management with respect to issues that particularly concerned him, such as the Irish Land Bill of 1881, the reform of parliamentary procedure in 1882, and the County Franchise Bill in 1884, he was apt to shun discussion of other issues which he found unpalatable, or which might involve him in a prolonged commitment to leading the government. In November 1884, nearly two years after he joined the government, Lord Derby noted in his diary that the Cabinet 'has been harmonious, though not very businesslike. The Premier listens with more patience, and speaks less, than anywhere else. He is far from being dictatorial'. Thus, on one occasion, when the Cabinet was discussing the despatch of a relief expedition to rescue General Gordon, Derby records that 'Our discussion was long, and as usual in such cases, rather desultory: quite amicable, no sign of temper on the part of anyone, but much perplexity, and no agreement as to what should be done.' Likewise, Derby found the Cabinet hopelessly divided on the question of Egyptian finance, at the beginning of 1885: 'every man has his own ideas, and no two of them are alike. The peculiar position of the Premier, who is always declaring himself to be on the point of retiring, increase the difficulty, for he is very unwilling to do anything that may bind him to stay longer in office, and we cannot act without him.'[44] In another diary entry, reflecting upon the state of the government towards the end of 1884, Derby provides a striking illustration of the way the government was being run, and makes an admission which is especially startling coming from the Colonial Secretary:

> Our chief administrative danger to my thinking lies in the careless, slipshod way in which Cabinet business is done: questions taken up, talked about, dropped with no decision taken, and then after some weeks one finds that they have been settled by the sole authority of some one department, perhaps with, perhaps without, the sanction of the Prime Minister. I trace in his speech and manner no sign of old age: but I can scarcely think that in his best days he would have let things slide as he does now. To this hour I do not know who was responsible for the sending of Gordon to Khartoum: nor when the expedition for his relief was finally settled.[45]

Joseph Chamberlain and the 'Radical Programme'

It is an historical commonplace to say that Gladstone's second ministry compares unfavourably with his first in terms of its achievements in the field of domestic policy. Apart from the electoral reforms of 1883–5, affecting corrupt practices, county franchise, and the redistribution of seats, the government's legislative record between 1880 and 1885 seems barren in contrast to the series of substantial measures enacted in the earlier period. This impression of legislative sterility is by no means inaccurate, but it is worth bearing in mind that the first session of the 1880 parliament had witnessed a promising start, with the implementation of a number of useful, if not spectacular, measures. To a large extent this was a case of paying off political debts incurred during the general election campaign: the Farmers' Alliance, which had assisted the Liberal cause in many county constituencies, was rewarded with the abolition of the tax on malt (a long-standing farmers' grievance), and with the Ground Game Bill, giving tenant farmers full powers over the destruction of hares and rabbits on their holdings, irrespective of the wish of landowners to preserve these creatures for sporting purposes. Nonconformists achieved a long-desired objective through the Burials Bill, permitting non-Anglican services to be conducted at burials in Anglican cemeteries, while the working men were favoured with an Employers' Liability Bill, which slightly extended rights to compensation for industrial accidents. An Education Bill was also passed, finally making elementary schooling compulsory. Even at this early stage, however, a great deal of parliamentary time was being taken up with other, unexpected problems, such as the case of Charles Bradlaugh, an avowed atheist whose right to take his seat in the House of Commons was disputed for several years, as well as the controversial Irish Compensation for Disturbance Bill. Unfortunately for the government's reputation, awkward distractions of this kind were to become a regular part of the pattern of politics over the next few years, and it proved difficult to find sufficient parliamentary time for major legislative undertakings, like the reform of local government in London and in the counties. What the Gladstone ministry might have achieved, if the good work of the 1880 session could have been followed up, can only be a matter for conjecture, of course, but it is at least worth knowing that this is a question that can reasonably be asked.

Nevertheless, the fact remains that during the early 1880s domestic political questions were largely obscured by the preoccupations with Ireland, the Transvaal, Egypt and other problem areas. This was a particularly frustrating situation for the leading representative of the younger generation of radicals, Joseph Chamberlain, who had looked forward to an ambitious programme of reforms which would help to consolidate the Liberals' hold on power and prevent any Conservative resurgence. The fact that Chamberlain had, for some years past, seen himself as the prime motivator behind a constructive domestic policy for the Liberal Party, although he had only been an MP since 1876, is indicative of the aggressive, ruthless and authoritarian traits in the character of this Unitarian businessman from Birmingham. For instance, the National Liberal Federation (NLF), founded in Chamberlain's home town in 1877, had been conceived as a means by which he could broaden his original power base in militant nonconformity into the leadership of a more generalised radical movement. According to its stated intentions, the NLF was to provide a forum in which grassroots Liberals could make their voice heard, and transmit their conclusions to the party leadership. Chamberlain's crude belief in democratic processes, expressing the 'will of the majority', is illustrated by the inaugural proceedings of the Federation:

> The Federation is designed to assist the formation of Liberal Associations, on a popular representative basis, throughout the country; to bring such organisations into union, so that by this means the opinions of Liberals, on measures to be supported or resisted, may be readily and authoritatively ascertained; and to aid in concentrating upon the promotion of reforms found to be generally desired the whole force, strength, and resources of the Liberal Party.
>
> The essential feature of the proposed Federation is the principle which must henceforth govern the action of Liberals as a political party – namely, the direct participation of all members of the party in the direction of its policy . . .[46]

In reality, the NLF was never, in Chamberlain's time, a truly national organisation, representative of all local Liberal associations, and many fellow radicals felt that it was being run by and for the benefit of a clique of Birmingham wirepullers. All the same, the Federation's presence was not something that the party leaders could afford to ignore, and it had certainly strengthened Chamberlain's claim for immediate admission to Gladstone's Cabinet, in 1880.

Writing to his close friend and ally, John Morley, in May 1883, Chamberlain was clearly conscious of the need for a new radical initiative now that the momentum gained from the 1880 victory had been dissipated. 'The time is coming', he declared, 'when our party (of 3 or 4) must have a programme and know exactly what it is aiming at.' However, as Chamberlain was only too well aware, the government's record in areas such as Irish and Colonial policy was not such as to inspire enthusiasm amongst the masses. 'The moral is that half policies never succeed and unfortunately in the present state of things whole policies are absolutely impracticable.'[47]

Chamberlain's concern was made all the more acute by his awareness of the fact that the first stirrings of interest in socialist ideas were becoming apparent around this time – Hyndman's Democratic Federation had been founded in 1881, and the Fabian Society was to arrive on the scene in 1884. Furthermore, radical ideas concerning land reform, associated with A. R. Wallace and Henry George, were also making an impact in Britain during the early 1880s. All of this pointed to the importance of developing a new domestic policy for the Liberal

Party as the most appropriate way of directing impulses for social change into safe channels. Thus, the *Radical Programme*, which first appeared as a series of articles in the *Fortnightly Review*, between August 1883 and July 1885, co-ordinated but not written by Chamberlain, can be seen as a response by the 'new radicalism' to the changing climate of thinking in Britain.[48]

In several important respects, the *Radical Programme* was merely reiterating the need for reforms which had long been advocated by radical politicians. John Morley's article on 'Religious Equality' – in other words, Church disestablishment – is an obvious case in point. An issue of such fundamental concern to many nonconformists could scarcely be omitted from a new radical manifesto, and Chamberlain's own Unitarian background dictated that it must be included. The same was true of Francis Adams's piece on 'Free Schools', which had been one of the demands of the Birmingham-based National Education League in the early 1870s, of which Adams had been secretary and Chamberlain the president. These two issues were in fact linked, as the Church of England was not only to be disestablished, but also disendowed, and the financial resources thereby released for use by the State were to pay for the provision of free education.

The treatment of the question of taxation in the *Radical Programme* did represent a more significant new departure in radical thinking, as it sought to establish the principle that taxes on income should be graduated, that is to say, levied at a rate that varied according to the level of an individual's income. Francis Adams, who also wrote this article, was more concerned to assert the legitimacy of the idea of graduated taxation than to indicate how the additional revenue raised from it ought to be spent, and he strove to present his case in the most cautious, reassuring language possible: 'No person will deny that a more equal distribution of wealth, if it could be effected without any revolutionary precedent, would be a gain to the whole community.' The implications of graduated taxation were, of course, ominous for all people on high incomes, but it is characteristic of the radicals' general approach to these matters that their main target was the landowning class. In a notorious speech made at Birmingham, in January 1885, Chamberlain had used language about landownership as a form of robbery, the denial of men's natural rights in the land of their birth, that might have come straight out of Henry George's *Progress and Poverty* (1879). And, while Chamberlain accepted that it was not possible to reverse centuries of custom, he had nevertheless posed the provocative question: 'What ransom will property pay for the security which it enjoys? What substitutes will it find for the natural rights which have ceased to be recognised?'[49] It is perfectly true that, in a sense, Chamberlain was merely re-asserting a widely accepted principle of taxation, that owners of property must contribute to the expenses of the State in return for the protection which the State affords them, but Chamberlain chose to express this idea in the most inflammatory manner imaginable. In fact, he was rebuked by Gladstone for making this speech, and he did not use this sort of language again, which may well explain the more measured tone adopted by Adams, whose article came out in the *Fortnightly* some months afterwards.

It was perhaps to be expected that, at a time when the agricultural depression caused by cheap foreign competition was hitting many landlords' incomes hard, making them a more vulnerable political target, and when drastic solutions to the land question were being proposed, such as Henry George's 'single tax', or Alfred Wallace's outright nationalisation, radicals seeking to put across more 'realistic' policies should also have focused on the problem of landlordism. The great advantage of such an attack was that by presenting to the population of the towns a common enemy, the landlords, who could be shown to be responsible for all of the problems afflicting the British people, attention could be diverted from the sources of tension which had the potential to create 'class' divisions within urban communities – that is to say, between employers and employees. Thus Jesse Collings, the author of the article in the *Radical Programme* on 'The Agricultural Labourer', argued that when elective county councils were established they should be empowered to purchase land compulsorily in order to provide allotments and smallholdings for the labourers. 'Three acres and a cow', as the popular slogan ran, was seen as a way of recreating a class of politically independent yeomen. But this plan could also be presented as a means of solving urban problems, such as overcrowding and unemployment, by stemming the large-scale migration of rural workers into the towns. Meanwhile, 'parasitic' urban landlords, extracting their 'unearned increment' from ground rents, could be depicted as the root cause of the problem of insanitary slum dwelling, and Frank Harris, in his article on 'Housing of the Poor in Towns', therefore advocated a number of additional responsibilities for local authorities, including the imposition of fines for the misuse of property, and powers of compulsory purchase for purposes of slum clearance (though, interestingly enough, the building of new dwellings was still to be left to private enterprise).

The *Radical Programme*, then, contained a mixture of traditional demands, mainly issues concerning nonconformists, and new or modified approaches to familiar radical concerns such as land reform and taxation, while at the same time addressing topical issues like slum housing. In principle, at least, it asserted the need for greater powers for publicly-elected bodies – though these were more likely to be municipal authorities than the central government – and made the case for a system of graduated taxation in order to help fund these new activities. Above all, the publication of the *Radical Programme*, in book-form in September 1885, was designed to exploit the atmosphere of impending change arising from the recent franchise and redistribution reforms, which had created some two million new voters in Britain and given substantial additional representation to the large towns (see Chapter 6).

It is important to emphasise, however, that the *Radical Programme* was the product only of a small coterie of radicals, centred around Chamberlain, who self-consciously regarded themselves as the vanguard of a broad radical movement. Indeed, they considered it necessary to discipline radicalism itself, by giving it a clear sense of direction, and avoiding being dragged into the personal jealousies and sectional rivalries that had so often in the past hampered the radical cause. As T. H. S. Escott, Chamberlain's principal collaborator, put it in an article entitled 'The Future of the Radical Party', published in the *Fortnightly Review* in July 1883, which served as a prelude to the series of pieces that made up the *Radical Programme*:

> Radicalism is not so much represented as it is burlesqued by politicians of the stamp of Sir Wilfrid Lawson, Mr. Cowen, Mr. Storey, and Mr. Henry Labouchere. The tendency of each of these gentlemen, and others who could be mentioned, is to identify it with some hobby or craze of their own, and by so doing frequently to discredit it. . . . We might perhaps say that Radicalism is the *general* opinion of the most advanced section of the Liberal party for the time being. . . . Above all things, Radicalism is a body of practical doctrines ready for immediate expression in legislation, seeking first and most earnestly the reforms which are nearest at hand and easiest to conclude.[50]

The 'Radical Programme' and the General Election of 1885

Before assessing the political impact of the *Radical Programme*, and of the election campaign which Chamberlain fought around it in 1885, it is necessary to establish more fully the context in which the *Programme* had evolved. First, it is important to remember that during the period when most of the articles were originally published in the *Fortnightly Review*, in 1883–4, it was not Chamberlain's intention that they should serve as a manifesto for the next general election. Rather, Chamberlain's anticipation had been that the question of franchise reform would remain at the forefront of political argument, with the House of Lords, hopefully, taking its resistance to the measure to such lengths that Gladstone's ministry would have no alternative but to dissolve parliament and launch a campaign on the cry of 'the peers versus the people'. The *Fortnightly Review* articles, therefore, were at best expected to have a long-term utility, by creating the impression that there was a long list of reforms waiting to be addressed once the immediate obstacle of the House of Lords had been dealt with. However, the fact that the franchise and redistribution bills were settled, as a result of an agreement between Gladstone and the Conservative leader, Lord Salisbury, in November 1884, created an unforeseen situation in which other domestic reforms had to be brought more quickly into view. In seeking to do this, though, Chamberlain was hampered by the obligations of collective responsibility, which made it difficult for him to launch out in new policy directions without incurring the wrath of the Prime Minister (and, behind him, of Queen Victoria).

The second surprise change in the political situation came, therefore, in June 1885, with the government's unexpected defeat on the budget and its consequent resignation. Whether ministers actually connived at their own defeat, in order to secure a welcome release from office, remains unclear, but it certainly suited admirably the purposes of Chamberlain, who was now free to campaign on a purely radical platform at the general election expected to take place before the end of the year, once the new electoral registers were compiled. It may well be the case that this unanticipated release from the restraints of office explains the improvisatory appearance of the *Radical Programme*, for the last two articles were only published in the *Fortnightly Review* in July, and the collected volume, which appeared in September, used for its introduction a separate article by Escott, 'The Revolution of 1884', written in January 1885 after the unexpected settlement of the franchise and redistribution questions. Hence the impression given by the published volume, that of a loose, somewhat unco-ordinated collection of essays, hurriedly repackaged to meet the requirements of an unforeseen situation.

Thirdly, it is essential to make the distinction between the *Radical Programme*, and the so-called 'unauthorised programme' – the latter being the three specific issues taken from the *Radical Programme*, free education, graduated taxation, and compulsory powers for local authorities to purchase land to provide allotments and smallholdings, on which Chamberlain actually fought the election campaign from September onwards. Contrary to the impression given by Chamberlain's official biographer, J. L. Garvin, the *Radical Programme* in its entirety was not used as an election manifesto in 1885.[51]

More interesting still is the fate of the 'unauthorised programme' which Chamberlain did put forward to the electorate. So far from sweeping all before him, and effectively establishing himself as the 'dictator' of what Liberal policy should be, Chamberlain's campaign backfired disastrously, and he was forced to retreat from the position he had staked out in September. One reason for Chamberlain's difficulties was that the public dispute which broke out between himself and Hartington, early in September, over the general direction of Liberal policy, provided Gladstone with the justification he was probably looking for to announce that he would continue to lead the party for the duration of the election, in order to restore unity. Gladstone's own manifesto, however, gave no encouragement at all to any of the issues being pressed by Chamberlain, concentrating instead on relatively uncontroversial matters like local government and registration reform. This made the position of Hartington and the moderates a great deal easier, for they had no problem in endorsing Gladstone's position and were therefore able to present themselves as party loyalists. Indeed, it was in order to emphasise this point that Chamberlain's most vocal critic within the Liberal party, G. J. Goschen, coined the term 'unauthorised programme' to describe Chamberlain's policies. With the Whigs and moderate Liberals happy to align with Gladstone in resistance to pressure for radical reforms, Chamberlain's immediate reaction was to demand that the three policies he had highlighted must be accepted by the next Liberal government if he was to participate in it (the so-called 'ultimatum speech', made at Lambeth on 24 September). But within a week he had retreated from this rash declaration, and merely asked instead that the three issues should not be specifically excluded from consideration by a Liberal government. For the remainder of the election campaign, therefore, Chamberlain pressed his reform proposals as 'open questions', a status that was, interestingly enough, accorded to them by Hartington, who was careful not to specifically rule out any of Chamberlain's ideas.[52]

Chamberlain's problems were not confined only to his relations with Gladstone and Hartington, though. What became clear, during the course of the election campaign in the autumn of 1885, was that even many radicals were either hostile, or lukewarm, to many of his proposals. This reflected the fact that by no means all of those who would have called themselves 'radicals' shared Chamberlain's views about the desirability of greater State or municipal intervention, and of graduated taxation to pay for it. In other words, many radicals still adhered to the older creed, of which John Bright was the living embodiment, which considered 'progress' to consist of the removal, or restriction, of the role of the State, not its extension. Thus, a man like Jeremiah James Colman, the Congregationalist mustard manufacturer and MP for Norwich, was never an admirer of Chamberlain, as he distrusted his authoritarian temper and sensationalist politicking: for him, self-help and voluntary effort provided the keys to social improvement, not legislative enactments, and any changes relating to taxation were to be approached with the utmost caution.[53] Another radical MP who disliked Chamberlain's 'socialistic' tendencies was also one of his closest political friends, John Morley. To Morley, the way forward for radicalism lay in the assault on the Established Churches, of which he had written in the *Radical Programme*: he was extremely reluctant to give any support at all to the 'unauthorised programme', and, in so far as he ever did, it was only half-hearted, and couched in language that was conciliatory towards the Whigs and moderates. In fact, with Chamberlain's other close ally, Dilke, prevented from taking a leading role in the election campaign because of the dark cloud of the impending Crawford divorce case hanging over his head (it was this that ruined his career the following year), and with other radicals loosely associated with Chamberlain's coterie, like Trevelyan and Shaw Lefevre, proving as lukewarm in their support as Morley, Chamberlain found himself fighting the battle for 'radicalism' almost alone.[54]

If Chamberlain's closest allies were of little help to him, in 1885, the response to the 'unauthorised programme' by many nonconformists was positively harmful. The demand for free education might have been expected to receive warm appreciation from nonconformist leaders, but instead it became entangled with the question of disestablishment and disendowment. Of course, Chamberlain, as a nonconformist himself, took care to reassert his credentials by declaring his support for the

principles of disestablishment and disendowment, but he was also keen
to put this subject to one side for the time being in order to concentrate
on the wider social issues incorporated in the 'unauthorised programme'. However, since one of the items in Chamberlain's programme
was free education, and since Church disestablishment, according to
him, was not an issue ripe for immediate settlement, this raised the
awkward question of how free education was to be paid for, if the pro-
ceeds of disendowment were not to be available. The only answer that
Chamberlain could give was that, for the time being, free education
would be financed out of general taxation; but this raised an additional
problem because, in an attempt to deflect criticism from the Church of
England, he had proposed that voluntary as well as Board schools
should be covered by his plan. From the nonconformist viewpoint,
therefore, the appalling prospect was raised of Church of England
schools, subject to no public control, receiving substantial extra financial
assistance from the State, which would be paid for out of taxes to which
nonconformists were compelled to contribute. For this reason, Chamberlain's plan provoked a storm of protest from nonconformists; many
Liberal candidates, such as Dilke, who had initially endorsed the idea,
were forced to retreat from it, and Chamberlain himself had virtually
dropped the issue by the end of the election campaign. This did not
prevent the Conservatives, of course, from capitalising on Chamberlain's
declared support for the principle of eventual disestablishment, by
raising their well-worn battle cry of 'the Church in danger'.[55]

The Outcome

The Liberal Party emerged from the general election of November–
December 1885 with almost exactly half of the 670 seats in the new
House of Commons. This was certainly a setback for the Liberals as a
whole, for they had expected to benefit rather more from the gratitude
of the electors for the recent franchise and redistribution reforms, and it
was a more severe blow still for Chamberlain, who had entertained
extravagant notions of a landslide victory – for which he would
undoubtedly have claimed the credit. Some Liberal gains were made in
the English counties, and Chamberlain naturally asserted that these
were due to the popularity of his 'three acres and a cow' proposals,
although it is far from clear that this was actually the case.[56] In their
traditional strongholds, the English boroughs, however, the Liberals

were stunned by the scale of the defeats which they suffered, as the Conservatives succeeded in capturing a slight majority of seats (114 out of 226). Chamberlain himself was forced to admit that 'The political condition of the Country is a disgrace to Radicalism.'[57] But there were many Liberals who saw Chamberlain's campaign as the cause of all the trouble. Sir Ughtred Kay Shuttleworth, one of the few Liberal survivors in Lancashire, wrote to one of his colleagues, as the scale of the setback suffered in the boroughs became clear, that 'I get letters daily from politicians of varying degrees of Radicalism, attributing their difficulties or disasters to our friend Chamberlain and his programme, and the spirit in which he thrust it forward.'[58] After all the results were in, Gladstone's former private secretary, Edward Hamilton, noted of Chamberlain in his diary that 'One hears on all sides that he has lost all his influence and incurred the enmity of his late followers.'[59]

What the general election of 1885 seemed to confirm, was that, if the Liberal Party was to continue to operate as an effective political force, it was crucial that it should remain a 'broad church', embracing the widest possible range of opinions. Chamberlain, in spite of his aggressive rhetoric, may never have seriously expected that it would be possible, or even desirable, to eliminate the Whig element from the Liberal Party, but events had in any case shown that it was unrealistic even to give the impression that the radicals could do without their aristocratic allies. Chamberlain was simply not in command of a united body of radicals capable of sweeping the Whigs into oblivion. The Whigs themselves were understandably jubilant at a result which demonstrated that they still had a vital role to play in Liberal politics. Lord Richard Grosvenor, the Liberal chief whip, estimated that only 101 out of the 333 or so Liberal MPs were radicals.[60] As for Gladstone, the friction between rival Liberals exhibited during the election campaign had served to reaffirm his belief that his leadership was indispensable for the preservation of party unity. In many respects, therefore, the first general election under the new electoral dispensation appeared to reinforce the Liberal status quo.

NOTES

1.   See T. A. Jenkins, *Gladstone, Whiggery and the Liberal Party, 1874–1886* (Oxford, 1988) pp. 39–50, for this climate of opinion.

2. Coleridge to Sir William Heathcote, 8 June 1877 in E. H. Coleridge, *Life and Correspondence of John Duke, Lord Coleridge, Lord Chief Justice of England* (London, 1904), vol. 2, pp. 267–8.

3. Richard Shannon, *Gladstone and the Bulgarian Agitation 1876* (2nd edn, Brighton, 1975) pp. 104–12.

4. Ann P. Saab, *Reluctant Icon: Gladstone, Bulgaria and the Working Classes, 1856–1878* (Harvard, 1991) p. 102 (and pp. 96–123 generally).

5. Ibid., p. 139 (and pp. 129–50 generally).

6. Ibid., p. 163 (and pp. 151–91 generally).

7. Hartington to Granville, 18 December 1876, in Bernard Holland, *Life of Spencer Compton, Eighth Duke of Devonshire, 1833–1908* (London, 1911) vol. 1, pp. 185–7.

8. Hartington to Spencer, 12 November 1876, in Peter Gordon (ed.), *The Red Earl: The Papers of the Fifth Earl Spencer, 1835–1910* (Northants Record Society, 1981–6) vol. 1, pp. 127–9.

9. Jenkins, *Whiggery*, pp. 69–71.

10. Ibid., Appendix I.

11. Ibid., pp. 82, 107.

12. Holland, *Devonshire*, vol. 1, pp. 249–54.

13. D. A. Hamer, *The Politics of Electoral Pressure* (Brighton, 1977) pp. 200–38.

14. See Jenkins, *Whiggery*, pp. 83–98.

15. See H. C. G. Matthew (ed.), *The Gladstone Diaries*, vol. IX (Oxford, 1986) pp. lvii–lxix.

16. M. R. D. Foot (ed.), *W. E. Gladstone: Midlothian Speeches 1879* (Leicester, 1971) third speech.

17. Richard Shannon, 'Midlothian: 100 Years After', in Peter J. Jagger (ed.), *Gladstone, Politics and Religion* (London, 1983).

18. Mundella to Robert Leader, December 1879, in Eugenio F. Biagini, *Liberty, Retrenchment and Reform* (Cambridge, 1992) p. 411. My italics.

19. See T. A. Jenkins, 'Gladstone, the Whigs and the Leadership of the Liberal Party, 1879–1880', *Historical Journal*, XXVII (1984).

20. This summary of the election is based on H. J. Hanham, *Elections and Party Management: Politics in the Time of Disraeli and Gladstone* (2nd edn, Brighton, 1978) pp. 30–2, 227–32.

21. K. O. Morgan, *Wales in British Politics, 1868–1922* (3rd edn, Cardiff, 1980) p. 56; I. G. C. Hutchison, *A Political History of Scotland, 1832–1924* (Edinburgh, 1986) pp. 134–49.

22. Jenkins, 'Leadership of Liberal Party', pp. 356–8.

23. Lord Derby's diary, 2 December 1882, Fifteenth Earl of Derby MSS (Liverpool Record Office).

24. Dilke's diary, 2 March 1881, BL Add MSS 43924. Courtney and Lefevre were other radical junior ministers.

25. Ronald Robinson and John Gallagher, *Africa and the Victorians* (London, 1961) pp. 207–8.

26. Dilke's diary, 22 September 1884, BL Add MSS 43926.

27. Robinson and Gallagher, *Africa and Victorians*, pp. 76–121.

28. Ibid., pp. 145–9.

29. Chamberlain to Morley, 11 and 15 February 1885, Chamberlain MSS (Birmingham University Library) JC5/54/607, 612. The subsequent Penjdeh crisis, which led to Gladstone's ministry making preparations for war against Russia in defence of the Afghan frontier, provided a smokescreen for Britain's evacuation of the Sudan.

30. These different perspectives are explored by J. P. Parry, *Democracy and Religion: Gladstone and the Liberal Party, 1867–1875* (Cambridge, 1986).

31. Jenkins, *Whiggery*, pp. 112–17.

32. Hartington to Gladstone, 19 December 1880, BL Add MSS 44145, f. 160.

33. Allen Warren, 'Forster, the Liberals and New Directions in Irish Policy, 1880–1882', *Parliamentary History*, VI (1987).

34. Jenkins, *Whiggery*, pp. 153–61.

35. Ibid., pp. 165–9.

36. See D. A. Hamer, *Liberal Politics in the Age of Gladstone and Rosebery* (Oxford, 1972) pp. 57–78, for this interpretation.

37. See Jenkins, *Whiggery*, pp. 230–41, for this paragraph.

38. Dilke's diary, 7 July 1882, BL Add MSS 43925.

39. D. W. R. Bahlman (ed.), *The Diaries of Sir Edward Walter Hamilton, 1880–1885* (2 vols, Oxford, 1972) entries for 29 August 1880, 3 April 1884, 31 August 1881, 14 May 1884, 14 April 1885.

40. Herbert, Viscount Gladstone, *After Thirty Years* (London, 1928) pp. 166–78, 195–7.

41. Jenkins, *Whiggery*, pp. 146–76, and Appendix II.

42. T. W. Heyck, *The Dimensions of British Radicalism: The Case of Ireland, 1874–1895* (Illinois, 1974).

43. For these motions, see respectively, *Daily News*, 15 June 1881, and *Manchester Guardian*, 16 June 1881; *Daily News*, 20 March 1884; *Leeds Mercury*, 24 March 1884; *Manchester Guardian*, 22 and 24 November 1884.

44. Lord Derby's diary, 27 November 1884, 21 April 1884, 8 January, 1885, Derby MSS.

45. Ibid., 7 December 1884.

46. National Liberal Federation, *Proceedings*, 31 May 1877.

47. Chamberlain to Morley, 19 May 1883, Chamberlain MSS, JC5/54/505.

48. D. A. Hamer (ed.), *The Radical Programme 1885* (Brighton, 1971).

49. J. L. Garvin, *Life of Joseph Chamberlain*, vol. I (London, 1932) pp. 548–52.

50. This article is included in Hamer's edition of *The Radical Programme*.

51. A point first made by C. H. D. Howard, 'Joseph Chamberlain and the Unauthorised Programme', *English Historical Review*, LXV (1950).

52. Jenkins, *Whiggery*, pp. 213–19.

53. Helen C. Colman, *Jeremiah James Colman: A Memoir* (privately printed, 1905) pp. 308–9, 356.

54. Jenkins, *Whiggery*, pp. 211–12.
55. See Alan Simon, 'Church Disestablishment as a Factor in the General Election of 1885', *Historical Journal*, XVIII (1975).
56. Ibid., pp. 818–19.
57. Chamberlain to Caine, 4 December 1885, in J. Newton, *W. S. Caine MP* (London, 1907) p. 124.
58. Kay Shuttleworth to Rylands, 28 November 1885, in L. G. Rylands, *Correspondence and Speeches of Mr. Peter Rylands, MP* (Manchester, 1890) vol. 1, pp. 352–3. See also Jenkins, *Whiggery*, pp. 227–9.
59. Hamilton's diary, 8 December 1885, BL Add MSS 48642.
60. Grosvenor to Gladstone, 12 December 1885, BL Add MSS 44316, f. 148.

6 The Crisis of Late-Victorian Liberalism

Introduction

While the overall result of the 1885 general election superficially confirms the Liberals' status as the natural majority party in British politics, it is impossible to ignore the reality that the social and political environment in which they were now operating was potentially inimical to their long-term success. The prosperity of the Liberal Party during the early and mid-Victorian years can be attributed in large part to the fact that it was the product of a specific stage in the development of British industrial society, one in which certain religious and occupational groups, heavily committed to the Liberal cause, possessed disproportionate electoral influence owing to the restricted nature of the franchise. By the late-Victorian period, however, as the British economy approached 'maturity', and as the electorate was further extended through the general application of the principle of household suffrage, major changes in the distribution of support for the political parties were making themselves apparent. The ability of the Conservatives, despite their defeat in 1885, to win a majority of English *borough* seats, was indicative of the way that the traditional basis of the Liberals' electoral hegemony was being undermined.

Changing Social and Electoral Patterns

There is a tendency to assume that the only victims of economic decline within the Liberal Party during the late-nineteenth century were the 'Whigs', those from aristocratic and landed backgrounds. It is certainly true that the agricultural depression of this period, brought about by the growth of cheap foreign imports, seriously eroded the incomes of many members of the traditional ruling elite. The effects of this depression were undoubtedly one of the reasons for the renewed decline in the proportion of Liberal MPs from aristocratic and landed backgrounds (there had been little change between 1874 and 1880), as an analysis of the 334 Liberals listed in *Dod's Parliamentary Companion* for 1886 indicates (Table 7).[1] The most interesting feature of these figures is that, while all of the component parts of the aristocratic and landed interest experienced a decline, their loss was accounted for not by any substantial increase in the proportion of businessmen in the party, but by a growing diversity of social backgrounds amongst Liberal MPs. Those listed in the miscellaneous category include four publishers or printers, four newspaper proprietors, three newspaper editors or journalists, four members of the Stock Exchange, five university professors, three scientists, five doctors or surgeons, and three farmers. In fact, if we add the twelve 'Lib–Lab' members to the miscellaneous group, this accounts for 15 per cent of the parliamentary party. Nevertheless, the aristocratic and landed Liberal MPs still constituted a substantial group in 1886, slightly more than one-third of the parliamentary party, if the 'Gentlemen' are included, and, with the ability of many such men to

Table 7　*Social Background of Liberal MPs, 1886*

			(1874)
Peerage connections	23	(6.9%)	(10.3%)
Baronets	25	(7.5%)	(8.2%)
Baronets' sons	8	(2.4%)	(3.3%)
Landed gentry	40	(12.0%)	(16.5%)
Heirs of gentry	2	(0.6%)	(1.2%)
'Gentlemen'	16	(4.8%)	(6.6%)
Merchants/manufacturers	102	(30.5%)	(29.6%)
Bankers	5	(1.5%)	(2.1%)
Lawyers	54	(16.2%)	(12.8%)
Working men	12	(3.6%)	
Miscellaneous	38	(11.4%)	(5.0%)
No information	9	(2.7%)	(3.7%)

diversify their investments in order to cushion the effects of the agricultural depression,[2] it must surely be a mistake to suppose that they could have had no future role to play in Liberal politics.

In any case, difficulties arising from the pressure of economic change were not confined to one section of the Liberal Party. Much is often made, for instance, of the fact that in 1885 the Liberals appear to have captured the support of many of the newly enfranchised agricultural labourers, but it must be observed that this too was clearly a declining occupational group. Another such group, with a longer association with Liberalism, included craftsmen and outworkers in industries such as woollen textiles, hosiery, and boots and shoes, who were gradually disappearing as a result of the tendency, throughout the second half of the nineteenth century, for factory-based industrial production to become the norm. Artisans in certain industrial sectors such as metal-working and engineering were also being squeezed, as a result of the growth of foreign competition. The slow demise of these varied occupational groups, all of which had strong connections with religious nonconformity, only served to exacerbate the general dilemma confronting the nonconformist sects, which, along with other religious denominations, found themselves being swamped in the rapidly expanding towns and cities, where the British population was increasingly coming to be concentrated. For one reason or another, therefore, many of the elements whose participation had enabled the Liberal Party to flourish in the past, were struggling to survive in the heavily urbanised and industrialised environment that characterised late-Victorian Britain.

The franchise and redistribution reforms of 1884–5 registered the consequences of these long-term economic and social changes, and an electoral system that had been seriously unrepresentative of the British nation was brought substantially up to date. Arguably the most important feature of the reforms was not the extension of household suffrage to the counties, but the large-scale redistribution of seats, which finally ended the gross over-representation of small boroughs in Southern England. In all, 132 seats (plus 6 newly created ones) were made available for redistribution, and the main area to gain was Greater London, whose representation increased from 22 to 62 MPs. Ominously for the Liberals, however, this was an area where the Conservatives had been making headway at elections since the late 1860s (it is surely no coincidence that there was little tradition of nonconformity in the metropolis), and it was the Conservatives who proved to be the beneficiaries of redistribution in 1885, winning 36 London seats. Indeed, their prospects had been further enhanced by a second feature of the Redistribution Act, the widespread creation of single-member constituencies. This had the effect, both in London and in major provincial cities like Manchester, Sheffield and Leeds, of constructing a number of predominantly suburban constituencies, dominated by the expanding 'white collar' workers in the tertiary sector, another distinct phenomenon of the late-Victorian period. The growing alarm amongst such voters at the radical tendencies within Gladstonian Liberalism had been evident since Disraeli's attempt to woo them in the early 1870s.

In so far as the Liberals managed to compensate for their losses in the boroughs through gains in the counties, this cannot be accounted for solely in terms of the agricultural labourers' vote. As a result of the Redistribution Act, 74 small boroughs, mainly in Southern England, were absorbed into their surrounding county constituencies, but it is significant that in 1880 these boroughs had elected 50 Liberal to 37 Conservative MPs. Liberal gains in the southern counties of England in 1885, therefore, were in part due to the incorporation into these constituencies of small boroughs, many of which had strong Liberal traditions. Furthermore, the redistribution of seats had brought additional representation to the more populous northern counties of England, and in these the voters newly-enfranchised by the third Reform Act included miners, potters, weavers, and other such occupational groups, living in industrial villages and small towns, as well as agricultural labourers. The picture that emerges, if we compare the 12 English counties north of a line from the Humber to the Bristol Channel (but excluding those counties on the Welsh border), and the 27 remaining 'southern' counties, is revealing. As Table 8 shows, over half of the seats won by Liberals in the English counties, in 1885, were in the 12 'northern' counties.

Table 8 *Election Results in the English Counties, 1880–85*[3]

| | 1880 | | 1885 | |
	Lib.	Con.	Lib.	Con.
27 Southern counties	21	87	63	66
12 Northern counties	29	33	69	33
Total	50	120	132	99

The reason for the sweeping redistribution of seats, and the creation of single-member constituencies, both of which seem to have worked against the Liberals' own interests, was that these were the terms demanded by the Conservative leader, Lord Salisbury, in November 1884, in return for his co-operation in allowing a franchise and redistribution package to pass through the House of Lords. Salisbury's determination to use the leverage provided by the Conservatives' domination of the upper House, in order to secure a drastic redistribution settlement, stemmed from his perception that there was really little point in maintaining an electoral system which – the 'freak' result of 1874 apart – had produced decades of Liberal majorities. Immediately after the Conservatives' defeat in 1880, for instance, Salisbury had expressed to Beaconsfield his view that no purpose would be served by preserving the small English boroughs, since these were predominantly Liberal, and later remarks show that he was well aware of the possibilities offered by the growth of what he called 'Villa Toryism' in the suburban areas[4] In spite of the misgivings of both Whigs and radicals, Gladstone accepted Salisbury's terms for the sake of obtaining a settlement and thus avoiding an unwanted conflict with the House of Lords. It would be true to say, therefore, that in 1884 Salisbury 'dished' the Liberals more thoroughly than Disraeli had the Whigs in 1867.

Intellectual Challenges

If the electoral foundations of the Liberal hegemony were being threatened, by the mid-1880s, other challenges were emerging, at the same time, to the principles underlying the Liberals' accustomed intellectual ascendancy. It was obvious that Great Britain no longer enjoyed an easy supremacy in the sphere of world trade, and that its relative position was being weakened by the emergence of competition from rapidly industrialising rivals, particularly Germany and the United States, which was hitting certain sectors of the British economy, like agriculture and the iron industry, very badly. The consequent sense of crisis – a Royal Commission was appointed in 1885 to inquire into what was being called a 'depression' in trade and industry – naturally prompted a rigorous questioning of the assumptions upon which British governmental policy had for so long been based. At one extreme, socialism first became a fashionable creed during the early 1880s, especially amongst educated young people, and there was a proliferation of organisations, such as Hyndman's Social Democratic Federation, William Morris's Socialist League, and the Fabian Society. Although the membership of these organisations was numerically small, their ideas and activities attracted a good deal of attention at a time when doubts were surfacing about the continued applicability of fundamental Liberal beliefs such as the autonomy of the individual, and the bias towards a policy of non-intervention by the State. On the other hand, the borough elections of 1885 revealed that many Conservative candidates were exploiting unease about foreign competition by espousing the heretical idea of 'fair trade', a policy of retaliatory tariffs designed to protect British producers. In this way, hard questions were being asked about the coping-stone of Britain's Liberal commercial policy – Free Trade.

The mid-Victorian Liberal gospel of progress was thus increasingly being called into question by the 1880s. Doubts were also growing amongst many members of the intelligentsia, who had been so enthusiastic in their advocacy of parliamentary reform and Liberal policy in the 1860s, as to the direction in which 'democracy' was taking the country. To men such as A. V. Dicey, Henry Sidgwick and G. C. Brodrick, who had seen parliamentary reform as a means towards the creation of a rational polity in which the wisdom of the educated elite would naturally exert a wide influence, it was alarming to witness the vulgar, irrational manifestations of democracy in practice. In particular, many intellectuals were becoming increasingly disillusioned with the demagogic style of leadership associated with Gladstone, who, through such episodes as the Midlothian campaigns, seemed to be gleefully pandering to the crudest instincts of the masses.[5] There is also a link here with a wider concern amongst much of the Liberal intelligentsia, about Britain's survival as a great imperial power in the face of hostile rivalry from France, Germany and Russia (and perhaps eventually the United States). A timely focus for such anxieties was provided by J. R. Seeley's widely read *The Expansion of England* (1883), which emphasised the need for Britain to strengthen the ties with her colonies in order to maintain her Great Power status. The stark message was that Britain needed to be strong if she was to survive, and there were already grave doubts as to whether the Liberal Party, headed by an idealist Prime Minister, and containing a substantial 'Little Englander' element, was equipped to provide the requisite firm government.

This issue was given greater immediacy by the impending crisis in Britain's relationship with Ireland. It was all too obvious, by the mid-

1880s, that the policy pursued by Gladstone's second ministry, of promoting land reform in an attempt to undermine popular support for the Home Rule Party, had been a failure. More seriously still, it was generally acknowledged that the inclusion of Ireland within the provisions of the country franchise reform of 1884, would serve to consolidate Parnell's grip in Ireland, an expectation that was duly fulfilled in 1885 when the Nationalists won 85 out of the 103 seats in Ireland. No Liberal was returned for an Irish constituency. The Liberals were thus to be confronted with an apparently insoluble problem: tradition suggested that they should be sympathetic to expressions of Irish Nationalism, in the same way as they had been in the case of more distant peoples like the Poles, Hungarians and Italians; but it was unclear how this could be reconciled with Britain's imperial concerns, which dictated that it was vital for Britain to maintain the Union with Ireland lest she precipitate the disintegration of her Empire.

Gladstone and Irish Home Rule

The motives behind Gladstone's Government of Ireland Bill, of 1886, which proposed the creation of a parliament in Dublin to deal with Irish affairs, remain a matter of considerable controversy. It is perhaps only fair to say at once that, given the sweeping success of the Parnellites at the 1885 general election, and the fear of a serious breakdown of law and order in Ireland if no action was taken, Gladstone was entitled to think that the British authorities had to do *something*. The 'Irish Question', it would have seemed to Gladstone, had become so pressing that it required a definite answer, one way or another.

An accusation frequently made by Conservative critics of Gladstone's policy at the time, and one which for many years after the event was widely accepted as an established fact, was that the commitment to Irish Home Rule was merely an unscrupulous bid by Gladstone for the support of Parnell, which he needed in order to regain the premiership. According to this view, Gladstone only became converted to Home Rule *after* the general election of 1885, which had left the Irish Nationalists holding the balance of power in the new House of Commons. The so-called 'Hawarden kite' of 17 December 1885, when Gladstone's youngest son, Herbert, leaked to the press details of his father's plan for Home Rule, was thus seen as a deliberate step designed to encourage Parnell to join with the Liberals for the purpose of removing from office Salisbury's minority Conservative government. Indeed this was precisely what happened, on 26 January 1886, and Gladstone was enabled to form his third ministry.

This cynical interpretation of Gladstone's conduct receives little support from historians nowadays. There is overwhelming evidence, notably in J. L. Hammond's monumental *Gladstone and the Irish Nation* (1938), to suggest that Gladstone's mind had been moving in the direction of Irish Home Rule during the summer and autumn of 1885, after the fall of his second ministry, but *before* the general election – at a time, in fact, when most Liberals were confidently anticipating that they would achieve an overall parliamentary majority. Indirect communications with Parnell, using his mistress, Katharine O'Shea, as an intermediary, had convinced Gladstone by early August that the Central Board plan proposed by Chamberlain in May was no longer a viable option, as it was not acceptable to the Irish Nationalists as a final settlement. 'Home Rule', in the sense of a legislative assembly for Ireland, was therefore seen by Gladstone as the only possible solution. During the summer and autumn, he cautiously revealed to a few of his Liberal colleagues the direction which his thinking on Ireland was taking. One recipient of Gladstone's hints was Lord Derby, who visited Hawarden Castle at the beginning of October, and recorded in his diary his conversation with the Liberal leader:

> He thought the question of the Irish Union one which must be studied seriously. He had been reading old debates upon it, including Pitt's speech in proposing it to Parliament [in 1800], and he was not satisfied with the argument in its favour. He had come to the conclusion that the Union was a mistake, and that no adequate justification had been shown for taking away the national life of Ireland. (These last words are nearly, if not exactly, those used by him.) . . . He did not agree in the assertion that the Irish would not be content with less than absolute legislative independence. . . . I asked whether he thought the English public would consent to repeal the Union on any terms – Whether the majority would not be against it? He shook his head, and said there was a vast amount of English prejudice to be reckoned with, and he did not know how that might be. One thing he saw plainly, that parliament could not go on as it had done: the Irish organisation had been perfected during the last ten years, the Irish had never been united as they were now . . . and it would be impossible to avoid coming to terms with them, if they returned

to the next Parliament 80 or 90 strong. . . . I listened with some surprise, for though I knew that he favoured the Irish claims, I was not prepared for what is in fact a declaration in favour of Home Rule.[6]

A great deal of confusion has arisen, however, owing to the fact that Gladstone refused to be pinned down as to precisely what his practical intentions were. His public speeches during the general election campaign, for instance, had little to say about Ireland, and what mention of the subject he did make was extremely general and vague. Similarly, when Herbert Gladstone flew the 'Hawarden kite', in December, Gladstone *père* still refused to confirm the accuracy of the revelations, and even when he came to form his third ministry, in January 1886, the basis on which he invited his colleagues to take office with him was that the government would simply 'examine' the question of Home Rule. All this has led some historians to argue that Gladstone really had no fixed intentions about his Irish policy, and that he was merely biding his time until circumstances revealed what would be the most expedient course for him to take.[7]

The great weakness of this interpretation is that it completely ignores the evidence about Gladstone's ripening opinions on Home Rule provided by Derby's diary and many other sources. Furthermore, it overlooks the possibility that Gladstone may have been deliberately vague about his plans precisely for the reason that he knew exactly what he wanted to achieve. In other words, the simplest explanation for the apparent contradictions in Gladstone's conduct is that while he had decided, before the general election of 1885, that Home Rule was the only answer to the Irish problem, he was aware that any sudden declaration of this opinion would be bound to split the Liberal Party, which was far from ready to embrace the idea of an Irish parliament. Gladstone therefore pursued a course of carefully refraining from publicising his intentions in the hope that he might gradually 'educate' his party, and indeed the country as a whole, into accepting his conclusion. What Gladstone seems to have been looking for, as he indicated in a letter to Lord Granville, in December 1885, was a 'healthful, slow fermentation in many minds, working towards the final product'.[8] From this perspective, the 'Hawarden kite' should be seen not as a calculated ploy by Gladstone, but as a blunder by his son, which only added to Gladstone's difficulties.

In his speech outlining the Government of Ireland Bill, when it finally emerged on 8 April 1886, Gladstone urged upon the House of

Commons the need for a break from the policies of past British governments, involving various mixtures of coercion and concession, which
had failed to get to the root of the Irish problem. A bold solution had
to be adopted, one that would recognise the legitimate aspirations of
the Irish people by establishing a legislative assembly in Dublin with
responsibility for Ireland's own affairs. It is essential to remember,
though, that the measure proposed by Gladstone did not grant Ireland
total independence. Although Irish representatives were no longer to be
sent to the Westminster parliament, that assembly would still have
retained control over such matters as foreign policy, defence and trade,
and Ireland was to have made an annual contribution to the Westminster parliament of £4,602,000 (equivalent to one-fifteenth of total
Imperial expenditure at that time). Nevertheless, Gladstone maintained
that his plan would serve to reconcile the Irish people to the Union
with Britain: 'the concession of local self-government is not the way to
sap or impair, but the way to strengthen and consolidate unity'.[9]

James Loughlin has demonstrated convincingly that Gladstone's perceptions of the nature of Irish society – of which his direct experience
was virtually nil – had been profoundly influenced by the historical
reading which he undertook during the summer and autumn of 1885,
once his interest in Ireland had been revived. The effect of this reading
was to produce in Gladstone's mind some rather eccentric ideas about
the consequences which Home Rule would have on Irish social life.
Gladstone managed to convince himself that there was nothing incompatible between Protestant landlordism and Irish Nationalism – had the
Protestant landowners not, after all, provided the leadership for the
nationalist movement in the late eighteenth century? This perspective
totally ignored, of course, the fact that recent Irish Nationalism had
been largely fuelled by agrarian grievances, but Gladstone was able to
believe that his Home Rule measure would serve to reintegrate the
landlords into Irish political and social life, encouraging them to reassert their position as the natural leaders of the Irish people.[10]

Peculiar as Gladstone's notions about Ireland may seem, there is no
reason to doubt his sincerity in pressing for the Home Rule Bill. But
this does not preclude the possibility that Gladstone's stance may also
have been influenced by other considerations, relating to the unity of
the Liberal Party and his authority over it. David Hamer, for example,
has suggested that Gladstone had one eye fixed on domestic political
concerns when he adopted Home Rule.[11] According to this view,
Gladstone saw the advantage of focusing his party's attention on some

single great unifying issue, as it encouraged the various Liberal sectional groups to subordinate their own particular projects – disestablishment, temperance reform and so on – for the sake of the greater cause which Gladstone had identified. The Home Rule commitment might thus be seen as another example of Gladstone's characteristic style of leadership: seeing how divided the party was on a wide range of domestic issues, during the protracted election campaign of 1885, he realised that the impending crisis over Irish policy could be used in order to divert the Liberals' attention away from their own quarrels. And of course there was the additional advantage that Ireland was a great moral cause, involvement in which would be spiritually beneficial to the Liberals in any case.

While certain episodes, like Irish Church disestablishment in 1868–9, and the onslaught against 'Beaconsfieldism' at Midlothian, seem to fit this model of Gladstone's leadership well, it is also necessary to stress the short-termism that helped to shape his strategy in the 1880s. In order to understand this, we have to remember that in April 1880 Gladstone had appeared to 'usurp' the Liberal leadership, which rightly belonged to Hartington. Gladstone rationalised his position by maintaining that he was only coming back for a specific purpose, to clear up the mess left behind by Beaconsfield's government, and that he would be retiring again as soon as this was accomplished, so that Hartington might be restored to his proper place. In practice, however, Gladstone succeeded in detecting a series of new problems, which he felt he needed to stay on a little longer in order to settle – he described them as 'specialities', issues which he felt only he was equipped to deal with effectively, such as the Irish Land Bill, the reform of parliamentary procedure, the franchise and redistribution bills, and the crisis with Russia in 1885.[12] If we follow this analysis through, Gladstone's renewed interest in Ireland, in 1885, fits into the pattern of 'specialities' which he always seemed able to discover at the requisite moment. Indeed, we can pinpoint the Cabinet crisis of May–June 1885, when Gladstone's colleagues were deadlocked over Chamberlain's plan for an Irish Central Board, as the decisive moment. After the Liberals fell from power, on 8 June, still with no decision having been reached as to the party's future Irish policy, Gladstone became convinced that it was imperative for him to carry on as leader for a little longer in order to preserve Liberal unity. Once this strategy was established, and Gladstone realised that the Central Board plan would not satisfy Parnell, he then moved towards the Home Rule solution.[13] If this interpretation is accepted, then the Liberal divisions manifested during the subsequent election campaign could not have prompted Gladstone's adoption of Home Rule: he had decided on this policy already, although the subsequent spectacle of Liberal disunity can only have confirmed his belief that his strategy was the correct one.

One other theory about Gladstone's behaviour which requires brief consideration is that put forward by Joseph Chamberlain in his *Political Memoir*, written in 1892 but only published in 1953.[14] Chamberlain alleged that Gladstone's adoption of Home Rule had been a deliberate stratagem designed to divert the public's attention away from Chamberlain's own programme of radical reforms. In the light of what was seen in the last chapter, about the difficulties into which Chamberlain's radical campaign had actually run during the autumn of 1885, his claim clearly has to be treated with scepticism. There may, all the same, be something to be said for Chamberlain's view if it is set in a wider context: Gladstone's Home Rule policy may not have been a direct response to Chamberlain's campaign, but it is possible that he may have regarded the Irish commitment as a useful means of setting the right moral tone for the new age of 'democratic' politics inaugurated by his third Reform Act. There is no doubt that Gladstone viewed with dismay the 'socialistic' tendencies apparent in the policies of the younger generation of radicals, like Chamberlain, as well as the leaning towards protectionism on the part of many Conservatives, and he took a very dim view of the vulgar brand of 'Tory Democracy' associated with Lord Randolph Churchill. It may well be the case, therefore, that Gladstone was tempted by the thought that it was his duty to postpone his retirement one more time in order to ensure that British political life, under the new electoral dispensation, got off onto the right footing. Certainly, this was an idea that was being expressed to him by others. Early in 1885, for example, when he had broached to Lord Acton the question of his retirement, Acton had responded urging him not to consider taking this step:

You mean that the new parliament, the first of our democratic constitution, shall begin its difficult and perilous course without the services of a leader who has greater experience and authority than any other man. You design to withdraw your assistance when most urgently needed, at the moment of most conservative apprehension and most popular excitement. By the choice of this particular moment for retirement you increase the danger of the critical transition, because nobody stands as you do between the old order of things and the new, or inspires general confidence.

Similarly, in the autumn of that year, as it became clear that Gladstone did intend to remain as leader, the response from his Whig colleague, Lord Kimberley, was carefully judged: 'the future of this Country will largely depend upon the impulse given at the commencement of the new political era. To give that impulse will be the fitting crown of your political career'.[15]

Gladstone himself was later to state, in a famous 'General Retrospect' written a year or two before his death, that he believed his initiative on Home Rule to have been one of those occasions during his career when he had exercised a 'striking gift', given to him by God. He described this gift as an ability to detect the elements necessary for creating a political movement in order to achieve some great objective. This was not the same thing, he insisted, as merely following public opinion: rather, it was 'an insight into the facts of particular eras, and their relations one to another, which generates in the mind a conviction that the materials exist for forming a public opinion, and for directing it to a particular end'.[16]

Whatever the conclusion one finally draws about Gladstone's perception of the nature of the 'Irish Question', or about the possibility that party and personal considerations also came into play, or even about the alleged role of 'Divine Providence', there is no reason to doubt that he was engaged in a genuine attempt to resolve the situation in Ireland. His strategy of public silence, maintained from the summer of 1885 until the spring of 1886, was intended to prevent the Liberal Party from breaking up, which it seemed bound to do if the issue was pressed too quickly. Gladstone seems to have believed, with characteristic self-confidence, that he could eventually persuade all Liberals, including recalcitrants like Hartington and Chamberlain, to fall into line behind his policy. Even when it became clear that a Liberal split of some kind was inevitable, there remained a possibility that this might not be fatal to the prospects of the Home Rule Bill. Only days before the critical division on the second reading, the uncertainty as to the course Chamberlain and his radical followers would take meant that the outcome was still in the balance, and it is worth speculating as to what might have happened if Gladstone's bill had narrowly survived this stage in the parliamentary process. In these circumstances, armed with the moral weight provided by a second-reading victory, there would have been no need for Gladstone to dissolve parliament: he might have proceeded, instead, by offering to drop the bill until the next session, and then relied on pressure from constituency associations and extra-parliamentary rallies to force the dissident Liberals to toe the line. Gladstone might still have hoped, in other words, that he could prevent any Liberal schism from becoming formalised. Whether he could then have overcome the resistance of the House of Lords, and of Queen Victoria, must remain in doubt, though the precedents of Irish Church disestablishment in 1869, and of franchise and redistribution in 1884, would have given Gladstone some encouragement. At the very least, Gladstone must have hoped that he could establish a firm Liberal commitment to Home Rule that would be his legacy to the party.

The Liberal Schism of 1886

In the event, of course, Gladstone's Home Rule bill was defeated at the second-reading stage, on 8 June 1886, by a majority of 341 to 311, with some 94 Liberal MPs voting against their own Prime Minister. Gladstone's response was to seek an immediate dissolution of parliament, and at the ensuing general election the dissident Liberals, known as 'Liberal Unionists', operated an electoral pact with the Conservatives in order to improve their chances of survival. Once the election was over, the Gladstonian Liberals were reduced to just 191 MPs, and the Conservatives, with 316 seats, were able to take office, buoyed up by the support of the 78-strong Liberal Unionist Party. This marked the beginning of a period of political ascendancy by the alliance of Conservatives and Liberal Unionists, which was to last for almost twenty years.

The explanation traditionally offered by historians for the schism in the Liberal Party was that this represented the formal 'revolt of the Whigs'.[17] In other words, those Liberals who deserted Gladstone in 1886 were thought to be the remaining members of the aristocratic and landowning classes, who, for some years past, had been increasingly alarmed by the growth of radicalism within the Liberal Party, with all that that implied in terms of social reform and redistributive taxation. The Home Rule crisis of 1886, so the argument goes, was merely a convenient pretext for a split that would inevitably have happened in any case, because of long-term developments within Liberalism. Opposition to Gladstone's Irish policy provided a fig leaf to conceal the ideological nakedness of the Whigs, who had long since ceased to play a positive role in Liberal politics. It should be noted that this interpretation was one to which Gladstone himself had given credence, when he attributed the actions of his opponents to selfish class-interest.

It cannot be denied that large numbers of Liberal aristocrats and landowners did rebel against Gladstone over the Home Rule issue. The situation in the House of Lords is complicated by the fact that in 1886 the Home Rule Bill was defeated in the Commons, and so it was not until 1893, when Gladstone produced his second bill, that the peers had an opportunity to vote on the question. At that time, only 41 peers, including a few Whig administrators such as Spencer, Kimberley and Ripon, supported Gladstone, while a record 419 voted against Home Rule, marking the virtual demise of the traditional Liberal aristocracy. In the House of Commons, however, matters were not so clear-cut. An analysis of the social composition of the 94 dissident Liberal Unionists, compared with the social composition of the Liberal Party as a whole, produces the results shown in Table 9. MPs connected to the aristocratic and landed interest clearly constituted the largest group within the Liberal Unionists, amounting to roughly 53 per cent (if we include 'Gentlemen') of the total, at a time when such men accounted for 34 per cent of all Liberals. There were somewhat

Table 9 *Social Background of Liberal Unionist MPs, 1886*

			(All Libs)
Peerage connections	11	(11.7%)	(6.9%)
Baronets	13	(13.8%)	(7.5%)
Baronets' sons	1	(1.1%)	(2.4%)
Landed gentry	16	(17.0%)	(12.0%)
Heirs of gentry	1	(1.1%)	(0.6%)
'Gentlemen'	8	(8.5%)	(4.8%)
Merchants/Manufacturers	26	(27.7%)	(30.5%)
Bankers	2	(2.1%)	(1.5%)
Lawyers	11	(11.7%)	(16.2%)
Miscellaneous	5	(5.3%)	(11.4%)

fewer lawyers among the Liberal Unionists than in the Liberal Party as a whole, and the Liberal Unionists were obviously a less socially diverse group in terms of members in the miscellaneous category. What is most striking, though, is that almost 30 per cent of Liberal Unionist MPs, including such prominent *radicals* as Joseph Chamberlain and John Bright, had backgrounds in business, a proportion that was almost the same as that for the whole of the Liberal Party.[18] In the light of these figures, it seems doubtful whether the notion of a 'revolt of the Whigs' provides an adequate explanation for what happened to the Liberal Party in 1886. If it is true that Hartington and many other Whigs did break away from Gladstone, it is necessary to explain why so many other Liberals went with them.

Furthermore, the conduct of Hartington and the 'Whigs' prior to 1886 also casts doubt on the assumption that their departure from the Liberal Party was only a matter of time. As was shown in Chapter 5, Hartington had proved to be a competent leader of the party, in the extremely difficult circumstances of the second half of the 1870s, and his decision to make way for Gladstone as Prime Minister, in 1880, had been intended as a temporary arrangement. His subsequent behaviour during Gladstone's second ministry, frequently fighting hard for his own position, but holding back from the drastic step of resignation, however distasteful some of the government's policies were, also indicates that he had not abandoned the ambition to lead the Liberals after Gladstone's – always apparently imminent – retirement. As late as December 1883, in a speech to his Lancashire constituents, Hartington had commended the merits and achievements of the Whig tradition:

> I confess I am not dissatisfied with the position that the Whig party have in former times occupied, and that I believe they occupy at the present time. I admit that the Whigs are not the leaders in popular movements, but the Whigs have been able, as I think, to the great advantage of the Country, to direct, and guide, and moderate those popular movements. They have formed a connecting link between the advanced party and those classes which, possessing property, power and influence, are naturally averse to change, and I think I may claim that it is greatly owing to their guidance and to their action that the great and beneficial changes which have been made in the direction of popular reform in this Country, have been made not by the shock of revolutionary agitation, but by the calm and peaceful process of constitutional acts.[19]

Although the impression is frequently given that the Whigs were already deserting the Liberal Party in sizeable numbers in the years leading up to 1886, there appear to be remarkably few cases which bear this view out. It is perfectly true, of course, that there were considerable political tensions within the Liberal Party, but it might reasonably be countered that this was a natural state of affairs for the 'party of progress'. During the 1885 general election, for example, much alarm was created by the tone of Chamberlain's radical campaign, and some Whig magnates publicly refused to endorse Liberal candidates who espoused Chamberlain's views, especially on land reform, but this generally seems to have been the limit of their alienation from the Liberal cause: abstention, rather than defection.[20] In any case, as we have already seen, Chamberlain's campaign ran into great difficulties during the autumn of 1885, which hardly suggests that he was strong enough to drive the Whigs out of the Liberal Party. On the contrary, the setback to Chamberlain's ambitions at this time ought to have given the Whigs *more* reason, not less, to continue to fight their corner within the Liberal Party. It is richly ironic, but also highly significant, that those Whigs who did leave the party in 1886 found themselves acting in alliance with the radical they were supposedly trying to escape from!

I. G. C. Hutchison's study of Scottish politics confirms the view that relations between Whigs and radicals had not reached breaking point in the mid-1880s.[21] As in the case of England, there certainly was friction between rival Liberal groups – though the main issue at stake here was the position of the Established Kirk – but these differences had not become irreconcilable, and there is little evidence of Whigs drifting away from the party before 1886. Even during the general election campaign of 1885, when the disestablishment crisis was at its peak, it appears that, in the final analysis, party loyalties prevailed over religious concerns. In fact, the election demonstrated that those Liberals sympathetic to the Kirk were too powerful to be ignored, and by the beginning of 1886 an accommodation had been reached between the Whig-dominated Scottish Liberal Association and the National Liberal Federation of Scotland (effectively a pressure group, campaigning for disestablishment). When the Liberal schism occurred, it again seems to have cut across existing lines of division: a number of prominent Whig peers were to be found supporting Gladstone's policy, such as Rosebery, Aberdeen, Elgin and Dalhousie, whereas the opponents of the measure included prominent nonconformist-radicals, like Duncan

McLaren, J. Boyd Kinnear, Cameron Corbett, and a crofter MP, Charles Fraser-Mackintosh.

If the Liberal schism of 1886 cannot be reduced merely to the level of crude economic determinism, we are left with the possibility that there may have been genuine ideological reasons for the refusal of many Liberals to follow Gladstone's lead. Hartington's speech on 9 April, following on from Gladstone's introduction of the Home Rule Bill, laid the groundwork for many Liberal attacks on their own leader's measure. The paramount duty of politicians, according to Hartington, was to preserve Imperial unity, and it was absurd to suppose that a bill which proposed to end Irish representation at Westminster, yet still subjected them to taxation for Imperial purposes (in effect, taxation without representation, as many other speakers pointed out), would provide a lasting settlement of the Irish problem. In Hartington's view, Gladstone's scheme would merely serve as a stepping-stone to the complete separation of Ireland from Britain, as Irish politicians would inevitably be tempted to use the institutions of self-government provided, in order to detach themselves completely. Given that the Irish were to have control over their own police force, Hartington argued that it would be impossible for the British government to prevent separation from taking place unless they were prepared to resort to large-scale military intervention. Hartington's response to the immediate situation in Ireland was that the Liberals must again show themselves to be the party of law and order, willing to apply coercive methods if necessary. While he did not rule out future concessions to the Irish in the direction of limited local self-government, this had to be a gradual process and could only be undertaken once social stability had been restored.[22]

Naturally, many other considerations were linked to this general concern for the preservation of Britain's Imperial greatness. For the Whigs, of course, the ultimate prospect of an independent Irish State raised fears about the despoliation of landlords, which would have included some of their own number. For many businessmen, on the other hand, the possibility that an independent Ireland would erect tariff barriers against British goods was an obvious cause for concern. In the case of Scotland, the preservation of economic ties with Ulster was certainly of great importance, but so too was the religious bond between Scottish and Ulster Presbyterians, and the prospect of the Ulstermen being persecuted by a Catholic-dominated parliament in Dublin therefore aroused passionate feelings.[23] Anti-Catholicism was undoubtedly a significant element in the Liberal Unionist equation, and this may have been particularly true in areas like the South West of England, where there was a large concentration of Wesleyan Methodists – a protestant sect notorious for its antipathy to Roman Catholics. Nor can we entirely rule out personal factors. Joseph Chamberlain, for example, while genuinely sharing the ideological concerns for the unity of the Empire, was clearly influenced by his anger at Parnell for not accepting his Central Board proposal of 1885, and his fury at the way Gladstone had proceeded to pre-empt his position by adopting a more radical policy. In the case of Hartington, it is hard not to believe that memories of the murder of his brother, Lord Frederick Cavendish, in Phoenix Park in May 1882, did not play some part in hardening his attitude.

Beyond this range of ideological, economic, religious and personal reasons why so many Liberals found the Home Rule Bill unacceptable, there was also considerable resentment at the way Gladstone had sought to impose his policy upon the party without consultation. As one Whiggish back-bencher saw it, Gladstone had suddenly commanded his party to desert its former policy and obediently adopt a radically different one solely on the grounds that he now declared it to be safe; but the Hon. Arthur Elliot was 'one of those who think that the Liberal Party did not find its principles for the first time on the 8th of April last', and he denounced what he saw as 'an entire break in the traditions of the Liberal Party'.[24] This feeling brought to a head the growing dislike of what was seen as the intolerably dictatorial tendency of Gladstone's leadership, something that was fundamentally alien to a party which gained so much of its identity from the belief in individual opinion. In 1886 even the veteran radical, John Bright, was complaining bitterly about Gladstone's authoritarian style, describing him as a 'Dictator' whose obstinate behaviour threatened to wreck the Liberal Party.[25]

This analysis of the reasons for the Liberal schism has proceeded so far on the assumption that what needs to be explained is why certain Liberals opposed Gladstone's Home Rule bill, but we might pertinently turn the problem round and ask why it was that the majority of MPs supported Gladstone in pursuing a policy for which they had no electoral mandate – most Liberals had played the Irish issue down as much as possible during the 1885 election campaign – and which no more than a handful of them had previously advocated. It is certainly a very striking feature of the Home Rule crisis that few of those who voted in favour of Gladstone's bill appear to have done so with any great confidence that the measure was right, or that it was likely to settle the Irish Question. Indeed, there was considerable lukewarmness towards Gladstone's plan, but this was tempered by a sense of helplessness, a feeling that, once Gladstone had publicly declared his opinion in favour of Home Rule, there was no realistic alternative but to go along with their leader's plan. As the future Liberal Prime Minister, Henry Campbell Bannerman, lamented, during the confused period in January 1886 when it was unclear whether or not there would be a Home Rule Bill, 'It is not as if any of us thought it a good thing in itself, or beneficial either to Ireland or England. . . . We regard Home Rule only as a dangerous and damaging *pis aller*.[26] Arguably, at the end of the day, loyalty to Gladstone, and loyalty to the Liberal Party as a whole, was the main determinant of the course adopted by the majority of MPs.

An interesting survey by the leading London evening paper, the *Pall Mall Gazette*, on 3 May 1886, suggested that the strongest support for Gladstone's policy came not from Liberal MPs, nor from the ordinary Liberal voters, but from the wirepullers who controlled the local party machinery:

> The Liberal associations throughout the Country are much more in favour of Mr. Gladstone than the members whom they return to support him in the House of Commons. . . . The caucus exists in a large measure to win elections, and anything and everything which threatens success at the next electoral combat is hateful in the eyes of the thoroughgoing Liberal association. . . . Neither the members of parliament at the top nor the rank and file at the bottom are so keen in support of Mr. Gladstone as the members of the Liberal hundreds who stand between the two. . . . Nearly all the resolutions of Liberal associations within the last ten days accept the principle of Home Rule . . . [but] While this is a somewhat remarkable phenomenon, it is perhaps less significant than the fact that, with all their devotion to Mr. Gladstone, the Liberal managers are wonderfully unanimous in expressing their acceptance of his bills in very guarded terms.[27]

Later the same month the National Liberal Federation itself declared its backing for Gladstone, and in so doing repudiated the authority of its own creator, Chamberlain. It would not be going too far to suggest that it was in 1886, rather than before, that the Liberal Party became, truly, the 'Gladstonian Liberal Party', as Gladstone finally succeeded in creating a party in his own image.

Consequences of the Liberal Schism

In the months immediately following the Liberal schism, there remained a possibility that the rupture need not prove to be a permanent one. The fact that the Liberal Unionists declined an invitation to enter into a coalition government with the Conservatives, indicated that men like Hartington and Chamberlain were unwilling to abandon their Liberal identity, and on the Gladstonian side, too, there is evidence, for instance in the Scottish constituencies, of continued affection and sympathy for the Liberal Unionists.[28] Reconciliation could only have taken place, however, in the event of Gladstone's speedy departure from the political scene; but, as it became clear that the veteran leader was determined to carry on and preserve the party's commitment to his Home Rule Bill, so the prospects for Liberal reunion faded. The pressure of events forced the Liberal Unionists into a closer association with the policies of Lord Salisbury's government, which included a rigorous enforcement of coercion in Ireland. The Gladstonian Liberals' instinctive dislike of coercion was intensified by the sight of the Conservatives applying it, though it is noticeable that Gladstone reserved his most violent attacks for the Liberal Unionists, who were helping to keep the Conservatives in office. The very nature of political partisanship thus ensured that the Gladstonian Liberals and Liberal Unionists were driven further apart, and it is probably true to say that, by the end of the 1887 session of parliament, Liberal reunion was no longer a realistic prospect. It now becomes necessary to consider the implications for the Liberal Party of the loss of the Liberal Unionists.

Some historians have expressed the view that the schism of 1886 had a distorting effect on the subsequent development of the Liberal Party. Richard Shannon, for instance, in his account of Gladstone's involvement in the Bulgarian agitation of 1876, suggested that the ultimate consequence of Gladstone's return to active political life was the 'ruin of radicalism', as the Liberals were prevented from following their natural destiny of becoming a party inspired and controlled by Chamberlainite radicalism. More recently, Colin Matthew seems to have adopted a somewhat similar view, arguing that if Liberal unity could have been preserved, and a settlement of the Home Rule question achieved, this 'would have cleared the way for the development of the Liberal party as a party of positive social welfare'.[29] After all, it was Chamberlain who, operating within the context of the Unionist alliance in the 1890s, was ahead of most Liberals in advocating new ideas of social reform such as old age pensions, industrial arbitration, and a universal system of accident insurance for workmen.

The obvious reservation about such lines of argument is that the fate of Chamberlain's radical campaign, during the 1885 general election, shows that he was incapable of carrying the radicals, let alone the rest of the Liberal Party, in support of a programme of measures which fell a long way short of his later Unionist social reforms. Chamberlain's 'Jacobinical' language, in 1885, which implicitly threatened the sanctity of all forms of property, and not just that of the monopolistic landlords, was clearly alien to the thinking of many fellow radicals, who regarded Liberalism as an essentially classless creed. An undiluted form of Chamberlainism, therefore, was not a viable option for the Liberal Party.

This still leaves the question of what role the Whig leader, Hartington, might have played in the hypothetical situation of a united, post-Gladstonian Liberal Party. Given the evidence suggesting that the revolt by many of the Whigs was by no means an inevitable event, it is worth considering the possibility that a Hartingtonian style of leadership might have presented certain benefits to the Liberals. Hartington's potential appeal would presumably have lain in his ability to please different sections of the party for different reasons: on the one hand, his imperialist views would have satisfied radicals of the Chamberlain–Dilke school, while on the other, his cautious but never entirely negative – approach to questions of domestic reform would have been reassuring to radicals of another school, like John Bright and John Morley, as well as to Whigs and moderate Liberals concerned for the rights of property. Exactly how far a Hartingtonian Liberal government might have gone in the direction of a programme of 'positive social welfare' is clearly impossible to say, but it is pertinent to observe that the social-reform issues of the 1890s revolved increasingly around the problems arising from the friction between capital and labour, and that in this sphere of policy it is unlikely that the Whig aristocracy would have been less sympathetic to the claims of labour than the large numbers of businessmen who continued to fill the ranks of the parliamentary Liberal Party even during the Edwardian era.[30] Clearly, a Hartington premiership would have been strongly 'Palmerstonian' in style, asserting the Liberals' claim to be a truly 'national' party, rather than one that was directed by class interests or 'faddist' pressure groups.

The greatest difficulty for a Hartingtonian Liberal government would undoubtedly have been how to deal with the problem of Ireland. It is unlikely that Hartington could ever have contemplated the creation of an Irish parliament, but, in the context of a post-Gladstonian Irish policy, it is impossible to tell how far he might have been prepared to go in the direction of local self-government as the price for maintaining Whig authority over the Liberal Party. One policy that the Whigs had become increasingly enthusiastic about, by the mid-1880s, was the one associated with Salisbury's Conservative governments, though it was also reluctantly proposed by Gladstone in 1886: land purchase. Providing Irish landowners with an opportunity to sell out, which many of them were only too glad to do, posed no threat to the sanctity of property, while the creation of a new class of peasant proprietors in Ireland could be seen as having a beneficial effect in terms of social stability. The greatest obstacle to this would have been radical dislike of a measure involving great expense to the British taxpayer, for the benefit of Irish landlords. Nevertheless, it is not entirely implausible to postulate a Whig version of 'killing Home Rule with kindness', during the 1890s.

Different conclusions can obviously be drawn as to what might have been the contribution to the Liberal Party of either Hartington's or Chamberlain's continued presence, but the fact is that the party lost both of them. At the same time, the Liberals were seriously weakened by the alienation of many influential leaders of Liberal opinion in the country. The defection to Liberal Unionism of such men as Dicey, Sidgwick, Goldwin Smith and Matthew Arnold, whose distaste for Gladstonian demagoguery had become increasingly marked since the 1870s, deprived the Liberal Party of much of that commodity for which it had always prided itself: heavy intellectual ammunition. Arnold, in an article for the *Nineteenth Century*, in May 1886, wrote of 'The Nadir of Liberalism', which he saw as the consequence of Gladstone's lack of Statesmanship, and over-readiness to respond to the crude attitudes of the 'philistines', whom he now equated as much with the working classes as with the middle classes. Meantime, at a more mundane but critically important level, the Liberals' Home Rule commitment cost them valuable support in the daily press. London newspapers in particular became heavily biased towards Unionism after 1886, but defections from Liberalism were spread across the whole country.[31]

Gladstone's Legacy

Gladstone's legacy to the Liberals was, like the man, complex and ambiguous. In the short term, it can be argued that the effect of the

Home Rule crisis was to augment the influence within the Liberal Party of the Cobdenite tradition of radicalism, at the expense of 'Palmerstonianism'. More precisely, late-Victorian Liberalism, as embodied in the person of Gladstone, may be described as an amalgam of Peelite–Cobdenism, representing the final assimilation by the parliamentary party of the wider impulses generated by the Free Trade movement of the 1840s. The fact that, in the late 1880s and early 1890s, a laissez-faire, 'Little Englander', anti-aristocratic (and scandalmongering) radical like Henry Labouchere, could have achieved a position of such prominence on the Liberal back-benches, is a good indication of the shift in the balance of forces within the party. It would be the object of Rosebery and the Liberal Imperialists, at the end of the century, to seek to reverse this process.[32]

Another concern of the Liberal imperialists was to be the need for a constructive programme of domestic reform. Certainly, there can be no serious suggestion that the shedding of at least part of the 'Whig incubus', in 1886, somehow liberated Liberal policy from the shackles of outdated, laissez-faire ideology, and enabled it to chart a new course. On the contrary, the notorious Newcastle Programme, compiled by the National Liberal Federation at its annual conference in October 1891, was notable mainly for the persistence of old, sectarian issues. Although there were proposals for the taxation of land values and the reform of death duties – reflecting the influence, in diluted form, of the ideas of Henry George – the 'omnibus resolution' was dominated by measures like Scottish Church disestablishment, temperance reform, the 'mending or ending' of the House of Lords, and 'Free Trade' in land. In any case, pride of place had to be given to Irish Home Rule, the policy for which Gladstone had hung on to the leadership. This was an explicit acceptance by the NLF of what has been called the 'obstruction theory' of Home Rule: that is, that none of the other reforms desired by Liberals could be achieved until the Irish Question was finally settled. Using characteristic imagery, which equated the 'party of progress' with that great symbol of Victorian material progress, the train, Gladstone and other Liberal commentators likened Home Rule to a tree that had fallen across the track, making it necessary for all Liberals, whatever their particular beliefs and priorities, to work together in order to clear the obstruction and get the Liberal train moving again.[33] Such an understanding of the situation clearly suited Gladstone, whose lack of sympathy for the Newcastle Programme was indicated by the fact that, in his own speech to the NLF conference, he scarcely mentioned any of the measures listed in the omnibus resolution. Returning to the premiership for the fourth and final time, in July 1892, Gladstone's energies were devoted almost exclusively to a second, abortive attempt to pass a Home Rule Bill.

When Gladstone finally retired, in March 1894, he left behind him a legend, a spectre that was to haunt his successors, rather than a positive programme for the future, pointing to a clear path forward for the Liberal Party. In a certain sense, nevertheless, the spiritual legacy of the Home Rule commitment was entirely in keeping with the peculiar nature of the Liberal mind. However considerable may have been the Liberal misgivings about Gladstone's policy in 1886, subsequent events, which served to reinforce the party's identification with the Home Rule cause, may also have exercised a strong appeal to the sacrificial mentality amongst many Liberals. Gladstone himself had once described 'true Liberalism' as 'the spirit of self-sacrifice',[34] and this evangelical notion, of suffering politically for the sake of a great moral cause like 'Justice to Ireland', evidently had a powerful emotional attraction for many nonconformists, as well as to the secular spirituality of a lapsed anglican like John Morley. Ireland thus became the sacrificial altar of late-Victorian Liberalism. It was no small achievement for Gladstone that he had managed to convince so many Liberals, including nonconformists, of the justice of his Home Rule policy, when they had so little natural sympathy for the Irish people. Moreover, the fact that Gladstone's Home Rule policy was never put into practice only enhanced its potency as a political symbol, something that was to survive for many years – and indeed has still not entirely died. The belief that Gladstone's Home Rule Bill represented a great missed opportunity to solve the Irish Question, thwarted by the stupidity of his fellow countrymen, who were unable to see the wisdom of his course, has given much comfort to Liberals during their long periods of political adversity.

Gladstone's other enduring contribution to Liberal mythology stems from his use of the rhetoric of 'class interest' in his attempts to explain the opposition to his Home Rule crusade. In a provocative speech at Liverpool, during the 1886 general election campaign, Gladstone referred to 'the case of the classes against the masses', regretting the sad fact that 'there is class against the mass, classes against the nation'.[35] It is important to clarify Gladstone's meaning in this respect, for what he was saying was that it was the privileged ruling elite, through their opposition to Home Rule, who were acting in their own selfish interests,

as a 'class'. The bulk of the people, 'the masses', according to Gladstone, were *not* motivated by class interest, and acted purely out of a
dispassionate concern to see justice done to the Irish nation. Putting
aside the obvious nonsense of Gladstone's analysis of the political views
of 'the masses' (especially in a place like Liverpool), what he was, nevertheless, seeking to assert was a characteristically populist view of the
essential classlessness of the common man. It is easy to see the advantage, for the Liberals, of believing in the superior morality both of their
cause and of their supporters in the country; and the endeavour to
convey the sense of shared identity between the mass of the people –
whether urban or rural, representing capital or labour – in the face of a
common enemy, the selfish 'upper ten thousand', continued to be a
part of the Liberals' rhetorical stock in trade during the age of Lloyd
George. It remains the case, however, that this distinctively Liberal
version of the 'class war' was likely to have only a limited political utility
in the face of 'real' class politics, in which capital confronted labour.

The Liberal Predicament

In electoral terms, the Liberal Party was seriously weakened by the
consequences of the Home Rule crisis, and its long-term position thus
rendered vulnerable. The Liberals suffered heavy defeats in the general
elections of 1886, 1895 and 1900, and though they were the largest
single party in 1892, they still fell a long way short of achieving an
overall parliamentary majority. A comparison of the results in 1885, the
first contest under the new electoral system, and just prior to the
Liberal schism, with those for 1895, gives a good indication of the
general trend, as is shown in Table 10.[36]

As these tables show, by 1895 the Conservatives had built substantially on the gains made in London and the provincial English
boroughs in 1885. No doubt the crisis of 1886 served to accelerate
defections from the Liberals by the urban and suburban middle classes,
but it is also clear that in some areas, especially London and Lancashire, the Conservatives were attracting the allegiance of large numbers
of working-class voters.[37] On the other hand, the inroads into the
English counties achieved by the Liberals in 1885 proved to be more
insecure, and, while they were still capable of doing fairly well in these
constituencies, as the 1892 results indicate (101 out of 231 seats), the
elections of 1886, 1895 and 1900 all confirmed the basic resilience of

Table 10   *British General Election Results, 1885 and 1895*

		1885			1895			
		Con.	Lib.	Nat.*	Con.	LU	Lib.	Nat.
England								
London	(62)**	36	26		51	3	8	
Boroughs	(163)	80	82	1	100	21	41	1
Counties	(231)	99	132		141	27	63	
Universities	(5)	4	1		4	1		
TOTAL	(461)	219	241	1	296	52	112	1
Wales†								
Boroughs	(12)	2	10		5	1	6	
Counties	(22)	2	20		3		19	
TOTAL	(34)	4	30		8	1	25	
Scotland								
Burghs	(31)	1	30		5	9	17	
Counties	(39)	7	32		12	5	22	
Universities	(2)	2			2			
TOTAL	(72)	10	62		19	14	39	
G.B. Total	(567)††	233	333	1	323	67	176	1

* An Irish Nationalist was regularly returned by the Scotland division of Liverpool.
** Including Croydon, West Ham North and West Ham South.
† Including Monmouthshire
†† No Liberal M.P. was returned by Ireland.

the Conservatives in their traditional strongholds. A greater determination on the part of landlords to exercise territorial influence was probably one reason for the Conservatives' recovery in the counties, after the shock of the 1885 result, but it is also likely that the activities of the Primrose League were of particular value in these areas. Wales, it is true, remained largely impervious to the attractions of Unionism, and this was one area where the Liberals' identification with Irish Home Rule may have been an electoral advantage, as many Welshmen were willing to support a measure which they hoped might subsequently be applied to themselves, to satisfy their nationalist aspirations. The situation in Scotland, however, was very different, and the unpopularity of Irish Home Rule (largely due, as we have already suggested, to the Scots' concern for the Ulster presbyterians) manifested itself in sizeable gains for the Conservatives in a country where they had always struggled since the Great Reform Act of 1832. Indeed, at the general election of 1900, the Conservatives, with their Liberal Unionist allies, succeeded in winning a majority of Scottish seats.

The loss to the Liberals arising from the Liberal Unionist revolt was particularly damaging because most of the successful Liberal Unionist candidates in 1886 were already the sitting MPs in their constituencies. There were strong regional concentrations of Liberal Unionist rebels, notably in Western Scotland, the West Midlands, where of course the influence of Joseph Chamberlain was decisive, the South West of England, the Western Marches, and to some extent East Anglia. As for the Gladstonian Liberals, their support, too, was heavily concentrated in certain areas, above all the West Riding of Yorkshire, the North East of England, parts of the East Midlands, rural Scotland and the whole of Wales. These areas provided a compact power-base for the Liberals, but not one that was sufficient by itself to guarantee an overall parliamentary majority.

That there was something fundamentally amiss with the late-Victorian Liberal Party is suggested by the evidence of demoralisation amongst the rank and file in many parts of the country. One obvious illustration of the problem of Liberal disorganisation was their inability to run candidates at all in many constituencies: in this way, 116 Unionist MPs in 1886, 117 in 1895 and 149 in 1900, were elected without facing a contest. This was due in part to the financial difficulties faced by the Liberals as a result of the loss of many of their wealthiest supporters in 1886. Another symptom of the Liberal malaise seems to have been the almost habitual tendency of many Liberals, in Scotland as well as in England, after 1886, simply not to bother to vote at all. The Conservatives thus seem to have benefited from low turnouts at many late-nineteenth-century elections.[38] Precisely what the reasons for this were in different parts of the country is a subject that awaits detailed investigation, but a number of partial explanations have been put forward: the disenchantment of the newly enfranchised agricultural labourers, who had voted Liberal in 1885 in the belief that this would bring tangible improvements to their living standards, only to be frustrated by the Liberals' subsequent preoccupation with Irish Home Rule; the fact that all four general elections between 1886 and 1900 occurred during the harvesting period, when taking time off work to vote was difficult for agricultural labourers – especially if they were feeling disillusioned with the Liberals in any case; the probability that large numbers of electors, in all types of constituencies, disliked the Home Rule commitment, and therefore preferred to abstain, either because they could not bring themselves to vote for a Unionist candidate, as their consciences told them they should, or else because they were dismayed at the way Gladstone's obsession with Ireland was relegating a range of domestic reform issues which they desired to see given higher priority.

Arguably the most worrying aspect of the Liberals' chronic inability to tap their full potential voting strength, was the danger that the electoral vacuum thus created might be filled by an emergent, independent labour movement. It is certainly the case that in some constituencies, for instance in parts of Lancashire, it was the new Labour Party that had established itself, by the Edwardian period, as the most viable opposition to the Conservatives. Many voters, it seems, were prepared to switch from voting Conservative to voting Labour (and vice versa), but would not consider voting Liberal.[39] In spite of the Liberals' remarkable landslide victory at the polls in 1906, which ostensibly points to the conclusion that all was still well with the party, the fact is that in September 1903 they had felt sufficiently vulnerable to be willing to do a deal with the recently formed and trade-union-financed Labour Representation Committee. This Lib–Lab electoral pact, by which the Liberals agreed to give Labour candidates a free run in some forty or fifty constituencies in England and Wales (often ones in which the Liberals' own prospects were poor), in return for a promise that Labour would not intervene anywhere else, ensured that the anti-Unionist vote was maximised in 1906. Ironically, given the dramatic collapse of the Unionist Party between 1903 and 1906, it is probable that the Liberals would have won in 1906 without the Lib–Lab pact; but in the 1910 general elections, on the other hand, it is doubtful whether the Liberal government could have survived without it.[40] Whatever the case may be, the implication is clear that by facilitating the entry into parliament of 29 Labour MPs, in 1906, the Liberals had sown the seeds of what had the potential to become their own eventual destruction, once an unfavourable climate was created in which the pressures of wartime government left the Liberals in disarray, and where Labour, bolstered by the rapid expansion of trade unionism, was no longer prepared to act as the Liberals' junior partner.

NOTES

1. The figures given in Table 7 are a refined version of those given in my *Gladstone, Whiggery and the Liberal Party, 1874–1886* (Oxford, 1988) pp. 225–7.

2. See F. M. L. Thompson, *English Landed Society in the Nineteenth Century* (London, 1963) pp. 292–326.

3. Figures derived from Michael Barker, *Gladstone and Radicalism: The Reconstruction of Liberal Policy in Britain, 1885–94* (Brighton, 1975) Appendix A.

4. Richard Shannon, *The Age of Disraeli, 1868–1881* (London, 1992) pp. 378–9; James Cornford, 'The Transformation of Late-Victorian Conservatism', *Victorian Studies*, VI (1963) p. 52.

5. T. Dunne, 'La trahison des clercs: British Intellectuals and the First Home Rule Crisis', *Irish Historical Studies*, XXIII (1982).

6. Lord Derby's diary, 1 October 1885, Derby MSS. See also Jenkins, *Whiggery*, pp. 241–9.

7. A. B. Cooke and John Vincent, *The Governing Passion: Cabinet Government and Party Politics in Britain, 1885–86* (Brighton, 1974).

8. Gladstone to Granville, 9 December 1885, in Agatha Ramm (ed.), *The Political Correspondence of Mr. Gladstone and Lord Granville, 1876–1886* (Oxford, 1962) vol. 2, p. 414.

9. Gladstone, House of Commons, 8 April 1886, *3 Hansard*, CCCIV, cols 1036–85.

10. James Loughlin, *Gladstone, Home Rule and the Ulster Question, 1882–93* (Dublin, 1986) pp. 180–96, 286–90.

11. D. A. Hamer, *Liberal Politics in the Age of Gladstone and Rosebery* (Oxford, 1972) pp. 108–23.

12. See Jenkins, *Whiggery*, pp. 230–3.

13. Ibid., pp. 239–49.

14. C. H. D. Howard (ed.), *A Political Memoir, 1880–92, by Joseph Chamberlain* (London, 1953).

15. Acton to Gladstone, 2 February 1885, in John Morley, *Life of William Ewart Gladstone* (London, 1903) vol. 3, p. 172; Kimberley to Gladstone, 13 September 1885, BL Add MSS 44228, f. 205.

16. John Brooke and Mary Sorensen (ed.), *The Prime Ministers' Papers: W. E. Gladstone. 1. Autobiographica* (London, 1971) p. 136. The

other occasions on which Gladstone claimed to have used this divine gift were the budget of 1853, Irish Church disestablishment in 1868, and his desire for a campaign against the House of Lords in 1894, after the peers had rejected his second Home Rule Bill.

17. Gordon L. Goodman, 'Liberal Unionism: The Revolt of the Whigs', *Victorian Studies*, III (1959).

18. Another analysis, using a more sophisticated method, arrives at fairly similar conclusions: W. C. Lubenow, 'Irish Home Rule and the Social Basis of the Great Separation in the Liberal Party in 1886', *Historical Journal*, XXVIII (1985).

19. Bernard Holland, *Life of Spencer Compton, Eighth Duke of Devonshire, 1833–1908* (London, 1911) vol. 1, pp. 405–6.

20. Jenkins, *Whiggery*, pp. 220–7.

21. I. G. C. Hutchison, *A Political History of Scotland, 1832–1924* (Edinburgh, 1986) pp. 154–68.

22. Hartington, House of Commons, 9 April 1886, *3 Hansard*, CCCIV, cols 1238–63.

23. Hutchison, *Scotland*, pp. 162–3.

24. Elliot, House of Commons, 18 May 1886, *3 Hansard*, CCCV, cols 1380–5.

25. Keith Robbins, *John Bright* (London, 1979) p. 257.

26. Campbell Bannerman to Lord Spencer, 8 January 1886, BL Add MSS 41228, f. 309. For other evidence of Gladstonian Liberal pessimism about Home Rule, see Jenkins, *Whiggery*, pp. 288–90; Loughlin, *Home Rule and Ulster*, pp. 48–50.

27. Cited by Loughlin, *Home Rule and Ulster*, pp. 51–2: 'his bills' refers to the fact that Gladstone's Home Rule Bill was supposed to be accompanied by a Land Purchase Bill, though the latter was subsequently shelved.

28. T. A. Jenkins, 'Hartington, Chamberlain and the Unionist Alliance, 1886–1895', *Parliamentary History*, XI (1992); Hutchison, *Scotland*, pp. 166–7.

29. Richard Shannon, *Gladstone and the Bulgarian Agitation 1876* (2nd edn, Brighton, 1975) p. 273; H. C. G. Matthew (ed.), *The Gladstone Diaries*, vol. X (Oxford, 1990) p. clxi.

30. See G. R. Searle, 'The Edwardian Liberal Party and Business', *English Historical Review*, XCVIII (1983).

31. Stephen Koss, *The Rise and Fall of the Political Press in Britain*: vol. I, *The Nineteenth Century* (London, 1981) pp. 286–92.

32. See H. C. G. Matthew, *The Liberal Imperialists: The Ideas and Policies of a Post-Gladstonian Elite* (Oxford, 1973).

33. See Hamer, *Liberal Politics*, pp. 126–35.

34. Lord Derby's diary, 28 January 1884, Derby MSS.

35. *The Times*, 29 June 1886.

36. Figures derived from the *Annual Register*, 1885 and 1895, with my corrections.

37. The account given in the remainder of this section is based largely on the following works: Neal Blewett, *The Peers, the Parties and the*

People: the general elections of 1910 (London, 1972); Henry Pelling, *Social Geography of British Elections, 1885–1910* (London, 1967); Michael Kinnear, *The British Voter: An Atlas and Survey since 1885* (London, 1968); Martin Pugh, *The Tories and the People, 1880–1935* (Blackwell, 1985); K. O. Morgan, *Wales in British Politics, 1868–1922* (3rd edn, Cardiff, 1980); I. G. C. Hutchison, *A Political History of Scotland, 1832–1924* (Edinburgh, 1986).

38.　Blewett, *Peers, Parties and People*, pp. 20–3; Hutchison, *Scotland*, pp. 165, 185. It was also a problem in areas where the Liberals were still strong: A. W. Roberts, 'Leeds Liberalism and Late-Victorian Politics', *Northern History*, V (1970) pp. 155–6.

39.　Duncan Tanner, *Political Change and the Labour Party, 1900–1918* (Cambridge, 1990); Hutchison, *Scotland*, pp. 179–80, 183–5, also notes this phenomenon, but does not think it quite so serious as in England.

40.　Blewett, *Peers, Parties and People*, pp. 408–9, 413–14.

Conclusion

Throughout this book, great emphasis has been placed on the diversity of the nineteenth-century Liberal Party. While this approach seems perfectly justified, given the broad spectrum of political opinions and the wide range of interest groups encompassed within what was very much a Liberal 'coalition', it is also necessary to consider what were the bonds that held the Liberals together for so long. Clearly, there had to be some common ground on which all Liberals could comfortably stand, if the party was to find an identity which would enable it to survive as a viable force for future political action.

Arguably the greatest source of inspiration, for Liberals of every kind, came from the party's rich mythological inheritance, which did so much to create a sense of shared pride in past triumphs and achievements. It did not matter that these mythologies involved a careful selection of historical facts, filtering out inconvenient evidence showing just how ambivalent their forebears had often been about precisely those issues which later Victorian Liberals took such pride in: what really counted was the Liberals' collective memory of how their own past had been. Thus, Liberals could congratulate themselves for being the party that had always stood for religious liberty, provided they recollected the Lord John Russell of the repeal of the Test and Corporation Acts, and overlooked the same Russell of the Durham letter and the Ecclesiastical Titles Act. Liberals liked to think of themselves as the party of electoral reform, which was not unreasonable in that they had carried the 1832 and 1884 Reform Acts, but this also led to a curious rewriting of history (as we saw in Chapter 4) so that it appeared to be they, and not the Conservatives, who were responsible for the household suffrage provision of the 1867 Reform Act. Free Trade, of course, played a major part in shaping the Liberals' identity, in spite of the fact that many had hesitated to support this policy in the early 1840s, and that much of what was accomplished was due to the efforts of the Conservative Prime Minister, Sir Robert Peel. Sympathy for the cause of Italian Nationalism, in the 1850s and 1860s, was the other great formative influence on the Liberal political character, and yet, as we saw in chapter 3, even this had only been possible at the time so long as the Liberals' commitment was confined to sympathy, and not extended to active military assistance. As late as 1879–80, the Liberals had managed to hunt as a pack when the prey was an increasingly vulnerable Conservative government, and fresh mythologies were subsequently created, such as the inevitability of their general election victory and of Gladstone's return to the premiership, when in fact, only a couple of years earlier, the Liberal leadership had found it impossible to unite the party in the face of the Conservatives' foreign policy, and many Liberals had condemned Gladstone's conduct in attacking Lord Beaconsfield.

A clear contrast has to be made, therefore, between the historian's view of the history of the Liberal Party, which sees that matters were rarely as clear-cut and straightforward as they later appeared, and perhaps inevitably presents a picture of the Liberals stumbling from one success to another, and the Liberals' own retrospective impression of a logical and orderly application of clearly-defined principles to a wide range of issues. For it was the latter view, after all, which helped to mould and motivate subsequent generations of the Liberal Party faithful.

If the past contributed so much to the Liberals' sense of shared identity, the present and future were always more problematic. Such was the diversity of Liberalism that there was little prospect of the party agreeing to a specific programme of reforms. Joseph Chamberlain tried to impose a programme on the Liberals in 1885, and failed; and when, beyond the period dealt with here, the National Liberal Federation did endorse the Newcastle Programme of 1891, this became a subject of controversy for years to come rather than a source of unity and strength. Much more effective were the great rallying-crys – sometimes constructive, sometimes negative – which enabled the Liberals, at certain times, to channel their energies in one direction and push into the background potential areas of internal dispute: Parliamentary Reform in 1831–2; the defence of Free Trade in 1852; Irish Church disestablishment in 1868, and the moral condemnation of 'Beaconsfieldism' in 1880, provided the focal points for Liberalism at its most formidable. Beyond these, there was often little to hold the Liberals together other than a reassuring faith in the inevitability of 'progress', and the mutual confidence of fellow travellers moving down the same track.

It was entirely characteristic of the Liberal Party that its two out-standing leaders, Palmerston and Gladstone, were both outsiders. The effectiveness of these recruits from Toryism – neither of them was finally ousted from the premiership, Palmerston dying in office, while Gladstone retired in his eighty-fifth year – owed much to the fact that they were not associated exclusively with one section or another of the Liberal Party. Palmerston's handling of foreign policy appealed to a cross-section of the political nation, including certain radicals and many Conservatives, while his cautious attitude towards questions of domestic reform was reassuring to the Whigs as well as to the Conservatives. Gladstone never attracted the same sort of cross-party support, but within the Liberal Party the ambiguity of his personal position meant that he was often able to secure the devotion of radicals and non-conformists, although his instinctive conservatism in most respects ensured that he remained close to many members of the Whig aris-tocracy, until 1886 at any rate. Furthermore, both leaders sought to extend their appeal beyond Westminster, through speaking tours in the provinces and careful cultivation of the press, and in each case the perceived ability to harness 'public opinion' greatly enhanced their authority over the Liberal Party. The *external* force generated by their role as national leaders provided at least some means of imposing dis-cipline on the Liberal ranks.

Though neither Palmerston nor Gladstone was, strictly speaking, a Whig, it is true that both men were keen to nurture the tradition of administrative leadership by the Liberal aristocracy. It was for this reason that, even after the eclipse of Lord John Russell in the 1850s, the Whigs were never reduced to the position of being a mere section, or 'wing', of the Liberal Party, and we have seen, for example, how the Whig duumvirate of Granville and Hartington provided capable leadership in the difficult circumstances of the 1870s. If the responsi-bilities enjoined on the Whigs by their own administrative ethic encouraged them to look to the wider interests of the Liberal Party, and prevented them from acting purely as leaders of a sectional group, so too, the complex nature of radicalism ensured that there was never a coherently organised radical 'wing' locked into a state of perpetual and terminal antagonism with the Whigs. More often than not, issues like imperialism and domestic reform served to divide rather than unite those who called themselves radicals, and herein lies the key, for example, to the frustrations of Cobden and Bright, and the failure of Chamberlain's attempts at radical leadership in the 1880s. It is seriously misleading, therefore, to describe the dynamics of the Liberal Party simply in terms of a constant Whig-Radical conflict, with leaders like Gladstone trying to mediate between them.

It was argued in Chapter 6 that the Liberal schism over the question of Irish Home Rule, in 1886, can only partially be explained in terms of a 'revolt of the Whigs'. The alienation of many Whigs, such as Hartington, from the Gladstonian approach to the Irish problem, certainly did occur, but it applied to many other Liberals as well, so that the schism largely cut across pre-existing social or political dividing lines. Home Rule, in other words, created a quite separate fault-line within Liberalism. However, this did not prevent the Gladstonian Liberals from claiming, after the event, that the schism was merely the result of class interest on the part of the Liberal Unionists, and in this way another tale was added to the growing body of Liberal folklore. Late-Victorian Liberals would learn to say 'good riddance' to the Liberal Unionists, and claim that their defection had been beneficial to the party – a cause for relief rather than of regret. Released from the shackles of Whiggery, or so it was claimed, the Liberals had willingly embraced Gladstone's morally elevated call for 'Justice to Ireland'.

The nagging question that remains concerns the political validity (leaving aside the historical accuracy) of the 'class' language employed by the late-Victorian Liberals. Once again, there was considerable ambiguity in the Liberals' position, for while they presented themselves as the party of 'the people', in opposition to the selfish aristocracy, the fact was that the Liberals at Westminster were by now predominantly a party of businessmen and middle-class professional groups. Apart from the dozen or so 'Lib–Lab' MPs elected in 1885, the Liberals did nothing in practice to facilitate the increased representation of working men in parliament. It is perfectly true, of course, that there had been an equal degree of ambiguity about the Liberal Party earlier in the nineteenth century, when the aristocratic Whigs had continued to provide leadership for a party representing the interests of large sections of the urban middle classes. In that case, however, it can be argued that these potentially conflicting forces were reconciled because the Whigs were prepared to govern along lines that were generally acceptable to the middle classes, most obviously through the implementation of Free-Trade principles, and that, in return, the middle classes showed relatively little interest in trying to seize the levers of political power for themselves. The great peril facing the Liberal Party by the end of the nineteenth century, on the other hand, was that a new climate of feeling was being created which encouraged the demand for the election of more working men to parliament, for no other reason than that they were working men, and certainly not because they advocated different policies from the Liberals. While a formidable case has been made by historians for the view that the 'New Liberalism' of the early twentieth century represented a successful attempt to adapt Liberal ideology to meet the requirements of a 'collectivist' age, it can be suggested that this was largely irrelevant to the situation. The cry of 'men, not measures', was ultimately to prove fatal to the Liberal Party.

Bibliography

General Works

Donald Southgate, *The Passing of the Whigs, 1832–1886* (London, 1962), though looking increasingly dated, is full of information, and it is still the nearest thing to a history of the Liberal Party, for the pre-1868 period at least. For the later nineteenth century, D. A. Hamer, *Liberal Politics in the Age of Gladstone and Rosebery* (Oxford, 1972), is the most useable account: Michael Bentley's more recent *The Climax of Liberal Politics: Liberalism in Theory and Practice, 1868–1918* (London, 1987), is pitched at too high a level for undergraduates. Michael Winstanley, *Gladstone and the Liberal Party* (London, 1990), provides an excellent brief introduction.

Paul Adelman, *Victorian Radicalism: The Middle Class Experience, 1830–1914* (London, 1984), is a useful starting-point for this aspect of Liberalism. There is a mine of material in Simon Maccoby (ed.), *English Radicalism* (5 vols, London, 1935–61).

The two outstanding general works on the electoral system are by Norman Gash, *Politics in the Age of Peel* (2nd edn, Brighton, 1977), and H. J. Hanham, *Elections and Party Management: Politics in the Time of Disraeli and Gladstone* (2nd edn, Brighton, 1978). Derek Fraser, *Urban Politics in Victorian England* (London, 1976), is an important study of the provincial towns. There is also a useful regional study by T. J. Nossiter, *Influence, Opinion and Political Idioms in Reformed England: Case Studies from the North East, 1832–74* (Brighton, 1975). For the Celtic fringe, see: K. O. Morgan, *Wales in British Politics, 1868–1922* (3rd edn, Cardiff, 1980); I. G. C. Hutchison, *A Political History of Scotland, 1832–1924* (Edinburgh, 1986); K. T. Hoppen, *Elections, Politics and Society in Ireland, 1832–1885* (Oxford, 1984).

On constitutional matters, G. H. L. Le May's *The Victorian Constitution* (London, 1979) provides a helpful survey. There is a provocative essay on the monarchy by David Cannadine, 'The Last Hanoverian Monarch? The Victorian Monarchy in Historical Perspective', in A. L.

Beier et al. (eds), *The First Modern Society* (London, 1989). On the development of political parties, there are suggestive articles by Angus Hawkins, ' "Parliamentary Government" and Victorian Political Parties, c.1830–c. 1880', *English Historical Review*, CIV (1989), and Hugh Berrington, 'Partisanship and Dissidence in the Nineteenth Century House of Commons', *Parliamentary Affairs* XXI (1968). See also, D. E. D. Beales, 'Parliamentary Parties and the Independent Member, 1810–60', in Robert Robson (ed.), *Ideas and Institutions of Victorian Britain* (London, 1967), and D. H. Close, 'The Formation of a Two-Party Alignment in the House of Commons between 1832 and 1841', *English Historical Review* LXXXIV (1969).

For religious questions, two volumes by G. I. T. Machin are indispensable: *Politics and the Churches in Great Britain, 1832–1868* (Oxford, 1977), and *Politics and the Churches in Great Britain, 1869–1921* (Oxford, 1987).

On the Liberal Party and the press, see Stephen Koss, *The Rise and Fall of the Political Press in Britain*, vol. 1: *The Nineteenth Century* (London, 1981), and Alan J. Lee, *The Origins of the Popular Press in England, 1855–1914* (London, 1976).

For Liberal philosophy, there are two convenient collections of documents: Alan Bullock and Maurice Shock (eds), *The Liberal Tradition from Fox to Keynes* (London, 1956), and Robert Eccleshall (ed.), *British Liberalism: Liberal Thought from the 1640s to the 1980s* (London, 1986).

1. The Spirit of Reform

Austin Mitchell, *The Whigs in Opposition, 1815–30* (Oxford, 1967), is the best study of the Whigs prior to the Great Reform Act. Whig ideology has received considerable attention in recent years: see Abraham D. Kriegal, 'Liberty and Whiggery in Early-Nineteenth Century England', *Journal of Modern History*, LII, (1980); E. A. Wasson, 'The Great Whigs and Parliamentary Reform, 1809–30', *Journal of British Studies*, XXIV (1985); L. G. Mitchell, 'Foxite Politics and the Great Reform Bill', *English Historical Review*, CVIII (1993), and the same author's *Holland House* (London, 1980).

There is now a useful general account of the Whig governments after 1830 by Ian Newbould, *Whiggery and Reform, 1830–1841: The Politics of Government* (London, 1990). Two stimulating, but conflicting, attempts to delineate Whiggery are by Richard Brent, *Liberal Anglican*

Politics: Whiggery, Religion and Reform, 1830–1841 (Oxford, 1987), and
Peter Mandler, *Aristocratic Government in the Age of Reform: Whigs and
Liberals, 1830–1852* (Oxford, 1990). All of these authors are critical, for
one reason or another, of Norman Gash, *Reaction and Reconstruction in
English Politics, 1832–1852* (Oxford, 1965), although this work remains a
classic.

For the 1832 Reform Act, see John Cannon, *Parliamentary Reform,
1640–1832* (Cambridge, 1973); Michael Brock, *The Great Reform Act*
(London, 1973); Norman McCord, 'Some Difficulties of Parliamentary
Reform', *Historical Journal*, X (1967); J. Milton Smith, 'Earl Grey's
Cabinet and the objects of Parliamentary Reform', *Historical Journal*, XV
(1972). The views of a moderate-reform MP (George Staunton) may be
found in M. O'Neill and G. Martin, 'A Backbencher on Parliamentary
Reform, 1831–1832', *Historical Journal*, XXIII (1980).

The following articles deal with various aspects of Whig politics and
policy after 1832: Abraham D. Kriegal, 'The Irish Policy of Lord
Grey's Government', *English Historical Review*, LXXXVI (1971); I. Gross,
'The Abolition of Negro Slavery and British Parliamentary Politics,
1832–3', *Historical Journal*, XXIII (1980); Peter Dunkley, 'Whigs and
Paupers: The Reform of the English Poor Laws, 1830–1834', *Journal of
British Studies*, XX (1981); Abraham D. Kriegal, 'The Politics of the
Whigs in Opposition, 1834–1835', *Journal of British Studies*, VII (1968);
G. B. A. M. Finlayson, 'The Politics of Municipal Reform 1835',
English Historical Review, LXXXI, (1966); Richard Brent, 'The Whigs
and Protestant Dissent in the Decade of Reform: The Case of Church
Rates, 1833–1841', *English Historical Review*, CII (1987); J. L. Alexander,
'Lord John Russell and the Origins of the Committee of Council on
Education', *Historical Journal*, XX (1977).

E. A. Smith, *Earl Grey, 1764–1845* (Oxford, 1990), is the first
biography of the Whig premier for seventy years. Studies of other
senior ministers include E. A. Wasson, *Whig Renaissance: Lord Althorp and
the Whig Party, 1782–1845* (New York, 1987); Philip Ziegler, *Melbourne*
(London, 1976); John Prest, *Lord John Russell* (London, 1972); Kenneth
Bourne, *Palmerston: The Early Years, 1784–1841* (London, 1982); Robert
Stewart, *Henry Brougham, 1778–1868: His Public Career* (London, 1985).
See also Abraham D. Kriegal's edition of *The Holland House Diaries*,
(London, 1977).

For the position of the radicals, see William Thomas, *The Philosophic
Radicals* (Oxford, 1979), and the same author's essay on this subject in
Patricia Hollis (ed.), *Pressure from Without in Early-Victorian England*

(London, 1974). Ronald K. Hutch and Philip R. Ziegler, *Joseph Hume: The Peoples' MP*, (Philadelphia, 1985), is a useful recent biography of a prominent radical. An essential work on nonconformity is Alan D. Gilbert, *Religion and Society in Industrial England: Church, Chapel and Social Change, 1740–1914* (London, 1976). A. D. Macintyre, *The Liberator: Daniel O'Connell and the Irish Party, 1830–1847* (London, 1965), deals with the Irish repealers.

Several good studies of individual constituencies in the post-Reform-Act era have appeared in the journal *Northern History*: Norman McCord, 'Gateshead Politics in the Age of Reform', IV (1969); D. G. Wright, 'A Radical Borough: Parliamentary Politics in Bradford, 1832–1841', IV (1969); Derek Fraser, 'The Fruits of Reform: Leeds Politics in the 1830s', VII (1972); and J. A. Jowitt, 'Parliamentary Politics in Halifax, 1832–1847', XI (1976).

2. The Slow Birth of Liberal England

There is very little on the Whigs for the period 1841–52. Some information can be gleaned from Southgate's *Passing of the Whigs*, Gash's *Reaction and Reconstruction*, Prest's *Lord John Russell*, and Mandler's *Aristocratic Government*, all cited above. In addition, see F. A. Dreyer, 'The Whigs and the Ministerial Crisis of 1845', *English Historical Review*, LXXX (1965), and Roland Quinault, '1848 and Parliamentary Reform', *Historical Journal*, XXXI (1988).

Norman McCord, *The Anti-Corn Law League* (London, 1958), is the standard work on the subject. See also McCord's essay, 'Cobden and Bright in Politics, 1846–57', in Robert Robson (ed.), *Ideas and Institutions of Victorian Britain* (London, 1967). G. R. Searle, *Entrepreneurial Politics in Mid-Victorian Britain* (Oxford, 1993), is a valuable new assessment of the difficulties confronting middle-class radicalism after 1846. See also N. C. Edsall, 'A Failed National Movement: The Parliamentary and Financial Reform Association, 1848–54', *Bulletin of the Institute of Historical Research*, XLIX, (1976). Recent biographies include Keith Robbins, *John Bright* (London, 1979), Nicholas Edsall, *Richard Cobden: Independent Radical* (Harvard, 1986), and Wendy Hinde, *Richard Cobden: A Victorian Outsider* (Yale, 1987).

On the nonconformists, R. G. Cowherd, *The Politics of English Dissent, 1814–1848* (London, 1959), is still useful. See also G. I. T. Machin, 'The Maynooth Grant, the Dissenters and the Establishment, 1845–7',

English Historical Review, LXXXII (1967), and Derek Fraser, 'Voluntaryism and West Riding Politics in the Mid-Nineteenth Century', *Northern History*, XII (1977). Clyde Binfield, *So Down to Prayers* (London, 1977), has interesting chapters on Edward Miall and on the Baines family.

For the Peelites, see J. B. Conacher, *The Peelites and the Party System, 1846–1852* (Newton Abbot, 1972). Two biographies of leading Peelites are Muriel Chamberlain, *Lord Aberdeen* (London, 1983) and Richard Shannon, *Gladstone*, vol. I *(1809–65)*, (London, 1982).

3. Lord Palmerston and Mid-Victorian Liberalism

Most of the literature listed for Chapter 2 is relevant. Muriel Chamberlain's *Lord Palmerston* (Cardiff, 1987), is a useful introduction, covering his whole career. Donald Southgate, *The Most English Minister* (London, 1966), examines the domestic impact of Palmerston's foreign policy. See also, Kingsley Martin, *The Triumph of Lord Palmerston* (2nd edn, London, 1963).

For the impact of the Crimean War, see Olive Anderson, *A Liberal State at War* (London, 1967), and her essay on 'The Administrative Reform Association' in Patricia Hollis (ed.), *Pressure from Without in Early-Victorian England* (London, 1974). More generally, there is J. B. Conacher's monumental *The Aberdeen Coalition, 1852–55: A Study in Mid-Victorian Party Politics*, (Cambridge, 1968).

A recent assessment of Palmerston's leadership is essential reading: E. D. Steele, *Palmerston and Liberalism, 1855–1865* (Cambridge, 1991), but see also, the important article by P. M. Gurowich, 'The Continuation of War by Other Means: Party and Politics, 1855–1865', *Historical Journal*, XXVII (1984). The high politics of the late-1850s is covered by Angus Hawkins, *Parliament, Party and the Art of Politics in Britain, 1855–1859* (London, 1987). Derek Beales, *England and Italy, 1859–60* (London, 1961), deals with an important formative influence on the Liberal Party. David F. Krein, *The Last Palmerston Government: Foreign Policy, Domestic Politics and the Genesis of Spendid Isolation* (Iowa, 1978), is a useful brief study of the 1859–65 ministry. A back-bench Liberal's view of the Palmerston era is provided by T. A. Jenkins (ed.), *The Parliamentary Diaries of Sir John Trelawny, 1858–1865* (Royal Historical Society, Camden Series, 1990). Walter Bagehot's classic, *The English Constitution* (London, 1867; 1963 edn with introduction by R. H. S. Crossman), is very much a description of the Palmerstonian regime.

D. G. Wright has written two useful articles on provincial cities in the early 1860s: 'Bradford and the American Civil War', *Journal of British Studies*, VIII (1969), and 'Leeds Politics and the American Civil War', *Northern History*, IX (1974).

4. The Rise and Fall of Gladstonian Liberalism

The two outstanding recent studies of Gladstone are H. C. G. Matthew's *Gladstone, 1809–74* (Oxford, 1986), a compilation of his introductions to the Gladstone Diaries project, and Richard Shannon's *Gladstone*, vol. I *(1809–65)*, (London, 1982). See also, the stimulating essay by Boyd Hilton, 'Gladstone's Theological Politics', in Michael Bentley and John Stevenson (eds), *High and Low Politics in Modern Britain* (Oxford, 1983), and the review article by Paul Smith, 'Liberalism as Authority and Discipline', *Historical Journal*, XXXII (1989). Agatha Ramm, *William Ewart Gladstone* (Cardiff, 1989), is a short biography covering the whole of Gladstone's career.

Two works by J. R. Vincent are of great importance for our understanding of grass-roots Liberalism: *The Formation of the British Liberal Party, 1857–1868* (2nd edn, Brighton, 1976), and *Pollbooks: How Victorians Voted* (Cambridge, 1967). A recent work adopting a different approach is Eugenio F. Biagini's *Liberty, Retrenchment and Reform: Popular Politics in the Age of Gladstone, 1860–1880* (Cambridge, 1992).

For the 1867 Reform Act, see F. B. Smith, *The Making of the Second Reform Bill* (London, 1966), and Maurice Cowling, *1867: Disraeli, Gladstone and Revolution* (Cambridge, 1967). For the Adullamites, see James Winter, 'The Cave of Adullam and Parliamentary Reform', *English Historical Review*, LXXXI (1966), and the same author's biography of *Robert Lowe* (Toronto, 1976).

Specific elements in the Gladstonian Liberal coalition of the 1860s are dealt with by G. I. T. Machin, 'Gladstone and Nonconformity: The Formation of an Alliance in the 1860s', *Historical Journal*, XVII (1974); Lawrence Goldman, 'The Social Science Association, 1857-1886: A Context for Mid-Victorian Liberalism', *English Historical Review*, CI (1986); and Christopher Harvie, *The Lights of Liberalism: University Liberals and the Challenge of Democracy, 1860–86* (London, 1976).

Aspects of Liberal policy between 1868 and 1874 are dealt with by the following: J. P. Parry, *Democracy and Religion: Gladstone and the Liberal Party, 1867–1875* (Cambridge, 1986); E. D. Steele, *Irish Land and British*

Politics (Cambridge, 1974); Bruce L. Kinzer, *The Ballot Question in Nineteenth Century English Politics* (New York, 1982); Thomas F. Gallagher, ' "Cardwellian Mysteries": The Fate of the British Army Regulation Bill, 1871', *Historical Journal*, XVIII (1975). Also relevant to this period is Jonathan Spain, 'Trade Unionists, Gladstonian Liberals, and the Labour Law Reforms of 1875', in Eugenio F. Biagini and Alastair F. Reid (eds), *Currents of Radicalism: Popular Radicalism, Organised Labour and Party Politics in Britain, 1850–1914* (Cambridge, 1991).

For the difficulties facing Gladstone's first ministry, see J. P. Parry, 'Religion and the Collapse of Gladstone's First Government, 1870–1874', *Historical Journal*, XXV (1982). D. A. Hamer, *The Politics of Electoral Pressure* (Brighton, 1977), is useful for the problems posed by mainly nonconformist pressure groups. See also, Paul McHugh, *Prostitution and Victorian Social Reform* (London, 1980), a case study of the contagious diseases agitation. Lawrence Goldman (ed.), *The Blind Victorian: Henry Fawcett and British Liberalism* (Cambridge, 1989), deals with one of Gladstone's radical critics. T. A. Jenkins (ed.), *The Parliamentary Diaries of Sir John Trelawny, 1868–1873* (Royal Historical Society, Camden Series, forthcoming, 1994), provides a critical account of events from the viewpoint of a Liberal back-bencher. Gladstone's 'retirement' in 1875 is covered by Matthew Temmel, 'Gladstone's Resignation of the Liberal Leadership, 1874–5', *Journal of British Studies*, XVI (1976).

5. Whigs, Radicals and Gladstonians

H. C. G. Matthew takes his study of Gladstone from 1875 to 1886 in the introductions to Volumes IX and X of *The Gladstone Diaries* (Oxford, 1986, 1990). The classic account of Gladstone's political re-emergence is Richard Shannon's *Gladstone and the Bulgarian Agitation 1876* (2nd edn, Brighton, 1975). See also Ann P. Saab, *Reluctant Icon: Gladstone, Bulgaria and the Working Classes, 1856–1878* (Harvard, 1991) and Marvin Swartz, *The Politics of British Foreign Policy in the Era of Disraeli and Gladstone* (London, 1985). On the Midlothian campaign, there is a stimulating essay by Richard Shannon, 'Midlothian: 100 Years After', in Peter J. Jagger (ed.), *Gladstone, Politics and Religion* (London, 1983). D. A. Hamer, 'Gladstone: The Making of a Political Myth', *Victorian Studies*, XXII (1978), is an interesting study of popular perceptions of the 'Grand Old Man'. On the other hand, the continued importance of Whiggery thoughout this period is asserted by T. A. Jenkins, *Gladstone, Whiggery and the Liberal Party, 1874–1886* (Oxford, 1988).

T. O. Lloyd, *The General Election of 1880* (Oxford, 1968), is the only study we have of a late-nineteenth-century election, though it is not entirely satisfactory. An interesting case study of the difficult relations between a Liberal MP (Gladstone's eldest son) and his constituents, is provided by Michael Bentley, 'Gladstonian Liberals and Provincial Notables: Whitby Politics, 1868–1880', *Historical Research*, LXIV (1991).

Ronald Robinson and John Gallagher, *Africa and the Victorians: The Official Mind of Imperialism* (London, 1961), remains the classic account of imperial policy in the 1880s. Irish policy, during the early years of the second Gladstone ministry, is the subject of Allen Warren, 'Forster, the Liberals, and New Directions in Irish Policy, 1880–1882', *Parliamentary History*, VI (1987). An inside view of Forster's Irish administration is provided by T. W. Moody and R. Hawkins (eds), *Florence Arnold-Forster's Irish Journal* (Oxford, 1988).

For radicalism, there is T. W. Heyck's *The Dimensions of British Radicalism: The Case of Ireland, 1874–1895* (Illinois, 1974), though his computational work needs to be treated with caution. There is a good modern edition of *The Radical Programme 1885* (ed. D. A. Hamer, Brighton, 1971). By far the best modern biography of Chamberlain is Richard Jay's *Joseph Chamberlain: A Political Study* (Oxford, 1981). The recent tendency to play down the effectiveness of Chamberlain as a radical leader is reflected in Alan Simon, 'Church Disestablishment as a Factor in the General Election of 1885', *Historical Journal*, XVIII (1975), and Roland Quinault, 'John Bright and Joseph Chamberlain', *Historical Journal*, XXVIII (1985).

6. The Crisis of Late-Victorian Liberalism

For the Third Reform Act, see Andrew Jones, *The Politics of Reform 1884* (Cambridge, 1972), and M. E. J. Chadwick, 'The Role of Redistribution in the Making of the Third Reform Act', *Historical Journal*, XIX (1976). A famous article by J. P. Cornford, 'The Transformation of Late-Victorian Conservatism', *Victorian Studies*, VI (1963), explores the impact of the 1884–5 reforms on the electoral system.

Several accounts now exist of Gladstone's Irish Home Rule initiative and its effects on the Liberal Party, offering a variety of interpretations. J. L. Hammond, *Gladstone and the Irish Nation* (2nd edn, London, 1964), takes an heroic view of Gladstone's conduct, while Gordon L. Goodman, 'Liberal Unionism: The Revolt of the Whigs', *Victorian Studies*, III (1959), applies a 'class' analysis to the Liberal schism. A. B. Cooke and John Vincent, *The Governing Passion: Cabinet Government and Party Politics in Britain, 1885–86* (Brighton, 1974), adopts an uncompromising 'high politics' approach to everything. W. C. Lubenow, *Parliamentary Politics and the Home Rule Crisis: The British House of Commons in 1886* (Oxford, 1988), and T. A. Jenkins, *Gladstone, Whiggery and the Liberal Party, 1874–1886* (Oxford, 1988), in spite of their differences of method, both arrive at anti-determinist conclusions concerning the Liberal schism. Other important recent contributions are Alan O'Day, *Parnell and the First Home Rule Episode, 1884–7* (Dublin, 1986), James Loughlin, *Gladstone, Home Rule and the Ulster Question, 1882–1893* (Dublin, 1986); H. C. G. Matthew (ed.), *The Gladstone Diaries*, vol X (Oxford, 1990); and Graham D. Goodlad, 'The Liberal Party and Gladstone's Land Purchase Bill of 1886', *Historical Journal*, XXXII (1989).

For the alienation of the Liberal intelligentsia, see Christopher Harvie, *The Lights of Liberalism: University Liberals and the Challenge of Democracy, 1860–86* (London, 1976), and T. Dunne, 'La trahison des clercs: British Intellectuals and the First Home Rule Crisis', *Irish Historical Studies*, XXIII (1982).

Attitudes towards Gladstone and his Home Rule Bill, among Liberal activists and the rank and file, are dealt with by P. C. Griffiths, 'The Liberal Party and the Caucus in 1886', *History*, LXI (1976), and Graham D. Goodlad, 'Gladstone and his Rivals: Popular Liberal Perceptions of the Party Leadership in the Political Crisis of 1885–1886', in Eugenio F. Biagini and Alastair F. Reid (eds), *Currents of Radicalism: Popular Radicalism, Organised Labour and Party Politics in Britain, 1850–1914* (Cambridge, 1991).

There are surprisingly few studies of constituencies, for the 1880s, but see Janet Howarth, 'The Liberal Revival in Northamptonshire, 1880–95: A Case Study in Late-Nineteenth Century Elections', *Historical Journal*, XII (1969), A. W. Roberts, 'Leeds Liberalism and Late-Victorian Politics', *Northern History*, V (1970) and E. Jaggard, 'Political Continuity and Change in Late-Nineteenth Century Cornwall', *Parliamentary History*, XI (1992). More generally, there is D. W. Bebbington, 'Nonconformity and Electoral Sociology, 1867–1918', *Historical Journal*, XXVII (1984). The best general survey of the post-1885 electoral system may be found in Part 1 of Neal Blewett's *The Peers, the Parties and the People: The General Elections of 1910* (London, 1972).

An optimistic assessment of policy developments during Gladstone's final years is provided by Michael Barker, *Gladstone and Radicalism: The Reconstruction of Liberal Policy in Britain, 1885–94* (Brighton, 1975). For a different view, see D. A. Hamer, *John Morley: Intellectual in Politics* (Oxford, 1968). See also T. W. Heyck, 'Home Rule, Radicalism and the Liberal Party, 1886–1895', *Journal of British Studies*, XIII (1974). For the post-Gladstonian years, Peter Stansky's *Ambitions and Strategies: The Struggle for the Leadership of the Liberal Party in the 1890s* (Oxford, 1964), is a blow-by-blow account. David Brooks (ed.), *The Destruction of Lord Rosebery: From the Diary of Sir Edward Hamilton, 1894–1895* (London, 1986), has a useful introduction. For the last years of the century, see H. C. G. Matthew, *The Liberal Imperialists: The Ideas and Policies of a Post-Gladstonian Elite* (Oxford, 1973). There is an excellent new survey of the Liberals after 1886 by G. R. Searle, *The Liberal Party: Triumph and Disintegration, 1886–1929* (London, 1992).

Index

Where the title 'Lord' is used, it should be understood that this was the courtesy title of a peer's son, and not a peerage in itself. Such individuals were therefore eligible to sit in the House of Commons.